Into Writing

Into Writing

The Primary Teacher's Guide to Writing Workshop

Megan S. Sloan

HEINEMANN
Portsmouth, NH

Heinemann
361 Hanover Street
Portsmouth, NH 03801–3912
www.heinemann.com

Offices and agents throughout the world

Library of Congress Cataloging-in-Publication Data
Sloan, Megan S.
Into writing : the primary teacher's guide to writing workshop / Megan S. Sloan.
p. cm.
Includes bibliographical references and index.
ISBN 13: 978-0-325-01228-5
ISBN 10: 0-325-01228-8
1. English language—Composition and exercises—Study and teaching (Primary). 2. Primary school teaching. I. Title.
LB1528.S56 2009
372.62'3043—dc22 2008048424

Editor: Wendy Murray
Production: Elizabeth Valway
Cover photo: Megan S. Sloan
Cover design: Night & Day Design
Composition: Publishers' Design and Production Services, Inc.
Manufacturing: Valerie Cooper

Printed in the United States of America on acid-free paper
13 12 11 10 09 ML 1 2 3 4 5

Dedicated to
Sam Sebesta
Our shared love for Alice in Wonderland *brought us together.*
You inspired me to be the teacher I am today.
You are my mentor, and my dear friend.

CONTENTS

View an additional chapter: Should I Be Teaching Writing During Science, Social Studies, and Math? *at* books.heinemann.com/sloan

FOREWORD

Some books you return to again and again—for wisdom, yes, but mostly because you feel at home in them. This is a book to feel at home in. From the first page, I felt myself having a conversation with Megan—two friends chatting about writing. I love a writer who takes down walls and just talks to me. Megan Sloan does that.

Whenever I do a workshop for teachers, I hope and trust that they will leave with one overwhelming thought: *I can do this.* That is precisely how I felt reading this book. Megan Sloan takes the mystery out of writing workshop without compromising any of the magic. It is easy to picture her beautifully orchestrated workshop flow, from the opening lesson through writing, coaching, and sharing. Her engaging, readable descriptions are so detailed, so vivid, you'll feel as if you're sitting right there in her classroom. Nothing is intimidating. Nothing is complicated. Everything feels so natural and familiar and *do-able* that you will say to yourself, "Why did I ever think writing workshop was hard?" Best of all, this is a *real* classroom, with *real student writers.* Some cannot wait to put pencil to paper. But others are nonreaders, or reluctant writers, or challenged by nothing—or bored with everything. As we meet them, one by one, we almost feel as if they are *our* students—and we have a stake in their success.

There's Jason, who can't sit in a chair—and has to write lying on a pillow. Here (hang onto your heart) is Alia, who doesn't write about her favorite weekend or favorite pet because home is not a place she wants to be. Meet Julia, who has a hard time (at first) with words, but can *draw*—and *tell* her story orally—and soon, with coaching, is producing writing she can proudly read. Say hello to Taylor, a challenged writer with minimal interest in the craft—until the day he discovers he's a poet. And then—there's Jimmy. Jimmy, who confesses in a whisper on the first day of school that he cannot read or write. How lucky for him that he, like the other children in this book, has come to *exactly* the right teacher. Megan tells him first not to worry—for it is her job to teach him. Gently, she builds a scaffold to literacy, starting with an easy book that he soon memorizes—and "reads." Letter sounds, high-frequency words, word cards, word walls, conferences, sticky notes with dictated stories all play a part in Jimmy's gradual transformation into a writer. But behind it all—and behind each child's success—is the teacher who believes, the teacher who searches for strengths in the humblest of efforts: This is teaching at its finest. This, in the end, is what makes writing workshop work.

For me, there was also enormous satisfaction in seeing how Megan interweaves process, workshop, and traits. I have struggled all my professional life to help teachers see that the six traits are not a silver bullet, not even a curriculum, but a way of thinking and talking about writing that enormously empowers revision—and therefore, both process and workshop. It is so gratifying to hear from a teacher who really understands this relationship, and sees how things work in harmony, rather than trying to replace one with the other.

Above all, I loved two things about this book. One is Megan's unrelenting commitment to modeling. Good writing instruction doesn't come, after all, from files of clever lesson plans. It comes from showing children writing in action: everything from choosing a topic to touching up pre-publishing details. Megan shows us, step by step, *just* how to do it—gracefully and fearlessly. Writing comes from who we are. So does teaching. In this book, a passionate teacher offers us a challenge: Dare to reveal what's "on your heart and mind" by putting it on the page, and the reward will be huge—children who love to write and who *get it*. She tells her students on the first day, "You are going to love writing workshop. It will become your favorite time of day." There. *There* is a writing goal worth aspiring to. You can always tell the best teachers, can't you? They're the ones to whom you wish you could send your own children.

The second thing that touched my heart? Megan not only loves her student writers, but she has profound *respect* for them. "I remember that all of my students are writers," she says. "They all have something to say." Having something to say is half the battle. Having someone who listens well is the other. Throughout this book, Megan shows us how to *listen* in writing workshop—literally, how to build a workshop centered on conversation. Her students create their own goals and rubrics, coach *her* as she writes, create meaningful, dialogue-rich conferences, and urge one another to take risks. They read with a writer's eye—and a critic's insight. With an understanding that will amaze you, *they* define and then create the classroom atmosphere that nurtures good writing. Want to know how writing workshop should look? Want to know how children learn to work independently? Just ask Megan's students. As we see from her remarkable example, we do our best teaching when we let our students lead us.

Long before I turned the last page, I knew this book would become a favorite. My copy is already well "loved," full of highlighting and notes—reminders of pages (like those that tell Jimmy's story) that I want to revisit. *Thank you*, Megan, for finally opening the door to writing workshop and inviting us all inside. Your book is a gift.

—Vicki Spandel
Author of
The 9 Rights of Every Writer (Heinemann)
Creating Writers, 5th edition and *Creating Young Writers*, 2nd edition (Pearson)
Creating Revisers and Editors (Pearson)
The Write Traits Classroom Kits (Great Source)

ACKNOWLEDGMENTS

The idea for this book began with teachers' questions about writing workshop. In small groups, during classes, after presentations, and in the hallways of my own school, teachers, including me, asked the same questions about how to run a successful writing workshop for our students. I collected these questions on sticky notes, posted them on chart paper, and studied them. I looked for questions that kept repeating themselves in the voices of teachers like me, and I decided to try to answer these questions—not as an expert, but as a teacher in the trenches, just like many of you. To these teachers, I am grateful. You inspired me to think critically about the way I teach writing to my students.

Many of my students (and their parents) shared writing for this book. Their stories, poems, letters, notes, books, and signs are amazing. I never cease to be dazzled by the talent of young writers. My wish is that you continue to write, write, write!

I am extremely indebted to Bonnie Campbell Hill and Nancy J. Johnson. You were the first educators who said, "You should really write this book." For your support, guidance, and friendship, I thank you. You have been wonderful mentors. I include Ralph Fletcher in this nod. Unbeknownst to him, he gave me the confidence to write this book when he said, "No one will tell your story like you."

Working with my editors, Wendy Murray and Maureen Barbieri, has been a wonderful experience. Wendy, you believed in me. You shared my vision, recognized that teachers still have questions about writing workshop, and believed that this book could serve as a huge support. Our original meeting was full of energy and I thank you for your incredible ideas, as well as your confidence in me to deliver.

Maureen, you are so knowledgeable about literacy and you have taught me much. Your detailed comments, along with your sheer will to make this book the best it could be, inspired me. I am indebted to you for your incredible questions and suggestions. You are a mentor and a new friend.

Elizabeth Valway, thank you for bringing this book together. Your hard work is appreciated.

A toast to the children's book authors as there are too many to name. You partner with me daily in my teaching and truly inspire my young writers.

I am grateful to all of the wonderful teachers I work with who inspire me every day: Barb Wagner, Stephanie Campbell, Cynthia Heffernan, Theresa McGrath, Tiffany Wilson, Juli-Anne Ask, and the rest of the crew at Cathcart Elementary School, including my principal, Casey Howard.

A special thank you to Julie Filer, Connie Roepke, and Brenda Wolf for allowing me to share your writing experiences in this book. You are truly remarkable and inspiring teachers, as well as wonderful friends. Julie—thank you for contributing your writing scoring form in Appendix B.

To my friends Toni, Jacque, Carrie, Letitia, Shelly, Kary, Corrine, Shelley, Hope, AnnAline, and Melissa, thank you for your interest and support in this project.

I feel lucky to have Cyndi Giorgis, Katherine Schlick-Noe, and Linda Dobbs as mentors and friends. Barry Hoonan and Janine King, you inspire me with your knowledge and your practice.

My parents, George and Jean Sullivan, could not be better parents, and teachers. Thank you for always believing in all of us and urging us to follow our dreams. And thank you for asking me continually, "How's the writing going?"

To my brothers and sisters, Bill, Tom, Kate, Dee, Nora, Steve, and in memory of Mike, I appreciate your support. To my nieces and nephews, Sarah, Sean, Steve, Kiele, T.J., Kaipo, Katie, Julia, and in memory of Keola, you have all brought me joy.

To my husband, Frank, I appreciate your notes of encouragement, the ones tucked into my suitcase and those that meet me when I get home. Thank you for your love and support, and for your confidence in me as a teacher and a writer.

CHAPTER 1

Okay, I Got the Twenty-Five Notebooks—Now What?

See if this sounds familiar: It is Labor Day weekend. The weather is warm and beautiful. Many of our friends have headed to a lake or the mountains, but we stay put, arranging to sneak in an evening barbecue as I put the last touches on my classroom and plan for the first day of school. A few hours before we are due at my sister's for a cookout, under the guise of needing more hot dog rolls and chips, I tell my husband I'll be back in a bit. He gives me a knowing smile.

Ten minutes later I'm standing in the home furnishing section at Target, my shopping cart already loaded with a bright area rug, spring pillows, and a jazzy lamp for my classroom. Down the aisle, I spot a colleague doing the same thing. We teachers are hopeless—hopelessly driven to making our classrooms warm, exciting places for our new students to be.

Tuesday morning, an hour before school. I've positioned the desks and tables, distributed the crayons, and grouped the sharpened pencils in decorative cans. I've arranged and rearranged the room to ensure a positive learning environment. My plan includes places for small groups to work together, as well as spots for individuals and partners. The new rug adds splashes of reds, greens, yellows, and blues over one corner of the room, providing space to gather as a whole class. Our Author's Chair, painted by a friend especially for this purpose, sits close by (Figure 1.1). Baskets grace the shelves with all kinds of reading material students will devour this year: books, magazines, newspapers, and more. A writing center with paper, a stapler, and other materials invites students to become independent writers. Quotes from famous readers and writers hang on the wall for inspiration, like Kate DiCamillo's "I put my heart on the page when I write." Students will absorb these quotes. A science table and shelf of math materials are ready. Last but not least, I've placed a welcome sign with every student's name in the window, inviting them in for a glorious year of wonder and learning.

I teach a multiage class. Last year it was first and second graders. This year, it is second- and third-grade children. (In this book, I will use examples from all three grades.) Today, some of the students are joining me for a second year; others are new. My room reflects the wide array of learners I will have in my class, such as Lonnie, who loves to read and write, but needs a quiet, away-from-others space to work; Jason, who struggles to sit in a chair but is able to complete tasks while lying on a pillow, with his stomach touching the floor; and Timothy, who excels when working with a partner or group of students. He is a real leader and needs opportunities to practice these skills.

My classroom environment is set up to meet all of my students' needs, providing different kinds of spaces for them to work in small groups, pairs, and alone. Those students here for a second year teach students who are just coming in about expectations and community. They lead the way with their enthusiasm and knowledge about "how things are done."

Donald Graves says, "Children want to write. They want to write the first day they attend school. This is no accident. Before they went to school

Figure 1.1 *Author's Chair*

they marked up walls, pavements, newspapers with crayons, chalk, pens or pencils . . . anything that makes a mark. The child's mark says, 'I am'" (1983, 4). I need to be ready to meet these eager writers.

I have been teaching for twenty-three years, but I know I must continue to learn. And although I have been using a writing workshop model for more than fifteen years, I vow to do it better this year. Over the summer, I reread books on writing by professional authors such as Regie Routman, Lucy Calkins, and Donald Graves. I participated in a book group that read *Boy Writers* by Ralph Fletcher. I found my well-worn, heavily tabbed professional books, including Fletcher's *What a Writer Needs* and *Awakening the Heart* by Georgia Heard, and studied them again.

Before Labor Day, I talked with colleagues about the books I reread. We traded ideas on how we've adapted things and shared new "aha's." We swapped leads on local bargains, such as wide-ruled composition books, three for a dollar, which I covered with decorative paper to make individual writers' notebooks. I stapled plain paper together to make journals for my younger writers.

Throughout the upcoming year, I will continue to reflect on where I have come from, where I am, and where I would like to be as a teacher of writing. I am determined to have the best year ever teaching writing. I have done everything to get ready. But getting ready is the easy part. Getting started is the challenge.

Why This Book Is Different

As I continue to make important adjustments and improvements after fifteen years of writing workshop teaching, I recognize the fallacy of thinking that a single book on writing workshop will be sufficient for teachers to "get it." There are wonderful books already out there by Donald Graves, Katie Wood Ray, Regie Routman, Ralph Fletcher, and other luminaries, yet questions remain. Teachers often say to me, "Yes, but how do you do workshop day to day? How do you begin? What do you say in a conference? What is the rest of the class doing while you confer? What kinds of minilessons are most effective? How do I motivate students to write for a variety of purposes and audiences?"

In this book I set out to answer these questions and more, and in general push the envelope in these four ways:

1. I emphasize differentiated instruction, focusing my teaching on individual student readiness as I explore the unique needs of grades K–3 writers.

2. I pay great attention to the sequence of teaching, including the daily flow and the minutes involved. Pedagogy won't "take" unless teachers have enough real-time guidance.

3. I share my genuine experiences teaching writing in the classroom. I take what I've learned about young writers and good teaching, and mesh them together in a way that will support primary-grade teachers as they work to make writing a priority in their classrooms.

4. I counteract the myth that children naturally read before they write, and that therefore reading should be emphasized over writing in first grade. Research supports that writing leads to reading.

Remind Me. What Is Writing Workshop?

It's gym day. After I drop off my students for P.E., I peek inside my colleague Connie Roepke's second-grade classroom and steal a moment to observe. They are in the middle of writing workshop. The scene is busy. Everyone seems to be on task; all of the students are working steadily. Walking around the room, I smile at what I see. Brenda writes intently and does not seem to notice I am there. Julia and Marcus sit in a corner. Julia reads her paper to Marcus, who asks a question. Two students work at computers, their drafts in front of them, helping each other navigate the keyboard. Jenny is making a book, stapling several papers together. I ask her, "What is your book going to be about?"

"Horses," she answers. "I love horses and I'm going to write a story about a horse that gets lost."

"That sounds great," I encourage her. "Maybe you could come read your book to our class when you finish it." Jenny smiles.

I continue to roam. I finally spot Connie, perched on a small chair, having a conversation with Mason, who struggles with writing. They are discussing the book he wrote. Mason reads a sentence aloud and then explains it further with another detail. Connie praises his ideas and suggests he add the detail to his book. Mason is not so sure, but Connie encourages him and he agrees to revise, with her help.

I glance once more around the room. Students work at tables, desks, even on the floor. Most are independent, but some work in pairs. One girl leans into her neighbor and shows her where to put a period. Jake uses his spelling card to spell a word. At the writing materials corner, a student picks out paper for his next piece. It is not silent, but students are productive. There's a low buzz. It's almost like seeing inside a bee's hive. Everyone has a job. They are busy working on projects (Figure 1.2). Students are in different places. Most write, but some share, some type, and some prepare to write.

Figure 1.2 *Writing Workshop in Progress*

What's Going On? Observations of a Second-Grade Workshop

- Students creating books with paper, stapler, scissors
- Student writing alone
- Students writing in pairs
- Students publishing work—typing on the computer
- Peer conferences (students reading to one another and asking questions)
- Teacher-student conferences
- Students drawing before writing and after writing
- Students using reference materials (books, spelling cards, thesaurus, other students)
- Student rereading and revising, editing work
- Students working on the floor, at desks, at tables, at a computer

So what is writing workshop? The experts all have a unique way of describing this time in the classroom, but they all agree that writing workshop should be an authentic experience for students. Donald Graves (1994) asks us to observe the process of real writers, and try to mimic those conditions in our classrooms.

Regie Routman (2005) challenges us to think of writing workshop as a "time in which everything that writers do to create a meaningful piece of writing for a reader takes place" (174). Key elements include teaching, exploring writing for purpose and audience, holding conferences, and allowing self-chosen topics.

It is, however, Ralph Fletcher and JoAnn Portalupi's definition that creates a truly vivid image for me. They liken writing workshop to a junior high industrial arts class, where students are "spread around the room working on their individual projects." Of course, the instructor may gather students for a short lesson, but the majority of time that students are working, their teacher roams the room, "complimenting, asking questions, making suggestions" (2001, 2).

My Journey to Writing Workshop

I remember back to early days of teaching when I simply stapled journals together and had students write first thing in the morning. I provided no instruction aside from starter sentences. I often wondered why they had a hard time writing and why their writing was not very interesting.

Alia, a struggling first-grade student, showed me that if I wanted students to write well, I must offer them choice. As Donald Graves (2003) explains, "Children need to choose most of their own topics. But we need to show them all the places writing comes from, that it is often triggered by simple everyday events" (xii). In contrast, my wonderful starter sentences, like *My favorite part of my weekend was . . .*, never inspired Alia to write. Each day, she produced a nearly empty page. When I finally asked her why she didn't write, she said, "I want to write about rainbows." I soon found out that Alia did not have a favorite part of her weekend. Home was not a favorite place to be. She did not like animals, so the prompt *My favorite pet would be . . .* did not inspire her either.

While other students were able to write about these topics, many wrote without detail or voice. When I realized that choice was crucial, I told students, "Write about anything. Write about the small things, the everyday things like playing hopscotch or climbing trees or watching a butterfly flit from flower to flower." The good news was that students began writing every day, and with more detail. The bad news was that I still wasn't teaching them anything, so they weren't advancing much. Occasionally, students were successful, through no effort of mine, writing about topics that were important to them. Some students grew as writers simply because they were writing every day.

After years of reading the experts and learning through my students, I synthesized all that wisdom into six key ideas about the workshop model, and what my young writers need. Students need to:

1. understand what makes writing come alive,
2. see lots of models of engaging writing,
3. learn writing skills and strategies through brief minilessons,
4. have time to draft (when they try out those strategies),
5. experience opportunities to talk one-to-one about their writing, and
6. have time to share and reflect about their writing.

What does the workshop schedule look like?

Many people have the idea that writing workshop is an unstructured kind of time in the classroom. Nothing could be further from the truth. It is a very structured time of day (Sloan 2008). I organize my writing workshop in three blocks, as suggested by the experts (Calkins 1994; Fletcher & Portalupi 2001; Routman 2005). Figure 1.3 shows a typical workshop schedule.

I begin writing workshop with a minilesson (Figure 1.4). I might model a piece of writing, thinking aloud my process and highlighting specific teaching points. Or I might read a picture book, pointing out something the author does especially well. Sometimes I use a student piece of writing as a model, with the student's permission.

Next we move to drafting and conferring time. This is the longest block of time. Students need time to practice. They choose their topics and begin

Minilesson	Drafting and Conferring	Sharing/Reflecting/ Author's Chair
(5–15 minutes)	(25–35 minutes)	(5–8 minutes)

Figure 1.3 *Workshop Schedule*

Figure 1.4 *Megan Teaches a Minilesson*

writing or drawing. Meanwhile, I meet with individual students, conferring one-to-one (Figure 1.5). This is when I celebrate students' progress and nudge them to try something new.

We end writing workshop with a sharing/reflecting/Author's Chair time (Figure 1.6). Now students have an opportunity to reflect on what they've learned about themselves as writers and share a line, poem, story, or book with their classmates.

How much time do I spend on writing workshop?

That depends. Figure 1.3 shows some times I typically spend on the three writing workshop blocks, but these are flexible. At the start of a new school year, if I am teaching first grade, my drafting time might be shorter. By late January, when we are in the groove of writing workshop, thirty minutes is standard. As for my minilessons, I try to keep them under ten minutes. Sometimes, they may be under five minutes, particularly if I am finishing up something that I taught the day before. When I use the minilesson period to read a picture book, pointing out interesting language along the way, my lesson might take longer.

Figure 1.5 *Megan Confers with Eleanor*

Figure 1.6 *Jackson Shares His Work*

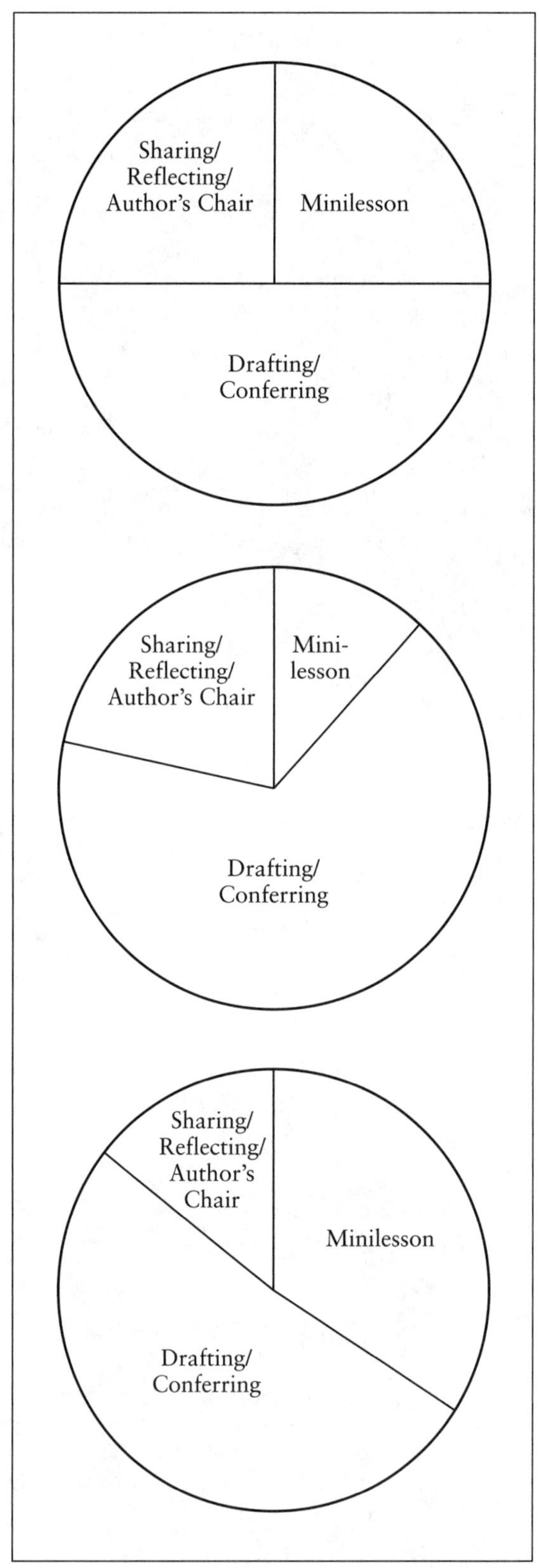

(Source: Fletcher & Portalupi 2001, 11)

Figure 1.7 *Possible Writing Workshop Schedules*

Think of writing workshop as a circle of time (Figure 1.7). A bit of that circle is devoted to a short minilesson. The bulk of the time is devoted to drafting and writing conferences. And the last bit is reflecting/sharing time (Routman 2005; Fletcher & Portalupi 2001; Calkins 1994). I decide how much time I have in my circle and then divide that into proportions that make sense for my students. Most important, I make sure they have time to write every single day.

Writing is one subject where the wide range of abilities and skill levels matters little. The writing workshop model is uniquely suited to meet the diverse needs of my students. I teach a minilesson (and yes, occasionally I pull students into small groups for this), and then students work at their individual ability levels to craft their stories, books, nonfiction pieces, or poems.

For example, I may teach a minilesson about elaborating on ideas. Everyone is expected to experiment with this, but while one student works to include an anecdote or several examples to elaborate, another student tries to add just one more detail as a way to tell more. In my conferences, while holding high expectations, I help students practice what I know they are able to do, and I help them set appropriate goals for themselves as writers. We support each other during drafting times, helping with spelling, thinking of interesting words, and listening for clarity. During sharing/reflecting time we celebrate individual milestones as they read their pieces and share both their accomplishments and challenges as writers.

Elements of Writing Workshop

- Workshop occurs at a specific time of day.
- Students choose the writing topic and teachers emphasize writing for an authentic audience.
- Workshop opens with a high-energy minilesson (such as modeled writing, examples from published books, shared writing, or interactive writing) that either expands the possibilities for writing topics and genres or hones in on matters of craft and skill, such as word choice, transitions, and punctuation.
- Students have adequate time to draft.

- Students work at different stages of the writing process as they develop their own pieces, which may include writing related to learning in math, science, social studies, art, and other subjects being studied.
- Students are encouraged to write in a variety of genres (nonfiction, fiction, personal narrative, poetry, and so on).
- Teacher-student conferences occur almost daily (during drafting time).
- Workshop closes with sharing/reflection time.

(Calkins 1994, Graves 2003, Fletcher 1993, Routman 2005)

How do I begin the year?

No matter what grade level I teach, the beginning of the year is an important time to develop a positive learning environment. My students and I learn to trust one another, and together we set the expectations everyone will follow as members of this class. To begin, I introduce a "Read to Self" time (Boushey & Moser 2006, 49).

On the first day, students are nervous. They come in wide-eyed and a little unsure. Robbie stops at the door, looks in, and says, "Ohhh." He stands there for a moment and then crosses the threshold. Robbie finds the coat rack, and then sits in a chair reading a magazine. I see him look up several times and scan the room with his eyes.

Adena comes in quietly. She doesn't know where to put her backpack. I help her unload her things. We then find her a place to sit. Adena sees the book basket on her table, but does not know what to do. I come over and suggest, "Why don't you read from Dr. Seuss." I choose *One Fish, Two Fish* for Adena, telling her it is one of my favorites. Adena opens the book and now seems at ease.

And then there is Davy. Davy bounds in with all the energy in the world. He runs over to the starfish sitting on the science table and picks it up to examine both sides. Then he darts over to a basket of books about snakes. "I love snakes," he says, with tons of enthusiasm. After redirecting him to hang up his coat and put away his supplies and backpack, I find a quiet corner for Davy to enjoy his book.

Miya and Tatum arrive next. They were students in my class last year and will be here for a second year as the "elders" (Boushey & Moser, 2006). After hugs and a quick chat, Miya and Tatum become my helpers, showing students where to put their things and helping them settle into "Read to Self" time. This is the way we will begin every morning. My returning students know this and they don't miss a beat. The younger students learn by example, and find a place to read.

Students aren't the only ones who are nervous. I too am feeling apprehensive. While I am excited about my new adventure, I still have jitters. Will I get to know these kids and learn to love them like last year's class? Will I meet their needs as writers? What are these students' strengths and interests? Will they learn to love writing like I do? I know I have a huge influence on the answer to that question. How will I help them become skilled writers who write with a clear and unique voice?

Getting to Know My Students

Before I venture into lessons on writing, I must first get to know my students. Who are these twenty-three first, second, or third graders I will have for the next 180 school days? What are their favorite books? What languages do they speak at home? Are they passionate about anything? Is it race cars or ballet? Hanna, a former student, loved dogs. I mean, *really* loved dogs. She talked every day about taking her dog to obedience school. She studied, wrote, and devoured a book about a dog named Balto who traveled across the Alaskan wilderness to bring much needed medication to sick people. Maybe one of my new students will feel the same way. Or maybe there will be another Nick, my dirt bike rider who occasionally came in with a scratch or two, and more often with an exciting story to tell, or Sarah, who loved to jump rope and could jump longer than anyone else in first grade.

Where will our conversations lead us this year? These conversations will inspire our writing. Is there a science expert in the bunch? Last year, Daniel knew everything about bats and taught the rest of us to love bats too. Will there be a Mariner fan who rattles off baseball statistics? And will there be someone like Emily, who quietly wondered about the world around her and shared the new things she observed?

As the first days of school tumble into weeks, I am keenly aware that I am getting to know these individuals, and it feels good. I ask questions, lots of questions. And I listen when they answer because I want my students to know I care and am deeply interested in their lives. I also observe and ask myself questions about these new and fascinating students.

Discovering Students: Some Questions to Consider

- Who is a quiet learner?
- Who asks questions?
- Who needs to hear directions and talk it through with others before trying it on their own?
- Who lacks confidence and needs that little boost to help them experience success?
- Who loves to share?
- Who is reluctant to get started?
- Who is a natural caretaker of others who can mentor peers?

There's a lot for me to learn about my students. Robbie is unsure. He lacks confidence. But Robbie watches others and is smart. He catches on quickly and has a desire to learn. Adena is a bit quiet. She does not say much, but when she does, you better listen. She really has something to say. Jarrett always has something to share with the group—usually an interesting science fact he has learned in a book. And while reading and writing are difficult for Hunter, he asks, "What's that mean?" every time we come to a new word while reading a book. He wants to know and is not afraid to ask. His vocabulary begins to grow immediately.

Vicki Spandel (2005) says, "Our sincere interest in students' lives and their opinions is one of the strongest motivators we have" (21). I believe that. The more I show interest in my students' lives, the more connected they feel to me and our classroom, and the more they want to learn. Alex plays football. His face lights up when I ask about his practices. Julie is a gymnast, and we often talk about new tricks she is learning. We have gymnastics in common, as I was a gymnast for many years. And Demetry lives with his grandfather. I enjoy hearing about their special relationship—the things they do together and the things they talk about. My students know I care because I know who they are outside of school too.

Children work hard when they are in an environment in which they feel loved. They try new things. They take risks. They become confident learners. When students feel a teacher's interest in them as individuals, something amazing happens. They invest in learning. In addition, when children feel that someone is listening, that someone cares about their worries and their triumphs they will trust enough to open up about their lives, and their lives are what they will write about.

Letting My Students Know Me

At the same time, I need to let my students get to know me. So I share about my own life: I love Thai food, and my favorite dish is Swimming Angel. My favorite book of all time is E. B. White's *Charlotte's Web*. I love *Survivor* and watch it faithfully each week. And my favorite section in the Sunday paper is the travel section. I save it to read last. My students know I love to travel, and I often talk about the places I have been and those I want to visit in the future.

I talk about my nieces and nephews, especially the two youngest, six-year-old Katie and four-year-old Julia. They know that Julia loves puzzles and that Katie is a first grader just like some of them. This sharing of my own life is essential. It tells my students I trust them. It is my return gesture when they share their lives with me.

But how exactly does it help me teach writing? My personal stories become my modeled writing. I don't have to invent ideas to write about. I already have a whole file full of topics in my brain, and this folder is growing each day. In fact, I keep a list in my journal. When I observe something of interest, I write it down as a possible topic for writing (Figure 1.8). I often pull this list out in front of my students so they see an example of how writers sometimes keep track of their ideas.

As I share the list, I explain how I can write about May, the silver-haired English woman who greeted me each day with "Hello, Love" when I visited my dad in a nursing facility. She couldn't remember much, but she recognized me over and over again. I tell students about the black cat I saw speed across the road as I was driving up the hill to school one day. I share the questions I had. Where was she hurrying off to? Where had she been all night? Where did the myth about how unlucky it is for a black cat to cross in front of you come from? I show how I can write about my observations of the world around me—feeling a chill in the air one day and tightening my scarf around my neck; observing that the trees suddenly seem to be naked, their bare branches cutting into the clear blue sky.

My stories are of great interest to my students, even though there is nothing extraordinary about them. We have real conversations about life. They begin to share more of their lives each day. These one-to-one, as well as whole-class, conversations become the stories my students write down.

- black cat running across road
Where is she going?
- May - always in pink, greeting each day - "Hello love"
- Black birds sitting in a row on telephone wire - six of them
Trees bare - leaves are gone - blue blue sky
- Julia - her giggle as she tells me about her day - "It was a blast"

Figure 1.8 *Journal Page*

What do I do the first day?

The hardest part about doing something new is getting started. I am often asked, "What do I do first? How do I begin setting up a writing workshop in my classroom?" My answer always comes back to this. Begin at the beginning. Find out what your students know and can do, and start there.

While I get to know my students as individuals, in a general sense, I realize I must also get to know them as writers. I need to find out what they know. What are their strengths? What can they already do? My students come in with skills. If I am going to teach them anything, I must learn to build upon what they already know.

On the first day of school I give students a blank piece of paper. I invite them to draw a picture of anything they want and then write about it. My goal is to observe with a watchful eye. My students will teach me. The sidebar lists some of the things I look for as I move around the room, observe, and confer.

Some Things I Look for in First-Day Writing

- What do students choose to write about? (This says a lot about who they are.)
- Do students find it difficult to settle on a topic?
- Can students elaborate upon an idea?
- How comfortable are students with letters and sounds?
- What is their spelling and punctuation like?
- Does their drawing match their text?

Meggan, a special needs second grader, gets right to work drawing a colorful picture of her family. She labels her mother, father, sister, and herself. She is very proud of her work. I take out my assessment notebook, a binder in which I keep anecdotal notes about my students, one student per section. As I roam around the room, I jot down my observations.

Ricky, a first grader, draws a yellow dog in the middle of his paper—nothing else. He tells me, "This is my grandpa's dog. His name is Dixie."

I encourage Ricky, "Why don't you write that down?"

"I don't know how," he replies.

"Then you tell me again and I will write it down for you." Ricky smiles as I record his idea. He reads his sentence back to me. Again, I take a moment to jot down what I notice and possible *next steps* for Ricky (see Figure 1.9).

Neil is a very capable second grader who did not enjoy writing last year. His previous teacher placed more emphasis on handwriting than creativity, and Neil rarely got to choose his topics. Today, Neil draws a quick picture and sits quietly. "How's it going?" I ask.

Observations	Next Steps
Drew picture of g-pa's dog. Topic means a lot to Ricky. Lacked confidence to write text. Dictated to me.	Ask more questions to get Ricky to elaborate. Share pencil and work on stretching out sounds. (Assess letter-sound knowledge.) Direct him to word wall for high-frequency words.

Figure 1.9 *Observations of Ricky*

"I can't think of anything to write."

"What do we have here?" I prod.

"This is a picture of my camping trip."

"That's a great first sentence," I encourage. "Why don't you start with that?" After a few moments I ask another question, prompting a conversation with Neil about his experience. Neil's eyes light up as he talks about his marshmallow, which caught fire while he was roasting it. I nudge him to focus on that detail and elaborate. Again, I stop to take notes (Figure 1.10).

Last, there's Miya, a quiet but confident third grader. She draws a picture of herself on a horse. By the time I stop to check on her, she has written several sentences reaching halfway down the page, detailing the first time she ever rode a horse.

All of my students are in different places. They need different things from me. Ricky needs me to be there for him: to praise him for his picture and idea, to boost his confidence, and to be his secretary. In a few days I will encourage Ricky to put pencil to paper and write himself. I will be there to help him sound out the words and to remind him that the word *is* appears on our word wall. I will guide Ricky to put finger spaces between his words so his writing will be easy to read. Then I will ask Ricky to reread his own writing to see if it makes sense.

Neil needs to be nudged with a different approach. Neil is very bright. He can tell you facts about almost anything and loves to share orally. Neil needs to see the power of writing by discovering that it is an effective way to communicate ideas. So I meet him where he is, using how he likes to communicate as a starting point, before he writes. I ask him to tell me his story, and I jot down his words on sticky-notes, recording important ideas. I give Neil these notes as reminders of all he has to say. I number his ideas to help Neil organize his writing. I won't leave without helping Neil think of a strong lead sentence.

Observations	Next Steps
Drew picture of camping but did not know what to write. Has a lot to say orally when asked questions. Does not elaborate much.	Help Neil find a focus for his writing and elaborate. Record his ideas during our conversation on sticky notes to remind him he has lots to write.

Figure 1.10 *Observations of Neil*

And Miya—I ask her to read what she has so far, listening intently as she talks about this important event. I praise her for her details and we chat about how it really felt to get on a horse for the first time. I encourage her to add those special details to her writing and talk about where those ideas may fit. As I move away, Miya is busy revising.

I am gathering precious information today. A few students write many sentences about their pictures, adding relevant details. They are confident writers. Most students write two or three sentences with varied knowledge of spelling, capitalization, and punctuation. Then, there are a handful of students who have never written their own thoughts on paper before. Their interest and confidence level is low.

I lament, remembering last year's class: Daryia, my thoughtful poet; Bobby, our word choice expert; and Matt, our king of details. All of them enjoyed writing and always had so much to say. They loved writing workshop and begged for extra time to write. Will my students reach a similar point this year?

After school I gather today's writing in front of me. I am determined to look for what is there, rather than what is missing. Robbie put a few letters down and used three colors in his picture. Kara wrote: *This is my dog. He is a wiener dog.* Kara has an idea and one detail. Tatum showed her ability to elaborate and spell most words correctly in her page about Disneyland. Her picture is quite detailed.

I file each paper in individual student folders. This will be my baseline for each young writer. I reflect on what I observed during writing time: eagerness, confidence, reluctance, uncertainty. This is the place from which we will start. I cannot think back about last year's class, or the class from the year before. I must meet this year's students where they are. Our journey begins here.

CHAPTER 2

What Do the First Six Weeks Look Like?

It is the second day of school. Sunshine and a crowd of eager children's faces greet me as I open my classroom door. Students tumble in today, knowing just what to do. I watch as they find spots around the room with piles of books at their sides. I say hello, and receive notes and pictures from students, already showing their love of school. As the noise quiets to a soft murmur, I take a moment to reflect about how quickly the year will go.

Before I know it Halloween and Presidents' Day will be here and gone, and I will find myself saying my June good-byes to twenty-five students and families. I know that all good teaching aims for specific end results. I want this class of students to love writing, to the point that it takes them in surprising directions, the way it did last year for Jackson and Ryan, who began a "Fascinating Haiku" club for students to read and write haiku. (And they did!) All of its members were boys. Then there was Eleanor. At the end of the year, her mother told me Eleanor's poems and stories were "everywhere in our house." And Jordyn. On the last day of school she chose writing as a way to deal with her emotions about the school year ending.

Last

The last bus to ride,
The last recess to have,
The last whistle to blow,
The last poem to write,
The last book to read,
The last song to sing,
The last bus to ride,
The last day of school.

This passion and excitement about writing is what I want for this year's students. I want them to become writers because they love it!

It is only Day 2, but what I do today, and tomorrow, and next week will affect the students I say good-bye to in June. Day 1 is under our belt. Now I need to choreograph my first week, and then my first month. My goal is to take small steps, encouraging a learning environment that will foster writing success.

The Reading-Writing Connection: A Good Starting Point

If I want my students to become good writers, I have to start by sharing what good writers do. Shelley Harwayne (1992) suggests that we "prepare fertile ground and do what the experts suggest: 'Bathe, immerse, soak, drench your students in good literature'" (1). What better way to do this than by providing lots of opportunities for students to read many different kinds of books? So my room is filled with great fiction, nonfiction, poetry, fairy tales, biography, word-play books, songbooks, and more (Figure 2.1). Students have many opportunities to read on their own and with others (Figure 2.2). I want them to discover books, both as readers and as writers. I want them to explore with

Figure 2.1 *Baskets of Books*

Figure 2.2 *Students Reading*

wonder the delight of a good book. I ask students, "What genres do you enjoy reading? Maybe these are the same genres you will enjoy writing. What topics do you enjoy reading about? Maybe you would like to write about these topics, as well."

We also read together (Figure 2.3). I read aloud and we do shared reading. As a class, we wonder at books like Denise Fleming's *Where Once There Was a Wood.* Fleming begins, "Where once there was a wood . . . " A rabbit hops across a wooded field.

I ask, "What does this author do to make us want to turn the page?"

Tatum answers, "She doesn't really finish the sentence."

Johnny adds, "You wonder what is going to happen."

"I agree," I say. "Good authors make us want to turn the page to find out what is going to happen next."

We continue reading Fleming's book and I ask, "What words create images you can see in your mind?" We ooh and aah at the words Fleming chooses: *unfurl, slither, rummage, roosted.* We talk about these energetic verbs and how the author must have chosen them carefully. I use the language of writers with my students (verbs, adjectives, simile, metaphor) interchangeably with other descriptors. Students learn these terms very quickly and begin to use them nat-

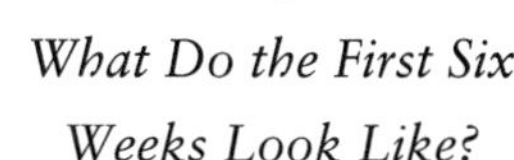

Figure 2.3 *Megan Reads to Students*

urally. We act out Fleming's verbs and decide to post some on our *Interesting Word Wall* to remind us to choose powerful words when we write. As we work our way through the book, students comment about the different animals Fleming includes and about the harsh reality that awaits us at the end of the story.

Key Lesson Points

This lesson:

- helps students recognize that an author makes choices
- illustrates the effectiveness of a good first sentence or lead (drawing the reader in)
- introduces students to great word choice in a piece of writing
- builds vocabulary

- provides a reference (chart or word wall) for future possible word choices
- offers an example of a complete story with a clear sense of order
- inspires students to want to write like Denise Fleming

Following the lesson, I encourage students to read books with writers' eyes. I ask questions such as: What does this author do to make the story interesting? How do the words in the poem make you feel? Why do you think the poet repeated that word? What kind of sentence did the author use to begin this nonfiction book about our solar system? If we train children to look for the details that make a piece of writing good, they will start to experiment in their own writing. Harwayne (1992) says, "Students need to value listening to good literature, talking about good literature, and owning good literature before they are asked to have a good lead or to use surprising details" (3). We need to provide tons of opportunities for our students to talk about good literature, not just as readers but as writers, so they identify what works in a piece of writing, and why it works. As assessment expert Rick Stiggins once said to a group of educators, "It's a funny thing; if you show kids the target, they might just hit it."

Professional Books for Learning About Read-Aloud and Shared Reading

- *On Solid Ground: Strategies for Teaching Reading K–3* by Sharon Taberski
- *The Read Aloud Handbook* by Jim Trelease
- *Reading Essentials* by Regie Routman
- *Reading Magic: Why Reading Aloud to Our Children Will Change Their Lives Forever* by Mem Fox
- *The Reading Workshop: Creating Space for Readers* by Frank Serafini
- *The Wonder of It All: When Literature and Literacy Intersect* by Nancy J. Johnson and Cyndi Giorgis

Sharing My Reading and Writing

My reading instruction for the year begins with a "show and tell" of sorts. I share with students all of the texts I am currently reading (Routman 2003). I bring in a basketful of books, magazines, catalogs, and newspapers. I share a novel, a few professional books, the travel section of the newspaper, a Pottery Barn catalog, a daily devotional, and an instructional pamphlet for my DVD player.

I introduce each text, sharing with students my purpose for reading, as well as how I go about working through each text. For instance, I read the novel from beginning to end. I skim for information in the pamphlet, and I look for an interesting chapter in one of the professional books and begin there. We talk about the variety of material I am reading, all in the same week. This demonstration promotes great conversation about all of the different purposes we have when we read and how important reading is to our lives.

Likewise, I want students to see how important writing is to *their* lives. I begin by sharing my own writing samples from the past week. These include emails, letters, a grocery list, a draft for an article, a to-do list, notes taken at my mother's last doctor appointment, a thank-you card, my journal, and a parent letter to go home this week. I don't read every piece, but I share with students my purpose and audience for each. I then talk about how purpose and audience are key factors I use to determine whether I will revise and edit or let a piece stay as it is first written.

I discuss which pieces were easy to write and which ones took a lot of thinking. For instance, my grocery list was easy to write. It is simply a list of words: *milk, eggs, cheese, ham, chicken, Cheerios, bananas, tea,* and *JELL-O.* I just had to think quickly about what I needed and write the items down.

My thank-you card was to my friend for a gift I received (Figure 2.4). I wanted it to flow so I took more time with it, thinking about my word choice and sentence length. My first draft would be my final, so I made sure I knew how to spell every word before I wrote them down. I also took time to write neatly since I wanted my friend to read it easily.

My article was about students self-reflecting on their writing. It took much more thought. I didn't worry about neatness. I crossed out whole lines and wrote in the margins. I reread and revised many times. I let students see my "scratch outs."

As for my parent letter, I tell students that I will ask another teacher to read it, to check for clarity and correct spelling, before I send it home. I talk about how important writing is in both my job and my personal life.

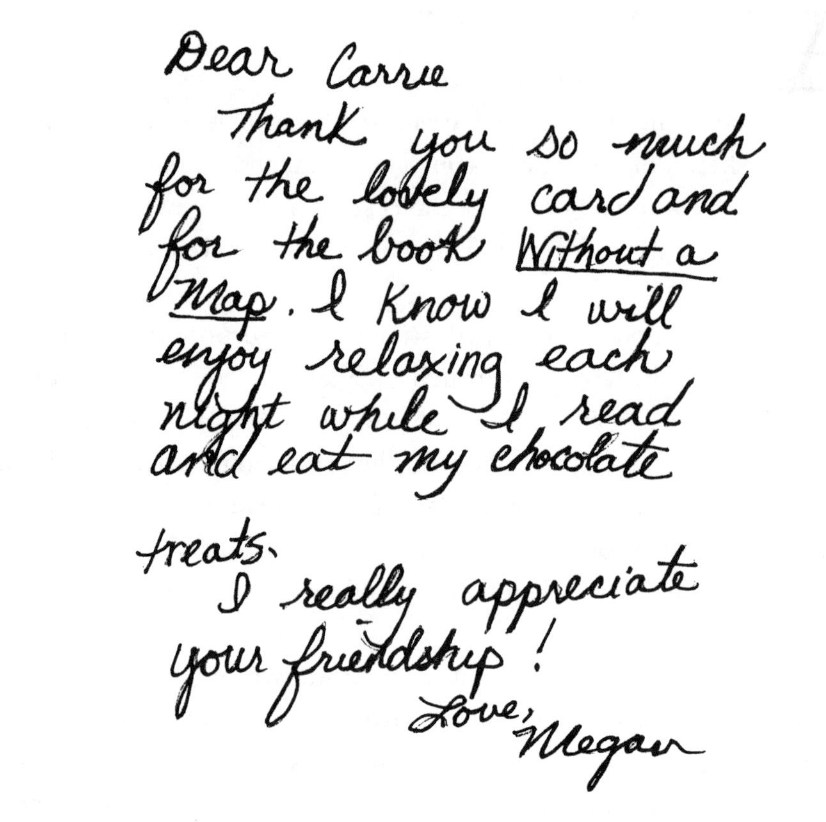

Dear Carrie
Thank you so much for the lovely card and for the book Without a Map. I Know I will enjoy relaxing each night while I read and eat my chocolate treats.
I really appreciate your friendship!
Love,
Megan

Figure 2.4 *Megan's Thank-You Card*

Sharing Student Writing

Then I challenge students to think of the writing they do at home and school. Emily shares, "I wrote a letter to my grandma yesterday."

Katie says, "I made a sign for my bedroom door. It says, *My room.*"

I ask, "Who just celebrated a birthday?"

"I did," Michael answers.

"Did you help write invitations?"

Michael nods.

I encourage students, "Let's think of all the ways we use writing in our daily lives. This can include anyone in your family." We record ideas on a class chart (Figure 2.5). This becomes a visible reminder of how important writing is to us.

Why Choice of Topic Matters

With all of our mandated assessments requiring students to write to a prompt, some might ask, "Why give students choice at all? If they don't choose topics for the test, why should they choose topics for daily classroom writing?"

Figure 2.5 *All the Writing We Do*

I would argue that we are not just teaching students to write well for a test, but to become effective writers throughout their lives. I agree that students should have the opportunity to practice writing to prompts. They will need this skill at various times in life: for interviews, job-related writing, and educational endeavors. However, if our goal is to teach students to be good writers, we must also afford them choice of topic. When I give students choice, they truly amaze me. I see writers shine. When students write about a topic of interest, they write about what's on their hearts and minds.

I recently visited a school that uses a scripted writing program. In one second-grade classroom, the prompt was set and students were carefully guided through each detail. At the break, I asked the teacher if students ever got to choose their own writing topics. "Not really," she answered, and then after a long pause she added, "But when they do choose their topics, their writing is so much better."

Author Mem Fox (1993) lists *choice of topic* as the "first consideration for writing or teaching writing." Fox argues, "Real writers choose their own topic; therefore, children should be allowed to do the same." She explains that when she has decided on a topic for a book chapter, her editor never tells her, " 'No, you can't write about that. Write about this.' " Instead, her editor shows interest in the topic (36). Likewise, Donald Graves (1994) includes *choice* in his list of conditions for effective writing (106).

I want students to learn to choose topics they know and care about so they will write well. I also want students to see their lives as worthy topics for writing. So as children come into the classroom, day after day, bubbling over with things to share—*I lost my tooth; my dog had puppies; we went camping*—I respond, "That would make a great writing topic," because it *will.* Vicki Spandel (2005) states, "Writers who discover their own topics write with voice and commitment" (18). I believe this because I see it every day. Still, students don't always know how to decide on a topic. So I model. This becomes one of my first writing lessons. I gather students and begin by thinking aloud the process I follow when choosing a topic for writing.

My Lesson for the First Week of School: Teaching Students to Choose Topics

"Today, I'm not sure what I will write about. I have lots of things on my mind. Yesterday I had to take my dad to the emergency room. I could write about that." I jot down *dad—emergency room* at the top right corner of my chart paper and continue, "I also could write about spiders because I know a lot about that topic and I just read a great book that could help me." I write *spiders* underneath my first idea. Then I say, "You know what is also on my mind? I've noticed that a few leaves on the tree outside our window are turning red." As I record this third idea, I say, "I think I will write about the start of fall. I am beginning to feel a chill in the air, too, so I'm thinking summer is coming to an end." I begin writing in front of my students.

> *I know there are seven days left of summer, but I am beginning to see early signs of Fall.*

I continue writing a short piece, modeling for students my process for elaborating; asking myself questions; talking about what I see, hear, and feel; rereading my text to make sure it sounds right and makes sense. Here is my finished piece.

> *I know there are seven days left of summer, but I am beginning to see early signs of Fall. There is a slight chill in the air, even when the sun is out. When I look at the trees I see glimpses of oranges and faint yellows, even a few vibrant reds, in the leaves. When I listen very carefully, I hear cheers of football fans and band music making their way toward me. It is so hard to say good-bye to summer, but if I have to, I will take this beautiful and exciting season of Fall.*

Key Lesson Points

This lesson:

- encourages students to consider different topics for writing
- shows students that "everyday happenings" can make worthy topics
- emphasizes the importance of liking your topic
- highlights the importance of rereading over and over to make sure your writing makes sense and sounds right
- models the helpfulness of "talking your story" first
- demonstrates that writers ask themselves questions as they write
- shows that a topic considered, but not chosen, can be written about another day
- explores what writers may be thinking as they write
- demonstrates how writers elaborate on an idea

I encourage students to write about what they know, what they like, and what's important to them (Figures 2.6 and 2.7). Over and over in the first weeks of school, I model, thinking aloud my process for choosing a topic. They see the choices I make: the everyday, ordinary, real-life topics. They see that I'm truly interested in my choices. These demonstrations encourage students to see the significance of their own lives, to recognize that simple ideas like washing dishes or taking in the garbage bins often make the best writing topics for young children.

Book for Poetry Writing

***Kids' Poems* by Regie Routman**

These short, practical books by Regie Routman (2000) are filled with illustrated poems written by students that teachers may read aloud and photocopy for their class. They also include a simple framework for guiding poetry. Grade-specific, there is a volume for kindergarten, first grade, second grade, and grades three/four.

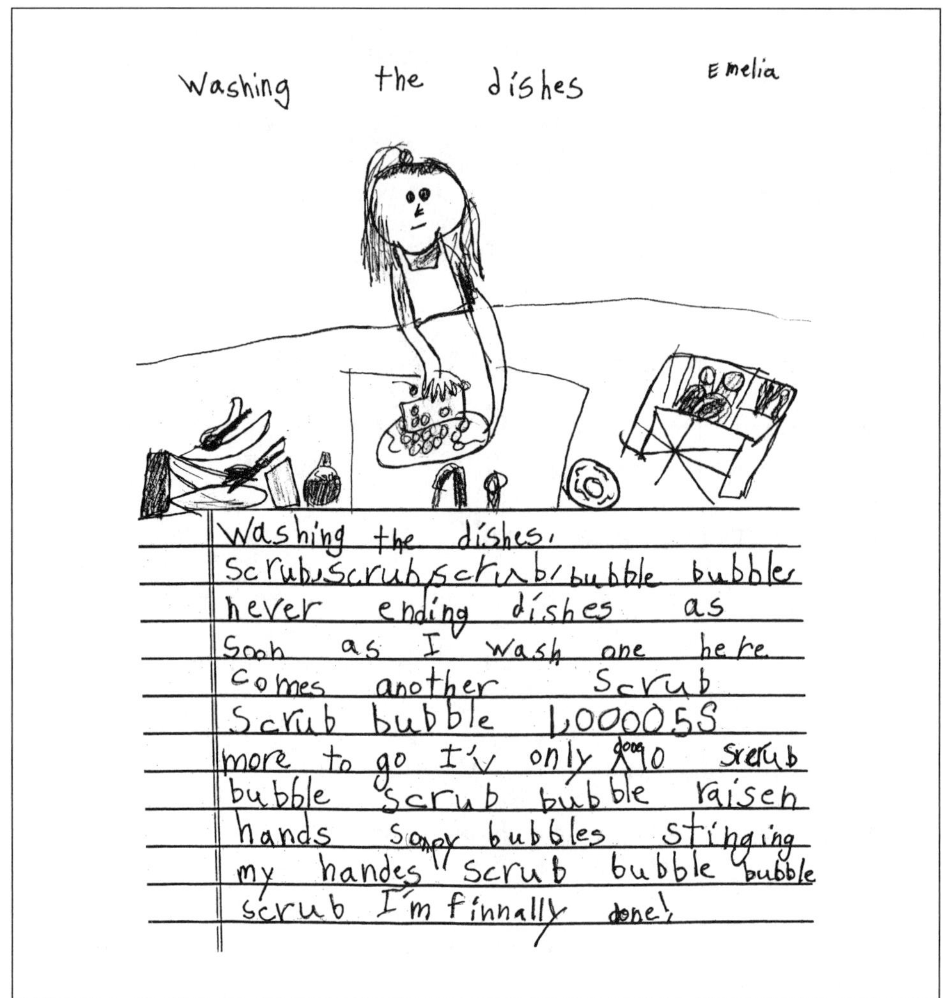

Figure 2.6 *Emelia Writes About Washing the Dishes*

When I feel students are ready, we create two class charts (see Figure 2.8). The first lists what makes a good writing topic:

- something you know about
- something you like (you're interested in it)
- something you have a book about
- something you wonder about

Taking in the Garbage Bins

Running outside.
Running very fast.
Trying to get it over with.
It seems like my dog is racing me.
As always,
She wins.
So when I finally get there,
I grab the garbage bins,
And use the way my brother
Showed me.
It makes them balance.
I grab them and run!
When I get inside the house,
My parents are very happy...
Because
I did my job!!!

Malcolm

Figure 2.7 *Malcolm Writes About Taking in the Garbage Bins*

The second chart lists how we get ideas:

- We have an experience.
- We read a book.
- We talk with someone.
- We notice something.
- We draw a picture.

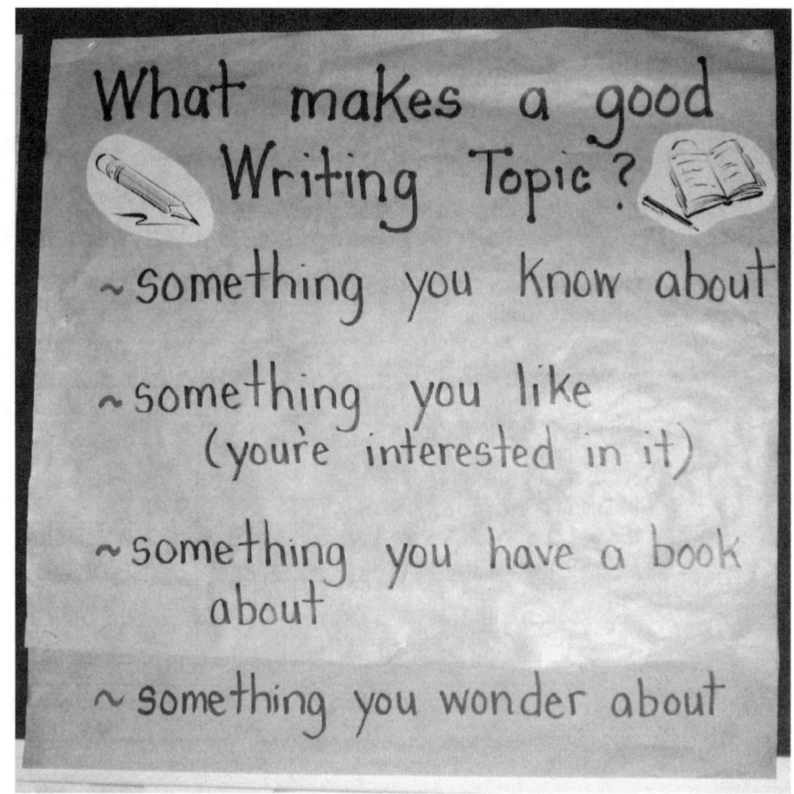

Figure 2.8 *Students Help Create Class Charts*

These hang on the wall all year as reminders for students as they write, and for me to refer to during minilessons.

On a subsequent day, we make a chart of *Great Writing Topics*. Students contribute subjects they might like to write about (Figure 2.9). This chart serves as an inspiration when students are deciding on their own writing topics.

How do I teach young students to be independent writers?

Now that we have established a positive writing environment and students have had some lessons in choosing topics, it is time for them to practice becoming independent writers. Teachers often ask me, "How do you get young students to write independently for a sustained period of time?"

My answer: "Like anything else, first you teach them; then you expect they can do it."

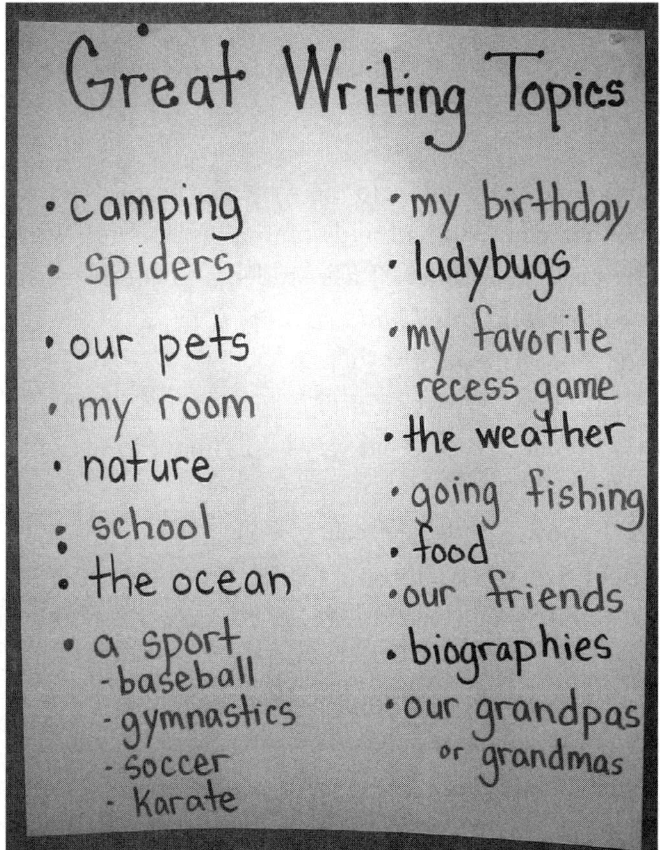

Figure 2.9 *Great Writing Topics Chart*

My Lesson: Building Writing Stamina

The drafting part of my writing workshop lasts roughly thirty minutes. But students do not begin writing this long on the first day. We start out slowly and build. Janet Angelillo (2002) suggests, "If you expect students to write for long stretches, you must help them build stamina" (26). Similarly, Gail Boushey and Joan Moser (2006) speak about "needing to teach children how to build stamina for independent work" (24).

I display and explain the word *stamina*, using the definition from the *Scholastic Children's Dictionary* (1996): "the energy and strength to keep doing something for a long time." I then compare the writer to a marathon runner. Here is a person who runs the ultimate race. She doesn't get up one day and run twenty-six miles. Instead, she trains for months, beginning with one mile, adding a mile or two each day. On race day, the runner needs certain things in order to run effectively. She wears the right shoes, and a visor to keep the sun from her face. Along the route, volunteers hand her cups of water so she will stay hydrated. All of these things, along with her steady training, contribute to the runner's stamina, resulting in success when she completes the race.

Like the runner, certain conditions will help the writer be more effective. So I ask the questions, "What will help us build stamina as writers? What will help us write for long periods of time?" I ask students to complete the statement: *During writing workshop I will build stamina if I . . .*

Adena raises her hand, "If I write quietly."

"Great idea, Adena," I respond. "Anyone else?"

Ben says, "If I use my spell-check card. That way I don't have to stop and ask."

"If I write about what I know," adds Rebecca.

"Yes, we've talked about that when choosing topics. It is much easier to keep writing if you write about what you know," I encourage. "Any other ideas?"

Luca says, "If I ask for help quietly so I don't bother others."

Nathan adds, "If I write the whole time."

I record student ideas on a class chart (Figure 2.10).

Now that we know what will help us build stamina, we get to work. On Day 1, students begin with five minutes of sustained writing. I praise children for work well done. On Day 2, we try adding two minutes, making our total writing time seven minutes. If we are successful, I ask students if they would like to increase our writing time on Day 3. Students are very eager and love the challenge. Ryan says, "I think we can do ten minutes." Amber looks a little unsure.

I ask, "What do you think? Is that too much of a challenge?"

Amber says, "I can try."

"Well, that's all I ask of you. Shall we give it a go?" Students agree and we actually write for eleven minutes that day. Amber is very excited. I praise her, along with the whole class, for their efforts.

We build our writing endurance each day by adding a few more minutes to our drafting time. Of course, students lead the way on this. It is important that they write the whole time. Things don't always go smoothly. There are times when one child or even several children find this difficult. When this happens, we slow down. We adjust. As soon as someone is not writing, we stop, gather together, and talk about what went well. This continues, even if the pace is slow, until students are able to write for twenty-five to thirty minutes. Sometimes this includes drawing pictures, but students are expected to work quietly and semi-independently, nonetheless.

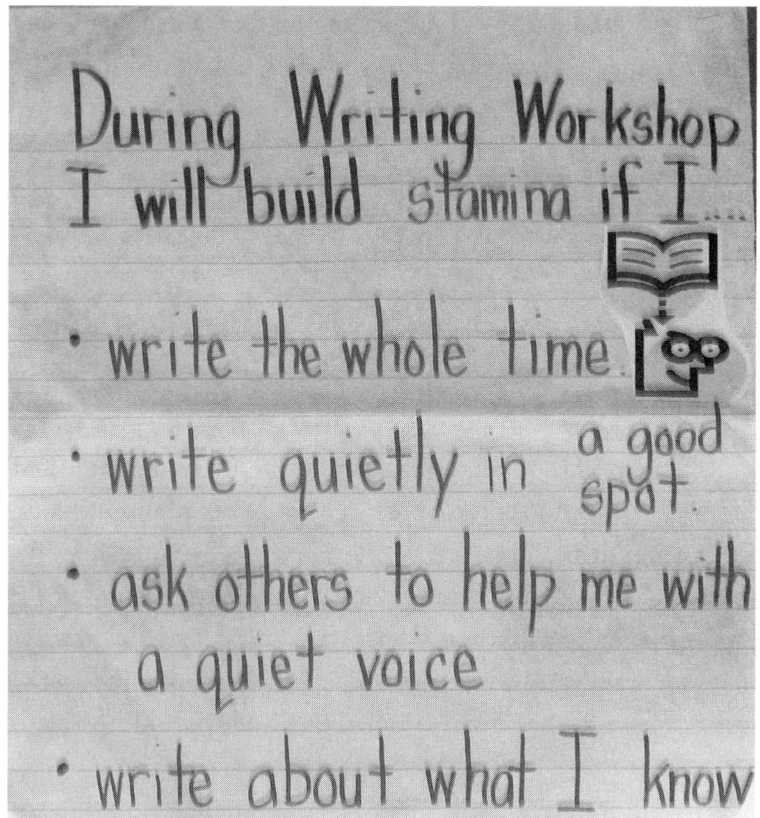

Figure 2.10 *Students' Stamina Chart*

During this time I "stay out of the way" (Boushey & Moser 2006, 25). This may sound funny, but if I am giving students positive reinforcement like "Great job writing quietly" or even just standing close by to encourage "good writing behaviors," students will expect this and they will not become independent. I want them to work without me, so that I am available to meet individually with students for writing conferences.

We keep our charts up in the room as reminders of our writing workshop expectations. We revisit these charts, talking about why it is important to find a good place to write and stay there, or why it is important to be quiet during this time. Students set the rule for conferring with a friend, getting supplies, or picking a writing spot. The rule is simple: you must do it quietly and without disturbing other writers.

We practice these things too. For instance, one student models getting supplies the wrong way (making noise, talking with a friend along the way, and taking too much time), and then another student models the correct way to get supplies (quietly, quickly, and without disturbing others). We talk about our expectations and why they are important. Students practice again and get positive feedback for "doing it right."

While I want students to develop endurance for writing, I also want them to continue to love writing. The writing workshop is a precious gift of time to write about what interests students. It is important for me to keep the joyfulness of this time intact. If anything interferes with this, I must regroup, and reflect on what I need to change.

What about materials? Notebooks? Paper? What else do I need?

Materials and management of those materials can really bog us down. Deciding whether to use spiral notebooks, composition books, or plain old paper can leave us feeling confused and unsure if we're "getting" the workshop idea correctly. Before we get too excited about which materials to use, however, we need to remember one thing: It's not so much what students write on that's important; it's that they write, and write often. Then, the students and teacher need to feel comfortable with the choice of writing materials and be able to manage them with ease.

We all have different preferences. My choice mostly depends on the students' grade level. For kindergardeners and first graders I choose paper. I realize that students at this age need choices, so I set up a slotted box with all kinds of paper: plain paper, paper with lines, paper with half space/half lines, full size, and half sheets. I have some ready-made books stapled together, but I also provide a stapler, tape, sticky-notes, and glue sticks so students can create their own books.

Katie Wood Ray and Lisa B. Cleaveland (2004) describe writing workshop for young writers as "a happy place where we make stuff" (1). Young children are creators. Show them how to fold paper and make a book and they get excited. It may not look perfect. The edges might not line up neatly, but it is authentic. They own it. I think of Robbie, who wrote a series of books: *The Car Ride 1* through *The Car Ride 10*. I helped him staple together the first few books in the series, but then he took over, cutting, folding, and stapling his books on his own. And he was proud! His first book was three pages, along with a title page:

The Car Ride

We went past a school.
We went past a truck.
We went past a boat.

I watched as Robbie wrote each of his car ride books (Figure 2.11). His language expanded as I encouraged him to use specific words to tell his story. Robbie's spelling of high-frequency words improved as Robbie began to use the resources available to him. My conversations with Robbie included encouragement and teaching about using his spelling card and our class word wall. I showed Robbie how to use word families to help him figure out the spelling of different words with similar patterns.

For second graders, again I provide a selection of paper (Figure 2.12). Students at this age love to create artsy books as well. (I often think they should start a Crafts Guild together; they are so engaged with the fine art of bookmaking!) They need many different kinds and sizes of paper for their various books. Grant recently asked me to help him find the exact kind of paper he wanted to use. He needed a certain shade of red for his cover and he wanted the paper to have a certain kind of lines. I loved that Grant was so particular in his plan for his writing.

I also make writer's notebooks available toward the middle of the year. Some students request this and are ready to keep their writing in a notebook. I often begin with a notebook just for poetry. This provides a nice segue for students as they learn to use a writer's notebook. I prefer the composition

Figure 2.11 *Pages from Robbie's First* Car Ride *Book*

Figure 2.12 *Writing Center with Materials*

books because the pages stay together and students have a hard surface to write on if they are not writing at a table or desk. Some teachers love using spiral notebooks for their students' writing journals instead.

Third graders tend to prefer writer's notebooks right away, but they also like to create books and write on single sheets of paper (Figure 2.13). Again, I use composition books but spiral notebooks work great too. The notebook provides a place for students to collect new thoughts and ideas for writing, as well as a place to revisit those ideas they want to revise and possibly publish.

Writing Folders

Because I choose to let students write on individual sheets of paper and create their own books, I must have a place for their work. I use two folders. First, each student has a writing workshop folder. This folder has two pockets and holds writing that students are currently working on, as well as a spelling card for editing (Figure 2.14). Students keep their writing workshop folders in their desks or cubbies.

Next, when students are finished with a piece of writing (whether it has been published or not), they also need a place to keep their work. I could choose to send these writing pieces home, but I like students to keep them in

Figure 2.13 *Joelle Selects Paper During Writing Workshop*

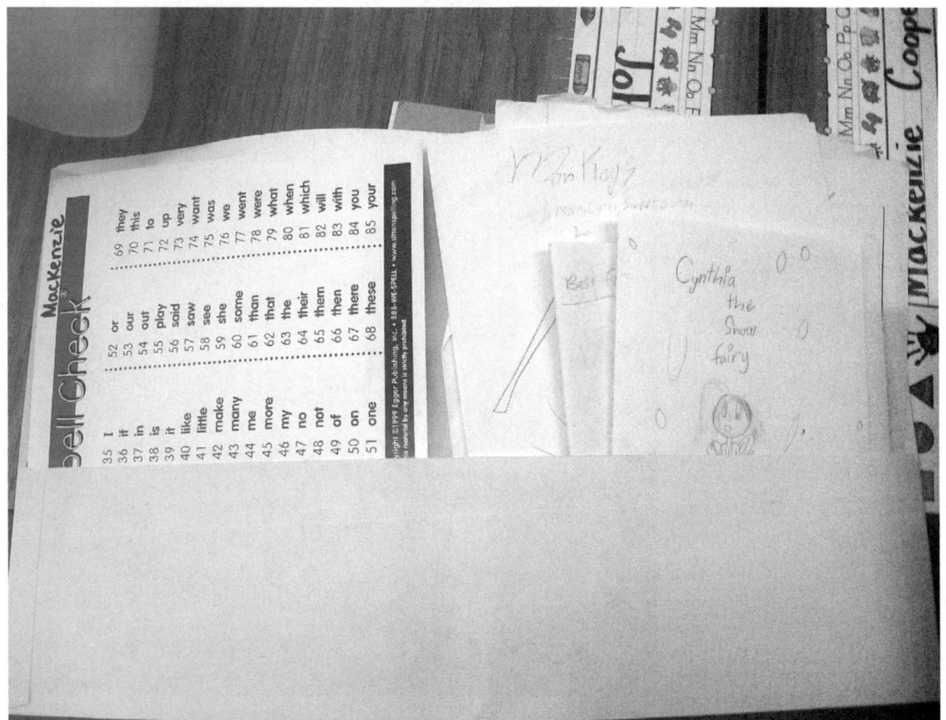

Figure 2.14 *Writing Workshop Folder*

the classroom as a record of how they've grown as writers. I fold and staple large pieces of chart paper to make two-pocket folders that are fifteen-by-fifteen-inches square (see Figure 2.15). We keep these folders in a crate in the classroom, and students visit their folders to choose pieces for portfolio picks, to look over their work during reading and writing times just for fun, and to share their writing with other students (Figure 2.16).

I ask students to design and decorate their folder covers the first week of school. For third-grade students using writing notebooks, I either let them choose already covered notebooks, picking out designs and colors they like, or I let students help cover the notebooks themselves.

Time to Write

I try to set a schedule that works for my students, and for me. Each year I look at my entire day and see where I can carve out forty-five minutes to an hour for writing workshop. What time will work? I try to keep this time consistent. Students will write best if they can anticipate their writing time. Once, I heard

Figure 2.15 *Writing Folders in Crate*

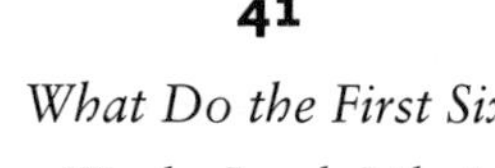

Figure 2.16 *Students Share Their Writing*

a student say, "I know I get to write right after first recess so I'm not always asking the teacher, 'When is writing workshop?' I just know." As Donald Graves (1991) says, "Each morning, children from all these backgrounds—which differ in family and ethnic customs, in their uses of space and time, in their understanding of the meaning of speech and print—enter the classroom. You prepare for their entrance with a predictable classroom which encourages highly creative, unpredictable, and delightful expression to flourish" (34).

I give students time to write. I let them practice choosing topics, writing text to go with pictures, adding more to their stories, and writing freely in their notebooks. These first few weeks tell me a lot about which students love to write and which ones will need me to "sell it to them": to model an excitement and love for writing.

We have incredible power to persuade our students that writing is fun. I always tell students the first day of school, "You are going to love writing workshop. It will become your favorite time of day." Some students look at me with odd expressions, but I am always right. Because I love to write, and I show students every day how exciting and powerful writing is, they start to love writing too. It is inevitable.

Final Thoughts

There's a lot to do to get a writing workshop going in our classrooms. It seems overwhelming as every task appears to be urgent, but we can't do everything the first week. It's important that we remember to take things one step at a time. We need to prioritize. We need to start with one necessary task and build upon that. We must be patient and believe it will happen. We will build writing workshops with our students. It will be productive and fun. Students will look forward to this time each day, and not only will they succeed as writers, they will thrive!

What to Do the First Six Weeks

The First Week

1. Encourage a positive learning environment:

   Get to know students as individuals.

   Let students get to know me.

2. Get to know students as writers. Have students write. Record my observations.

3. Set up writing materials. Have students decorate writing workshop folders, long-term writing folders, and/or writing notebooks.

The First Four to Six Weeks

1. Connect reading and writing. Show students what good writing looks like. Include picture books in minilessons about what makes good writing.

2. Share my own writing: emails, letters, journals, and so on. Talk about purpose for writing and variety of writing.

3. Teach students about choosing topics. Create class charts.

4. Teach students to be independent. Build writing stamina. Create a class chart. Practice being independent writers.

5. Give students ample time to write. Set a schedule.

6. Begin meeting with students for writing conferences.

CHAPTER 3

How Do I Teach Writing?

Planning Minilessons

I've set the tone and created expectations. Students have learned about writing stamina and have practiced writing for sustained periods of time. They've learned about choosing topics and reading books with a writer's eye. We've discussed materials. Students have their own writing notebooks, or they have access to and are learning to manage paper, books, and writing folders. Now what? How do I dive deeper? What is the next step to keep writing workshop going with my students?

What Do I Teach Now? Diving Deeper into Writing Workshop

I believe students should lead us in what we teach. Their interests and needs should guide us as we plan and teach our lessons. What we see in one-to-one conferences or whole-class shared writing experiences reveals a lot about what students need. I plan my lessons with a watchful eye, but I also have a sense of order in mind, especially at the beginning of the year, as to the minilessons I will teach my young writers.

Revisiting What Has Been Taught

I don't abandon what I have already taught, checking it off as though it is completed for the year. Just because I've taught students about stamina and choosing topics does not mean we do not revisit these throughout the year. Our charts stay posted and I refer to them often. If I see that students need another lesson in choosing topics, I teach one, either to the whole class or to a small group. If I notice that students are struggling to stay in one spot and write the whole time, we revisit stamina and smart writing behavior in a lesson with those who need it. Likewise, there are always students who benefit from reminder lessons on how to choose the right paper for their writing projects.

Lessons in modeling and reading books with a writer's eye happen all year. Our best models are the books in our classrooms. As we move to different writing skills and strategies, I read books that show an author's strength and we ooh and aah all over again, noticing what the author does well.

As students progress, I add new minilessons that focus on new skills and strategies: using a picture as an inspiration for elaborating with text; elaborating on ideas by giving examples or including anecdotes; stretching moments (Calkins & Oxenhorn, 2003) by telling what someone says or feels; using senses to add description; writing different kinds of leads (bold statements, questions, sentences that start with an incredible fact); expanding sentences or phrases to create fluency; and ending with what Regie Routman calls a "satisfying conclusion" (2005). I also teach students to use text features such as labels, bold print, and captions in their writing, especially their nonfiction pieces. Figure 3.1 offers a list of sample minilesson topics and books that showcase these strategies.

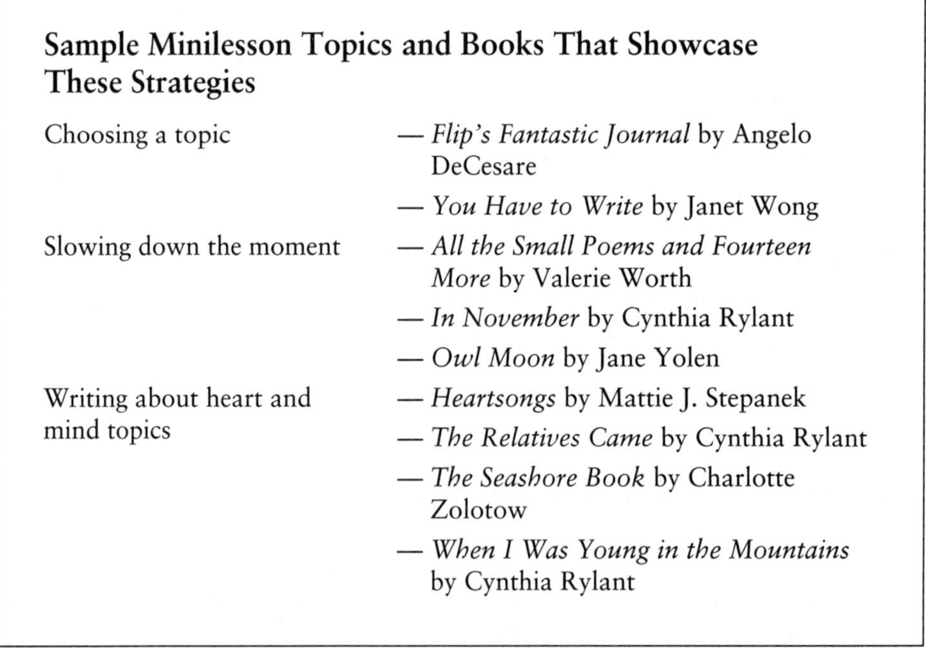

Sample Minilesson Topics and Books That Showcase These Strategies

Choosing a topic	— *Flip's Fantastic Journal* by Angelo DeCesare
	— *You Have to Write* by Janet Wong
Slowing down the moment	— *All the Small Poems and Fourteen More* by Valerie Worth
	— *In November* by Cynthia Rylant
	— *Owl Moon* by Jane Yolen
Writing about heart and mind topics	— *Heartsongs* by Mattie J. Stepanek
	— *The Relatives Came* by Cynthia Rylant
	— *The Seashore Book* by Charlotte Zolotow
	— *When I Was Young in the Mountains* by Cynthia Rylant

Figure 3.1 *Sample Minilesson*

Using anecdotes to elaborate	— *Who is Melvin Bubble?* by Nick Bruel — *A Picture Book of Harriet Tubman* by David Adler — *Abe Lincoln's Hat* by Martha Brenner
Using different kinds of leads	— *All About Deer* by Jim Arnosky — *Enemy Pie* by Derek Munson — *Gross Out! Animals That Do Disgusting Things* by Ginjer L. Clarke — *My Ol' Man* by Patricia Polacco
Using energetic verbs	— *Time to Sleep* by Denise Fleming — *Where Once There Was a Wood* by Denise Fleming
Using simile, metaphor, and other interesting language to create fluency	— *All the Places to Love* by Patricia MacLachlan — *Counting in the Garden* by Kim Parker — *The Eyes of Gray Wolf* by Jonathan London — *A Grand Old Tree* by Mary Newell DePalma — *Hoops* by Robert Burleigh — *Pumpkin Circle: The Story of a Garden* by George Levenson — *Sebastian: The Story of Bach* by Jeanette Winter — *Walk with a Wolf* by Janni Howker
Using interesting text features	— *Deserts* by Gail Gibbons — *Scaredy Squirrel* by Melanie Watt
Including a satisfying conclusion	— *Enemy Pie* by Derek Munson — *A Grand Old Tree* by Mary Newell DePalma
Writing from a different perspective	— *Barefoot: Escape on the Underground Railroad* by Pamela Duncan Edwards — *It's an Ant's Life: My Story of Life in the Nest* by Steve Parker
Organizing nonfiction text	— *Wolves!* by Christopher Nicholas — *Night Creatures* by Wade Cooper
Organizing fiction by time	— *The Paperboy* by Dav Pilkey — *Diary of a Worm* by Doreen Cronin

Figure 3.1 *Sample Minilesson*

How do I structure my minilessons?

Minilessons should be brief and highly focused. Young students have limited attention spans. Their minds wander and their bodies wiggle. I sometimes teach a minilesson over several days. I break the lesson into parts to keep students sitting for shorter periods of time.

We want to teach clearly and concisely and then let students try it out in their own writing. In *How's It Going?* Carl Anderson (2000) describes four components of an effective minilesson: connecting, teaching, having-a-go, and linking. My minilessons follow a similar structure.

1. Connect to the needs of students.
2. Teach.
3. Provide quick student practice or experience.
4. Encourage students to "have-a-go" with their own writing.

Connect

Good teaching always includes connecting the new skill to the students' needs. I might start a minilesson by saying, "During writing conferences over the last few days I've noticed many of you are having a difficult time elaborating or telling more."

Teach

During the teaching phase, I continue, "Today I am going to review a technique for elaborating that we notice some authors use when they want to tell more. It is called including an anecdote or 'story within a story.'" I show an example of how an author uses an anecdote to elaborate or I model using an anecdote in my own writing. I teach key words for starting an anecdote, such as *one time, once,* or *sometimes.*

Practice

Practice and experience are important. Here I give students a line such as "Playing baseball can be dangerous. One time . . . " I invite students to finish the line (orally or in writing) with an anecdote, telling about a time something dangerous happened while playing baseball. For instance, "One time the ball hit me in the face and I had to get seven stitches." We might even make a list of student ideas on a class chart. This practice/experience time is short (maybe three to five minutes) but allows students to experiment with support from the teacher and their classmates.

Have a Go

Last, I encourage students to "have-a-go" with their own writing. Depending on the strategy, a few will try right away, while others might take a few days or even longer to have-a-go. As students share their experiences, they are encouraged by one another's examples. The domino effect comes into play.

Strategies for Minilessons

Within the structure for minilessons, I realize I have choices as to how I will teach. Here are some of the strategies I use during my minilessons.

1. Demonstrate with my own writing.
2. Demonstrate with student writing.
3. Share a picture book or excerpt from a chapter book, thinking aloud what I notice and admire.
4. Use shared writing.
5. Use interactive writing.

What I want to teach informs the strategy I choose. Am I introducing a new skill or strategy? Maybe I demonstrate this for students. Is this a follow-up? Perhaps, as David Pearson and M. C. Gallagher (1983) suggest, I can release some of the responsibility to students, engaging them in a shared writing experience, so they get one step closer to trying it independently. Or perhaps this lesson involves beginning first graders and is focused heavily on conventions of print. Interactive writing might be my choice.

Some of these strategies involve more time than others. Engaged students will sit longer when they listen to a picture book than when a teacher demonstrates writing. Lesson times will vary depending on the strategy I choose, as well as student attention.

With some strategies the teaching and practice stages might happen simultaneously. Because they are heavily involved in shared and interactive writing, students practice as I teach; then they may practice again, on their own. In this chapter I define and show examples of modeled writing, shared writing, and interactive writing. I will also discuss sharing picture books to recognize aspects of good writing

What is modeled writing?

So what is modeled writing? It's the same thing as demonstrating writing. In modeled writing teachers use a think-aloud technique while writing or sharing writing in front of students. This might occur on a large chart or in a notebook projected on a screen for students to see. During modeled writing, teachers might also read something they previously wrote, such as a journal entry, poem, list, or letter, thinking aloud in order to teach something about writing to students.

Modeled Writing

Teachers use a think-aloud technique as they write or share their writing in front of students.

I also include sharing student writing and reading picture and chapter books as forms of modeled writing. While the teacher is not actually writing, these two forms of sharing can serve as wonderful models for students as they learn about good writing.

How important is modeled writing?

I always say, if you do three things only when you teach writing to children, make sure it's these: Model, model, and model some more.

Donald Graves (1994) encourages us to model in front of our students when teaching writing. He likens the teacher who does not model writing to the artist who does not demonstrate for students. Graves notes, "Writing is a craft. It needs to be demonstrated to your students in your classroom, which is a studio, from choosing a topic to finishing a final draft. They need to see you struggle to match your intentions with the words that reach the page" (110).

With his last line, Graves invites us to let students see our struggle. Let them observe us as we stop to wonder what to write next, or as we grapple to find that perfect word. Graves wants us to be vulnerable.

At the same time, it is important not to "write down" to children. I don't invent errors. That would be dishonest and disrespectful. They need to see the real me, working my way through my piece as I try to make it right.

A teacher once told me that she didn't like writing in front of her students because she didn't feel confident as a writer. She made mistakes and often struggled with what to write next. What a gift for us to show students that this is what writing is all about. It's about the struggle to write with a purpose and make our words sound good. It's about choosing language that describes exactly what we mean and elaborating in ways that will reel our reader into our story. It's about checking resources to be certain our conventions are correct. Writing is not about being perfect the first time. It's about working to reshape our thoughts over and over until we get it right. That's what students need to see. That's what we need to show them.

What kinds of things do I demonstrate?

My answer to this question is *everything, a little at a time*. A few years ago I observed an exemplary teacher who was modeling writing for first graders. She brought in a photograph she had recently found of a bird's nest that was built in a nook outside her garage. She explained that the photograph brought back memories, and she talked about how she first noticed this nest after hearing slight chirping from two baby birds. After she told her story, the teacher began writing, asking students for help with letters as she wrote. She demonstrated how to use fingers to add space between words. She also looked to the class word wall to spell the words *the* and *saw*. She stopped from time to time to reread, saying, "Let me read this again. I want to make sure it makes sense." At one point, the teacher asked students to help think of a word or two to describe the baby birds. She also stopped to ask the question "How?" after writing about taking a picture of the nest. Here is her finished piece.

> Last spring I found a birds' nest in the outside corner of my garage. I noticed it after hearing a slight chirp from above. When I looked up I saw two little bald birds, poking their heads up. I climbed on a ladder to take a picture.

Key Lesson Points

In this short lesson the teacher demonstrates the following for students:

- Use your own experiences for topic ideas.
- Write for a purpose and audience.

- Tell your story first.
- Write left to right on the page.
- Use spaces between words.
- Sound out words to spell them.
- Look to the word wall to spell high-frequency words.
- Reread your story to see if it makes sense.
- Revise to add details and to add descriptive words.
- Elaborate by telling how.

The teacher keeps the lesson moving, inviting students to help her so they will stay involved and focused. After teaching the lesson, she asks students to think of something they would like to write about. She invites students to draw their ideas first, saying, "Sometimes drawing our ideas helps us think of what we want to write."

Of course there are many skills and strategies that can be modeled for students during any writing lesson, from topic choice to editing for publication. Figure 3.2 contains a partial list.

Writing Skills and Strategies to Model

- considering purpose for writing
- considering the audience
- choosing a topic
- forming letters/handwriting
- applying phonics skills (sound-symbol correspondence)
- using resources to spell words or find information
- revising
- editing
- using correct conventions (capitals, punctuation)
- applying concepts of print (left to right, spacing)
- elaborating on ideas or adding details
- matching text to drawing
- using interesting language (words, phrases, similes, metaphors)
- extending and combining sentences for fluency
- including lead sentences and satisfying conclusions
- rereading for clarity
- publishing

Figure 3.2 *Writing Skills and Strategies to Model*

What is shared writing and when do I use it?

Throughout the year, I continue to model with my own writing the skills and strategies I want students to learn. However, as students gain in knowledge and skill level, I want to get them in on the process of trying some new writing strategy or genre immediately, and so I turn to shared writing.

In shared writing children join in contributing to the story, poem, or expository piece. The teacher records student ideas. Discussion and participation are key elements. Regie Routman (2005) describes shared writing like this: "In shared writing, the teachers and students compose collaboratively, the teacher acting as expert scribe for her apprentices as she demonstrates" (83). So, what does this look like?

Shared Writing

- The teacher records student ideas.
- Discussion and participation are key elements.

My Shared Writing Lesson: Nonfiction

It is early November. A *Scholastic News* featuring bats inspires us to read other texts about this night creature. We read *Amazing Bats* by Seymour Simon and *Bats* by Gail Gibbons. Following our study, I ask students if they would like to write their own book about bats and they agree.

I ask, "What is our purpose and who is our audience?" Students decide to write an informational book for another classroom's library.

We begin by taking notes. I ask, "What have we learned about bats? Let's take some notes to remind us of the facts we might want to include in our book."

Immediately students chime in. Tatum says, "They are mammals." I start taking notes, modeling the use of a recently learned text feature, bullets.

Johnny adds, "They live in caves and attics."

Joelle says, "Some of them migrate."

I continue to encourage ideas, recording them on a chart. We finally have our list (Figure 3.3).

I say, "Okay, we have our notes. We only wrote a word or two for each idea. Now we need to elaborate on these ideas in our piece of writing. How should we start? We need a solid lead sentence."

Josh suggests, "How about: *We like bats. Bats are very interesting animals.*"

Figure 3.3 *Notes About Bats*

I answer, "That sounds great. It's clear and tells our readers what our book is about." I record our first two sentences. "Now what? What should we say next?"

Reilly raises his hand. "Bats are mammals."

"Okay." I record Reilly's idea. "Alright. This is a great sentence to start with."

Linnae adds, "In fact, they are the only mammals that fly." I record both sentences.

Then I ask, "How can we elaborate or add a detail?"

Ricky says, "We could tell what a mammal is."

"Yes," I agree. "We could add a definition. Remember we learned that's one way to *tell more*. Or we can tell what makes a bat a mammal."

Jarred says, "They have fur and they feed their babies milk, just like us."

I add Jarred's words to our piece and then say, "Let's look at our notes again. What should we write next?"

Bobby suggests, "We should tell where bats live."

I ask, "Okay, what should our sentence say?"

Jessica answers, "Bats can live in caves and attics."

"They also live in trees and in bridges," adds Tyler.

As I begin to write, Miya says, "They live in farmhouses too." Students agree that we should combine these into one sentence: *Bats can live in caves, attics, trees, bridges, and farmhouses.*

Our discussion continues and students decide to add: *They hibernate in buildings and some fly south for the winter.* At this point, Taylor says, "Not all bats hibernate, so we should change *they* to the word *some.*"

At this point I add, "You know, our sentence says that bats *fly* south for the winter. Is there a more interesting word we can substitute for *fly*?"

Students agree to change *fly* to *migrate.* Our new sentence reads: *Some hibernate in buildings and some migrate south for the winter.*

We continue to read over our notes, deciding which facts should be used, and how to elaborate on each one. After writing about *echolocation,* I suggest we read this part to see if it makes sense. Tatum says, "It's kind of confusing."

Students agree. I say, "I think we need to explain *echolocation* differently. Maybe we should reread how Seymour Simon and Gail Gibbons explain *echolocation.*" We revisit excerpts from both books and then make our revisions.

We go on to add a fact about what bats eat and how this can help trees grow. Then we make sure we have an ending sentence that will tell the reader our book is finished. We reread our piece for clarity, making additional revisions. The following day students decide on page breaks and we mark our text (see Figure 3.4).

Then I project the computer screen onto the wall, ready to type our final book. Students read the chart to me as I type with a watchful eye. They act as editors, catching any convention errors I make, as well as deciding on page layout. I ask, "Should the text go at the top of the page, the bottom of the page, or be split?" We also continue to revise, adding and deleting words, as well as changing small ideas. When the typing is finished, we make one final read and then print our copy. Students illustrate the pages and covers for each book and we now have our published copies, ready for delivery and our own classroom reading (Figure 3.5)

Two wonderful byproducts come from this shared writing project. The first is that we receive three shared writing thank-you notes from both primary and intermediate classrooms. One is an email, one is a handwritten letter, and one is a poster with individual notes. These other teachers have used this opportunity to teach about thank-you letters with a real purpose and audience in mind. And my students get to see that thank-you notes come in different forms (see Figures 3.6 and 3.7).

The other additional benefit that comes from this shared writing experience has to do with reading. Students read this book over and over, reading

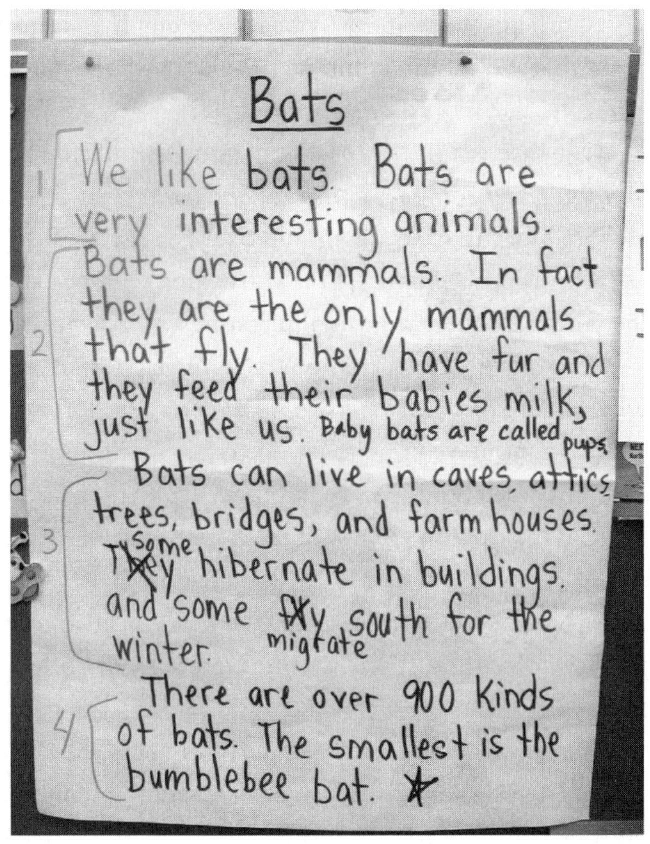

Figure 3.4 *First Part of Shared Writing Chart About Bats*

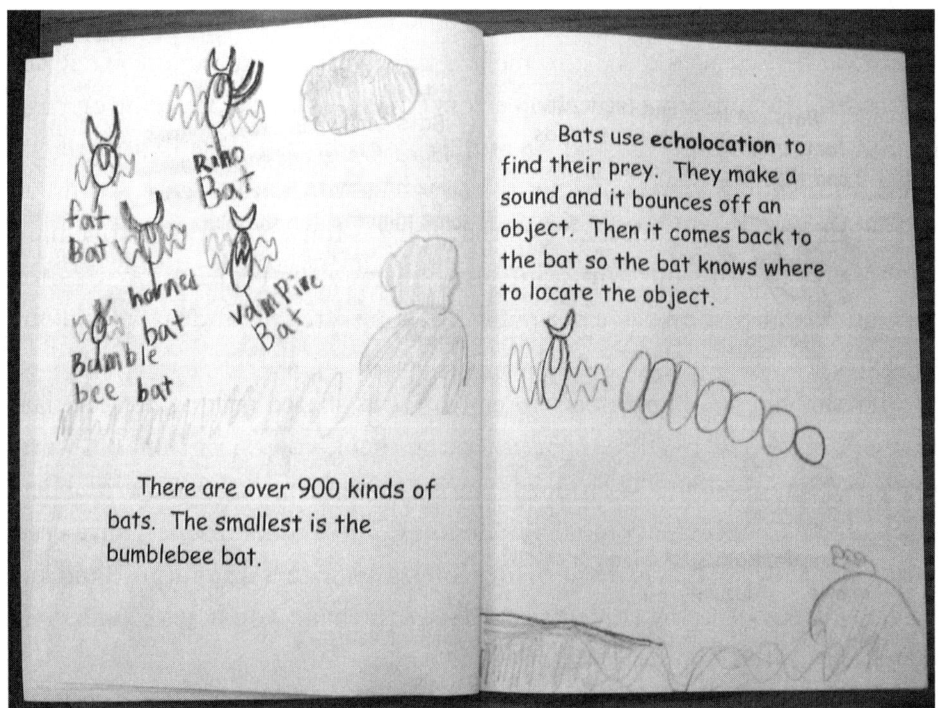

Figure 3.5 *Sample Page from Published Bat Book*

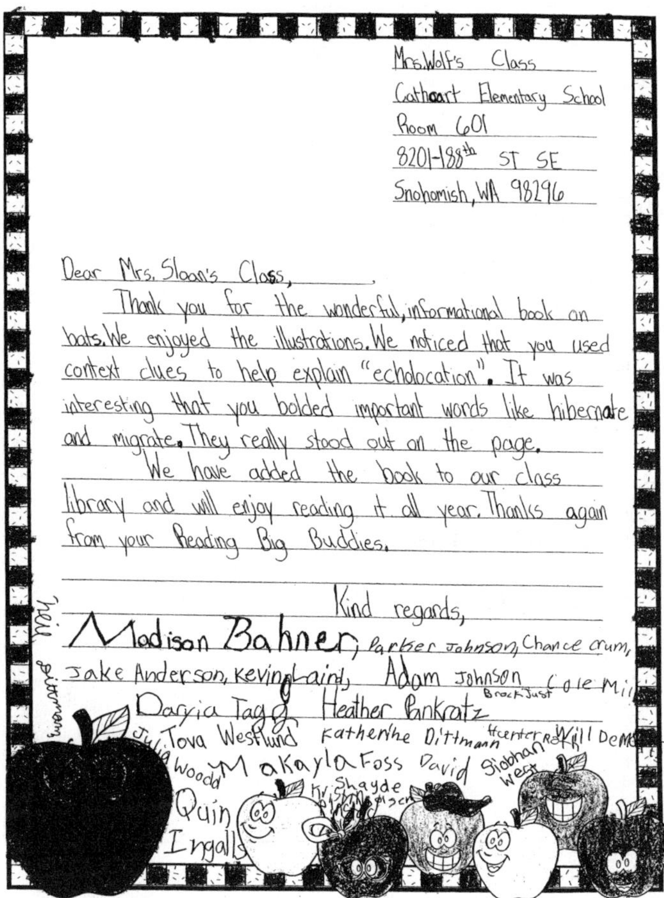

Mrs. Wolf's Class
Cathcart Elementary School
Room 601
8201-188th ST SE
Snohomish, WA 98296

Dear Mrs. Sloan's Class,

Thank you for the wonderful, informational book on bats. We enjoyed the illustrations. We noticed that you used context clues to help explain "echolocation". It was interesting that you bolded important words like hibernate and migrate. They really stood out on the page.

We have added the book to our class library and will enjoy reading it all year. Thanks again from your Reading Big Buddies.

Kind regards,

Madison Bahner, Parker Johnson, Chance crum, Jake Anderson, Kevin Laird, Adam Johnson, Daryia Tagg, Heather Pankratz, Tova Westlund, Katherine Dittmann, Makayla Foss, David, Siobhan West, Quin Ingalls

Figure 3.6 *Shared Writing Thank-You Letter from Third and Fourth Graders*

with much greater accuracy and fluency than I have seen earlier. It brings back my true belief in language experience (students reading their own writing) as part of the reading program.

Interactive Writing

- Teacher and students "share the pen."
- Ideas come from students and teacher.
- Focus centers on ideas and conventions.

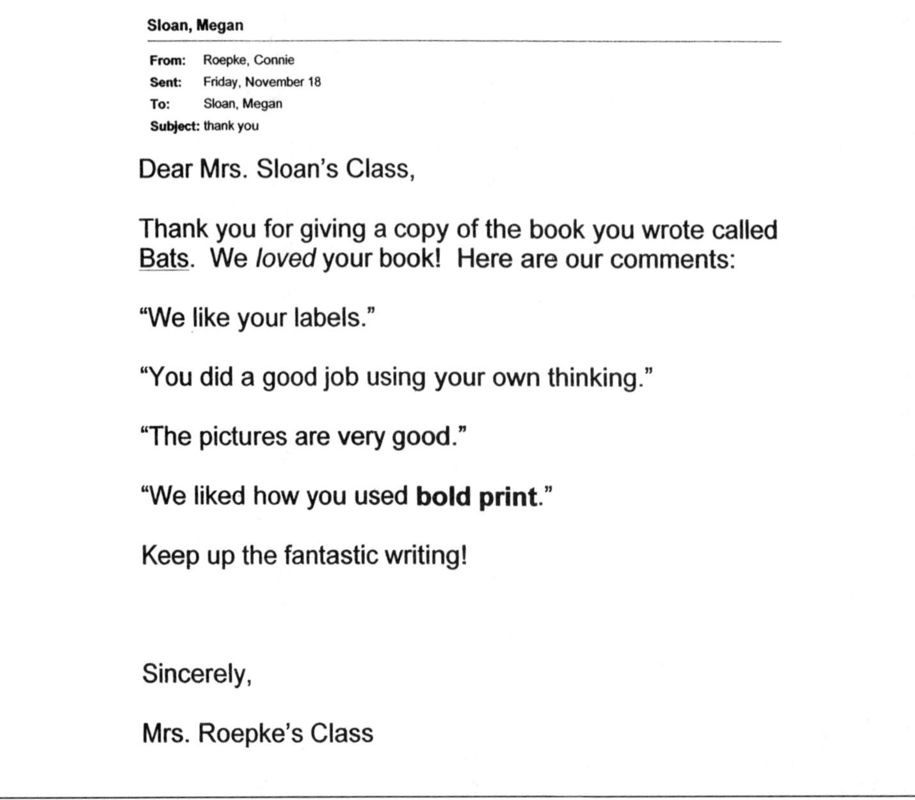

Sloan, Megan

From: Roepke, Connie
Sent: Friday, November 18
To: Sloan, Megan
Subject: thank you

Dear Mrs. Sloan's Class,

Thank you for giving a copy of the book you wrote called Bats. We *loved* your book! Here are our comments:

"We like your labels."

"You did a good job using your own thinking."

"The pictures are very good."

"We liked how you used **bold print**."

Keep up the fantastic writing!

Sincerely,

Mrs. Roepke's Class

Figure 3.7 *Email from Second Graders*

What should I consider when choosing interactive writing?

As Regie Routman (2005) explains, "Interactive writing is a form of shared writing in which the teacher and a student or students share the pen. The student writes the letters he or she can write, the teacher writes the rest" (87). When I choose interactive writing, I work with either small groups or individuals; it is usually too time-consuming to do with my whole class. I use this strategy mostly with kindergarteners and first graders because they are learning so many conventions of print. Here is a place I can let students "try out" their knowledge, while guiding them to use the correct directionality, spacing, capitalization, punctuation, and spelling. Less frequently, I also use interactive writing with second and third graders to teach and reinforce these same skills, at a higher degree of difficulty.

An interactive writing lesson moves a bit slower than shared and modeled writing, simply because students share the responsibility of the actual writing.

As students record ideas, lots of talk occurs about which letters to write and how to use spacing, punctuation, capitalization, and spelling.

An interactive writing piece should be short. I try to keep the writing to just a few sentences, at most. This way, students stay involved and active, while focusing on a few specific skills.

My Interactive Minilesson: Using Our Experiences to Write

It is October and my first-grade students are learning to spell some high-frequency words, as well as sound out words less familiar, as they write down their ideas. I decide to teach a lesson on getting writing ideas from our own experiences as well as using our word wall as a resource when we want to spell familiar words.

I begin by taking students for a walk around the school grounds. We notice that the leaves are beginning to turn different colors. Some are falling to the ground. Fall is in the air. We return to our classroom and I suggest to my first-grade students that we write about our observations. I ask, "What should we say first about what we observed during our walk?"

Immediately, Josh says, "Fall is here."

I invite Josh up to the chart to help write our first word. Before he writes, I ask students, "Where do we begin, and how should we begin our first sentence?"

Josh points to the upper left corner of our chart paper.

Tatum says, "We start with a capital letter."

"Right," I say.

Josh says, "*Fall,*" and writes an *F.* I fill in the *all.* Next I ask, "Who can write the word *is*?"

Robbie raises his hand as I remind students that the word *is* appears on our word wall.

I remind Robbie to use his finger to make a space between words and he writes the word *is.*

"*Here*," I say. "Who knows the first letter in the word *here*?" Adena comes up and writes an *h.* I fill in the *ere* and now we have:

Fall is here.

"Okay," I say. Let's elaborate. How do we know fall is here? What did we see on our walk?"

Mina says, "The leaves on the trees are turning red, yellow, and orange."

"Wonderful," I encourage. "Would you like to come up and spell the word *The*? It's another familiar word from our word wall."

Mina comes up, uses her finger to make a space, and writes the word *The*. Again, I emphasize using a capital letter to start a sentence. I say the next word, *leaves,* and ask, "Who knows what makes the first sound?" I repeat the sound for *l*. Jenny comes up and writes the letter *l*. I take over with the pen, writing the rest of the word *leaves*.

Then I invite two more students to write the words *on* and *the*. Each time I encourage students to look to the word wall to spell these words. I remind students to think about spacing and neat handwriting. I write *tr* for *trees* and invite two students to sound out the rest, while writing *ees*. Again, I take the pen and write *are turning*.

To finish out the sentence we look at the color words displayed on our wall. Three different students agree to help with writing the rest of our sentence: *red, yellow, and orange*. I share the pen, filling in the commas.

I say to students, "Let's reread our sentences to see if they make sense."

> Fall is here. The leaves on the trees are turning red, yellow, and orange.

Then I say, "We learned a lot of important things today. First, we learned to sound out parts of words to see if we can match a letter to the sound. We also learned that some words we might want to write are on our word wall. This is a good place to look to help you spell these words. Also, when you want to spell a color word, you can look at the color words on our wall."

I continue, "As you write today, I will look for students who look to our word wall for words to spell. I will also look for students who really try to match letters to the sounds they hear as they say what they want to write."

As students show a sufficient command of conventions, spelling with greater accuracy and independence, as well as using capital letters and punctuation correctly, I move them away from interactive writing, spending less time on this strategy.

Final Thoughts

Each minilesson strategy has an effective time and place. As teachers we need to consider everything—lesson objectives, materials, time, and (most important) our students—when we plan and teach our lessons. Again, I plan my lessons based on what I notice in my students' writing and their conversations about writing. Do they need a repeat lesson in stretching moments? Are they ready to learn about using anecdotes as a way to elaborate? Sometimes

Modeled Writing	Shared Writing	Interactive Writing
Teacher uses a think-aloud approach while writing in front of students.	Teacher records student ideas. Discussion and participation are key elements.	Students and teachers "share the pen." Ideas come from students and teachers. Focus centers on ideas and conventions of print.

Figure 3.8 *Table of Writing Strategies*

we come across a strategy in a read-aloud and students are curious, like using a question as a lead sentence or the use of a simile to describe something special. Structuring lessons that flow, while giving adequate connection, teaching, and practice, is important. Choosing the strategy that will best meet the needs of our objectives and students is the key.

More Topics for Minilessons

More Topics for Minilessons

- Match text to picture.
- Add a detail to elaborate.
- Tell your story first, then write.
- Consider your purpose and audience.
- Choose a topic: Write what you know and like, write about what is on your heart and mind, research a topic and write.
- Choose the right paper. (Is this a book? Do you want to write in your journal?)
- Take notes, make lists, or draw to help with your ideas.
- Organize your ideas.
- Elaborate by telling how, when, why, who, and where.

- Elaborate by including an anecdote (*one time . . . , once . . . , sometimes . . .*).
- Elaborate by including examples, definitions, facts.
- Elaborate by using your senses (what you see, hear, smell, taste, and touch).
- "Slow down the moment" by 1) telling how you feel; 2) telling what someone said; 3) using your senses.
- Include a strong lead sentence (variety of techniques).
- Include a satisfying ending sentence.
- Include energetic verbs in your writing.
- Use simile, alliteration, and metaphor.
- Reread your writing to see if it makes sense.
- Edit your writing (use your spelling card, other resources).

CHAPTER 4

What Do I Teach?

Twelve Minilessons That Pave the Way to Wondrous Writing

We just completed our minilesson. We are now in the heart of writing workshop: drafting and conferring. Students find their materials to begin writing, and I prepare to confer with a second grader, Jason. I sit down next to him and notice that Jason is writing a comic story. I ask him, "How's it going?"

Jason says, "Good. Can I read it to you so far?"

"I would love to hear your story. It looks like a comic story. Is that right?"

Jason nods his head and begins reading. After several pages, Jason reads:

Spider Warrior climbs to top of the hill. He out his sword.

Jason says, "Wait, I forgot some words." He inserts the words *the* and *pulls* where they belong. He rereads:

Spider Warrior climbs to the top of the hill. He pulls out his sword.

I say, "You know, writers often catch missed words when they reread their stories in the middle of their writing. That's one reason rereading is really important."

Jason continues reading. At another point, he realizes he has forgotten to explain something and his reader might get confused. I suggest that he could add another sentence, drawing an arrow to where it should go. Jason adds: *Spider Warrior and Ant Man used to be friends.* I commend Jason for considering his audience and making sure his story is clear.

Jason is not the only student who benefits from rereading his piece today. Another student makes needed changes after rereading. Yet there are some students who never reread their writing for possible revisions or edits. They miss opportunities to make their writing clear, fluent, and complete.

Sometimes I plan minilessons based on student need, and sometimes I base them on what appears to be a natural next step. In this case, I decide that "rereading our writing" will make a great minilesson this week. It reflects what I have noticed in student writing, and it is based on a genuine need. For this lesson I will either model rereading my own text, or ask Jason to serve as a model and co-teacher, sharing his experience. Together, we will explore how writers reread their writing to make sure it makes sense.

Polar Bears, Letters, and Lovely Language

This chapter includes twelve minilessons I have taught to students at varying primary grade levels. The lessons can be adapted easily for younger or older students. I include modeled, shared, and interactive writing strategies, as well as ways to use literature as a model. I address different genres—personal narrative, poetry, letter writing, and nonfiction—as well as different skills such as elaborating on ideas, including interesting language, writing leads and endings, and using correct conventions. Some lessons are taught in one session; others take several days.

I continue to adapt lessons. Because minilessons must match children's talents and needs, I look to my students and plan lessons that will strengthen and challenge them as young writers.

Modeled Writing—Match Text to Picture (Grades K–1)

If you tell a five- or six-year-old child, "Write about something—anything you want," she will probably look at you with a blank stare. However, if you ask this same child to draw a picture of something—anything she would like—you will probably get a picture, and with that picture comes a story.

With very beginning writers, those who are just matching letters to sounds, I start by modeling drawing a picture and telling my story.

The purpose of this lesson is to help students:

1. Find a topic.
2. Match text to a picture.
3. Use what they know to match letters to sounds.

I begin my lesson. "You know, today I was thinking about the rain and how I don't like it. I drew this picture of me in the rain." I show students my picture, which I drew before the lesson to save time. I continue telling my story. "I'm getting wet because I don't have an umbrella. My dog is getting wet too."

I continue, "Now that I've drawn my picture, I would like to write about it. I think I will write: *I don't like the rain.*" I write *I* and use my finger to make a space on my page. Then I say, "*Don't.* Who knows how to begin the word *don't?*"

Several students say, "*D.*" I slowly sound out the word *don't,* writing the letters as I go. I move on to the word *like,* and students help me as I match letters with the sounds we hear. I finish writing my sentence, modeling spacing and writing a period at the end.

Then I say, "Let me go back and reread my sentence to see if it makes sense." I read, "I don't like the rain."

"Okay. My sentence matches my picture but I'm thinking I can add a detail. What else can I write?"

"You're getting wet," says Eduardo.

"Yes, I am," I say. "I can add: *I am getting wet.*"

Again, I write the letters as I slowly sound out each word. Students suggest letters and remind me about spacing and a period at the end (Figure 4.1).

Figure 4.1 *Megan Models Matching Text to Picture*

"Okay. I am proud of my writing. I like my topic. My sentences match my picture. I used what I know about letters and sounds to write."

"Today you are going to draw a picture of anything you like. When you are finished, tell the story of your picture to a friend, like I did for all of you. Use what you know to write your story. Remember to stretch the words out loud and write the letters you hear. If you already know how to spell a word, just write it. Remember, the story you write should match your picture. If you get stuck, ask a friend for help and I will also be here to help. Have fun! Remember, writing is fun!"

Jesse quickly begins to draw a dinosaur. When he is ready to write I will help him match letters to sounds.

I walk over to Julia. She is stuck. I sit down next to her and ask, "What do you like to do?" She's not so sure.

And then she says, "I like to swim."

I say, "Really? Tell me about that."

Julia tells me about the pool they use. She describes the pool and talks about how her mom watches her swim.

I encourage, "Oh. I would love to see a picture of you swimming."

Julia sets to work. She draws in great detail the pool with two ladders—including the lines that go across, cutting the pool into thirds. She draws a row of chairs with her mom sitting in one of them. And then she begins to draw circle after circle. I ask her, "What are those?"

She looks at me (as though I should know) and says, "Those are all the swimmers."

"Where are you?" I ask. Julia pens herself in darker than the rest and labels herself: *ME.*

I ask, "What would you like to write?"

"I don't know."

I prod, "Tell me what you want to say about your picture."

"I like to swim." I help Julia sound out the letters she hears as she writes them down.

I LiK T CAM.

Then I ask, "Do you swim alone?"

Julia giggles, "No. I swim with my friends."

I suggest, "Could we add that to your writing?" Julia is unsure. Her face and body language tell me she is finished writing, but she does have more ideas. "I am happy to write the rest of your sentence for you." I say.

Julia rereads, "I like to swim" and then adds, "with my friends." I add the last three words.

Figure 4.2 *Julia Writes About Swimming*

Then I ask, "Who is this?" I point to her mom.
Julia says, "My mom watches me."
I ask, "Could I add that idea?"
Julia nods. Then she rereads her writing one more time (Figure 4.2).

Interactive Writing—Write Informational Text (Grade 1)

As students begin to learn more about conventions of print (spelling, spacing, punctuation, and capitalization), I incorporate more interactive writing lessons into my teaching. Remember, with interactive writing, students share the pen and record some of the text written by the class (Routman 2005).

The purpose of this lesson is to help students:

1. Practice matching letters to sounds when spelling words.
2. Spell high-frequency words correctly.

3. Practice spacing, directionality, and punctuation.
4. Consider purpose and audience.
5. Elaborate on an idea.
6. Create an appropriate title.

For this lesson, I am working with a group of first graders in my first- and second-grade multiage class. We have been reading about frogs so I suggest this for a writing topic today. Students agree.

"Okay. How should we begin?"

Taylor suggests right away, "We should call our story *The Frog*." I record this title at the top of our page.

"Okay. What should we write next?"

Emma suggests *I like frogs*. I hand Emma the pen as we all remind her where we start writing on the page.

I ask, "What kind of letter will you write?"

Emma answers, "A capital "*I*." Emma writes the word *I* as she sounds it out aloud.

I ask, "Who knows how to write the word *like*?"

Tyler raises his hand. I suggest he look at our word wall for help. Tyler uses his finger to make a space and then writes the word *like*.

Malcolm says, "I can spell *frogs*." He comes up and writes the letters *f-o-g-s,* forgetting the *r*.

This provides an opportunity for me to say, "Let's say the word *frogs* together. Do you hear the *r* right after the *f*?" Malcolm realizes his mistake and we squeeze an *r* into the word. I add, "When we write, it is easy to forget some letters, so we need to stretch our words out loud and write what we hear."

We continue our story. I ask, "What should we write next? What do frogs do?"

Serena suggests, "Frogs hop from lily pad to lily pad." She comes up and writes the word *Frogs*. We continue with that sentence and add one more. I take turns writing to keep the lesson moving. We stop to stretch sounds and talk about spacing and punctuation. We end up with the following piece of writing:

The Frog

I like frogs. Frogs hop from lily pad to lily pad. Frogs are fun to play with.

"All right. Let's reread our writing to see if everything makes sense." We reread our text and it is very clear that our title does not match our writing. I ask, "Do you notice that our title suggests we are writing about one frog, but really our writing is an informational piece about frogs in general? How can we fix this?"

Taylor says, "We can change our title to *Frogs.*"

"That's a good idea." I cross out the word *The* and add the letter *s* to the word *Frog* (Figure 4.3). "You know, good writers revise their writing all the time. They reread to see if it makes sense, and when it doesn't, they make changes. That's what we just did. We are great writers because we revise."

During lessons like this, where students are sharing so many ideas, there are bound to be varying views about what should be recorded. We have firm rules. When one person begins to speak, others listen. They may disagree and we can discuss all ideas, but not all ideas will be recorded. This is a shared experience and students know this. That is why students have lots of opportunities for individual writing. I want students to know I value all of their ideas.

The next day, some first-grade students choose to write their own pieces about frogs (Figure 4.4).

Figure 4.3 *Interactive Writing About Frogs*

Figure 4.4 *Serena Writes About Frogs*

Shared Writing—"Welcome to Our Class" Letter (Grades 1–2)

One of the things I want students to know is that writers write for real purposes and audiences. Regie Routman (2005) says, "Our students need to see that our purpose for writing is genuine, that we write with readers in mind, even if the readers are ourselves" (42).

The purpose of this lesson is to help students:

1. Consider purpose and audience.
2. Learn about the letter-writing format.
3. Elaborate on ideas.
4. Practice learned conventions.

I begin my lesson by announcing that we will have a new student joining our class tomorrow. I suggest we write a welcome letter for Edgar. I tell students to think of the kinds of things we want to put in our letter to help Edgar feel welcome and also learn a little about our classroom and school.

I start by talking about letter format. I tell students that letters often have the date at the very top. I write *Sept. 18, 2008* at the top of a piece of chart paper. I then show students about skipping a line and ask, "Does anyone know how to begin a letter?"

Eleanor answers, "*Dear*, and then the person's name."

"Yes. Since we are writing this letter to Edgar, I will write *Dear Edgar* and I will place a comma after his name. Now, what do you think we should write first?"

Dylan says, "*Welcome to our class!*"

"That's a great first sentence," I say, as I record it on our chart.

"Okay. I asked you to think of some things that will help Edgar feel welcome and learn about our class. Who has an idea for our next sentence?"

"*You will like it here*," says Alex.

I record Alex's sentence. "Great. Let's elaborate on this idea. How can we tell more about why Edgar will like it here?"

Nolan raises his hand. "We do a lot of fun things and we learn a lot."

I ask, "Like what?"

Ryan answers, "Like read really good books and do science experiments."

I add Ryan's ideas and ask, "Anything else?"

Jamie adds, "We play math games and have writing workshop."

I write down Jamie's ideas and then suggest, "Let's reread our writing to see if everything makes sense."

Sept. 18, 2008

Dear Edgar,

Welcome to our class! You will like it here. We read really good books and do science experiments. We play math games and have Writing Workshop.

"How does this sound so far?" I ask. Students agree that our letter makes sense. "Okay, what else should we write? Should we say something about recess?"

"*Recess is really fun,*" suggests Taylor.

"Give me some reasons," I say.

"*There are lots of things to play,*" adds Amber.

I suggest, "Here's a great place we can tell more. Lots of things to play *like . . . ?*"

Amber adds, "*Like the moonclimber and basketball.*"

"Super. You are really elaborating. Good writers tell more." I record the students' ideas. "Okay, I think we are ready to end our letter. Think about how we should sign it." I give students several options: *Your friends, Sincerely,* or *From.*

Students settle on *Your friends* and then Eleanor suggests, "We should say *Your new friends.*"

"Great thinking, Eleanor. Let's make that change. Good writers change their writing to make it better. Remember, that's called *revising.*" We reread our letter one more time and students are happy with it (Figure 4.5). I ask, "Is there someone who would be willing to rewrite our letter very neatly on a special sheet of paper that will fit on Edgar's desk?" I choose a student to do this.

I end our lesson by saying, "We will put this letter on Edgar's spot when he comes in tomorrow and I know it will make him feel very welcome. Well done writers!"

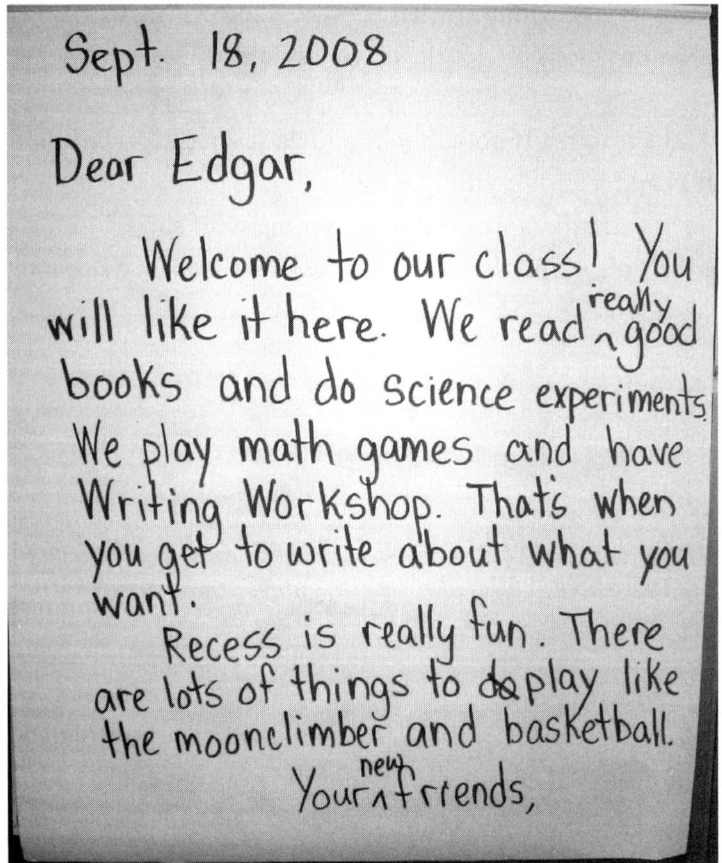
Sept. 18, 2008

Dear Edgar,

Welcome to our class! You will like it here. We read really good books and do science experiments. We play math games and have Writing Workshop. That's when you get to write about what you want.

Recess is really fun. There are lots of things to ~~do~~ play like the moonclimber and basketball.

Your new friends,

Figure 4.5 *Shared Writing: Welcome Letter*

Modeled Writing—Write About What's on Your Heart and Mind (Grades 1–3)

Teachers often tell me their students don't know what to write about. I always start with lessons on choosing topics (see Chapter 3). I refer to the chart we created earlier:

What Makes a Good Writing Topic?

- something you know about
- something you like (you're interested in it)
- something you have a book about
- something you wonder about

When students have had a chance to experiment with writing about what they know and like, I introduce the idea of writing about *what is on your heart and mind*. I post a quote by Kate DiCamillo: "I put my heart on the page when I write." We talk about what that means. I tell students that my best writing comes when I write about what is on my heart and mind.

The purpose of this lesson is to help students:

1. Choose topics that will stimulate good writing.
2. Think about or tell about their stories before they write.
3. Consider genre.
4. Reread, revise, and edit.

I begin today's lesson by telling students, "You know, I have been thinking a lot about my grandfather today. I'm not really sure why, but he is really on my heart and mind. I'm thinking that my grandfather might make a good writing topic for me today."

Regie Routman (2005) encourages us to tell our stories first: "Saying the story out loud engages the students, lets me clarify my thinking, and reinforces the importance of conversation before writing" (25). I begin telling students about my grandfather. "My grandpa had a wooden leg and he used to tell me a mouse lived in it. We loved going for long walks. He would sit in his lawn chair and I would bounce balls up against the concrete wall in the parking lot of his apartment." I show students a photo of my grandfather (Figure 4.6).

I begin writing in my journal. As I write, I think aloud (Figure 4.7). I reread, make revisions, and comment to students about what I am doing:

> *I remember my grandfather.*
>
> *Tom Gallagher was his name.*
>
> *I remember my grandfather's wooden leg—the way it clicked when he danced, and the mouse that lived there.*
>
> *"Sh! Meggie," my grandpa would say. "He's sleeping."*
>
> *I remember my grandfather's cane the way it went pet pet pet on the sidewalk during our long walks.*

After rereading, I say, "You know, this kind of sounds like a poem to me. I think I might like to put slash-lines in between words where I might like to break my lines." I do this, also making more revisions as I reread one more time (Figure 4.8).

I continue, "I think I would like to continue working on this piece about my grandfather. I need to think more about the things I remember about him."

Figure 4.6 *Megan Shares a Photo of Her Grandfather*

Figure 4.7 *Megan Reads Her Draft*

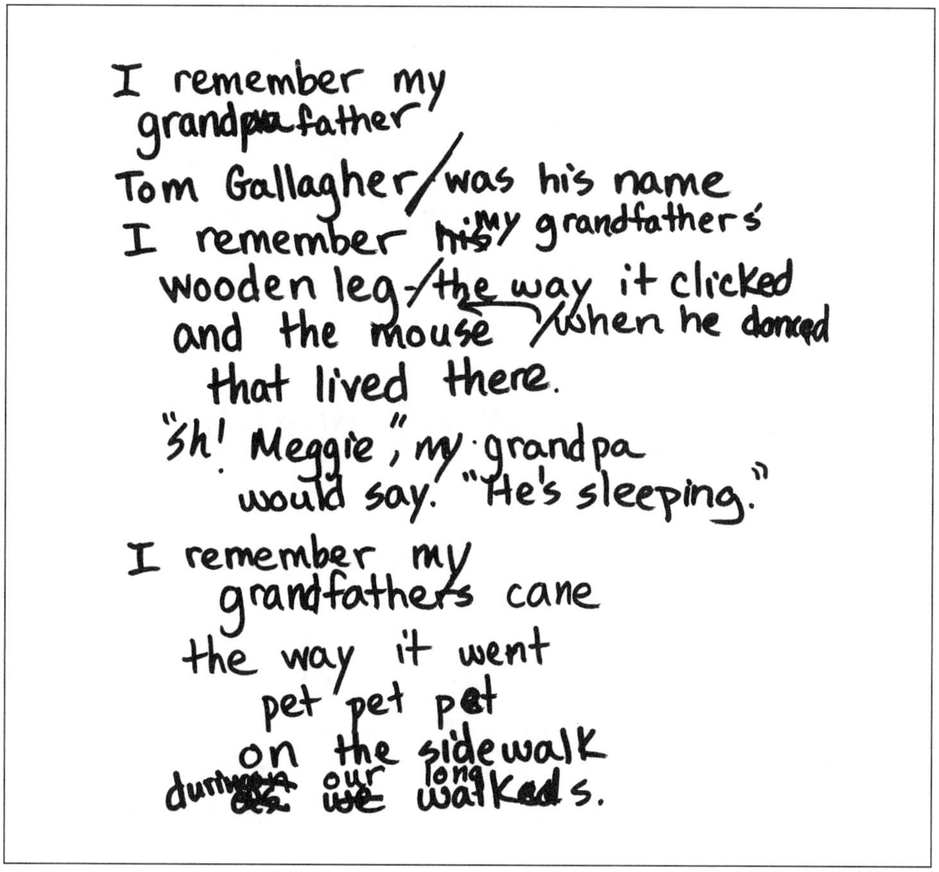

I remember my
grand~~pa~~father
Tom Gallagher / was his name
I remember ~~his~~ my grandfathers'
wooden leg / the way it clicked
and the mouse / when he danced
that lived there.
"Sh! Meggie", my grandpa
would say. "He's sleeping."
I remember my
grandfathers cane
the way it went
pet pet pet
on the sidewalk
during our long walks.

Figure 4.8 *Megan's Draft*

Then I challenge students, "Today, I would like you to think about what is on your heart and mind. It might be a person, like your grandfather or mom or brother or friend. It might be a pet, or a sport like baseball. It might be a hike you took with your family, or a book you are reading. It can be anything you are really thinking about and really caring about today." I continue, "Remember, my writing felt like a poem to me. You certainly may write a poem, but you don't have to. You might like to write a personal story about your topic."

I encourage students to turn and tell their neighbors about what is on their hearts and minds. What are they really thinking about today? If it helps to make a list, I encourage them to do that and choose from their list. When they are ready, I ask students to begin writing.

I ask students to share their topics. Emma says, "I'm going to write about my mom."

Dylan says, "Snakes."

Alex shares, "Our team won the football championship. I'm going to write about that."

And Ricky says, "I want to write about my dog Roxy" (Figure 4.9).

Of course, there are students who find it difficult to settle on a topic. Eduardo says, "I don't know what to write." For Eduardo, and others like him, I invite peers to ask questions that might lead to a topic. I also may hold a "topic-finding conference" with either individuals or a small group of students. We talk about what is on their hearts and minds. I ask, "What's going on in your lives? What are you interested in?" These conversations lead to writing. For younger writers, I ask them to draw something. This often catapults them into a topic worthy of their writing.

Shared Writing—Nonfiction Writing (Grades 1–3)

I want students to experience writing a nonfiction piece together from beginning to end. This way they will have support from both their classmates and me as we research, draft, revise, edit, and publish our piece. Since we will be working through the stages of the writing process, this lesson will take several days. To support our writing project, which is about polar bears, we have been reading several books about them. Among these are *Polar Bears* by Gail Gibbons, *Powerful Polar Bears* by Elizabeth Bennett, and *Polar Wildlife* by Kamini Khanduri.

Roxy Girl
the love
the puppy
the dogs we love
the fur
the wiggling her tail
the turning her head
the love
the puppy

Figure 4.9 *Ricky Writes About His Dog Roxy*

The purpose of this multiday lesson is to help students:

1. Learn about researching a topic.
2. Reflect upon what good writers do.
3. Plan and record writing ideas.

4. Take ideas and form them into sentences and paragraphs, then pages in a book.
5. Revise and edit.
6. Reflect upon the writing process, asking, "Are we doing what writers do?"
7. Publish our piece.

Day 1: Reviewing What Good Writers Do

I have been modeling all the things good writers do for a couple of months. I reread to make certain my writing makes sense. I model spacing and looking to my spelling card to spell words. I think aloud as I try to use interesting language, and I show students how writers revise their work to make it better.

Before beginning our writing project, I decide this would be a great time to reflect upon what good writers do. I tell students, "Before we begin our writing project later today, I would like us to think about what good writers do. I have a big piece of chart paper here and I would like you to turn and tell your neighbor two things you have watched me do, or noticed an author of a favorite book do, or some things you do as you write. After you turn and talk, we are going to record our ideas on this chart paper." (To learn more about "turn and talk," see Harvey & Goudvis 2007.)

Students share their ideas with students around them. After a minute or two, I gather students back together and ask, "What do good writers do?"

Students begin sharing. Tatum says, "They reread their writing."

Tatum knows this because she hears me say it every time students go to their writing folders to continue a piece they have started. I always say, "If you already have a piece started, make sure you reread your writing so you know where you left off and you can get your brain ready to continue."

I record Tatum's idea. "Okay. What else?"

Taylor says, "When they don't like a word, they scratch it out and change it."

"Yes," I say. "That is called *revision*. When writers do that, they are revising. May I write the word *revise* next to your idea, Taylor?" Taylor tells me yes and I record his idea.

We continue. Johnny adds, "They use spaces between their words."

Amber says, "They add details."

Miya adds, "They tell more."

Students continue sharing ideas and I record them. I am impressed at their level of understanding about what good writers do. I have to tape another paper onto our first one because students are so enthusiastic about sharing.

Finally, we have a complete list for now.

What Do Good Writers Do?

- They reread their writing.
- When they don't like a word they scratch it out and change it— REVISE!
- They use spaces between words.
- They add details—they tell more.
- They ask questions. (Does this make sense?)
- They get ideas from books, people, and their lives.
- They use interesting words.
- They check their spelling.
- They use capitals and periods.
- They write quietly.
- They write about what they know.
- They think about what they will write about.
- When they run out of ideas, they ask other writers for help or look in books.

We reread our list and decide this should remain on the wall (see Figure 4.10) to remind us to do these things as we write.

Day 2: Recording Ideas—Prewrite

We review our list, "What Do Good Writers Do?" Then I remind students of our topic: polar bears. We talk about all we have learned about polar bears. I have the books nearby for reference.

I begin our lesson by telling students, "We have been learning so much about polar bears over the last week. We have read some books together and I know many of you have been reading books about polar bears during reading workshop. Now I would like you to work with a partner to write two facts about polar bears on sticky notes."

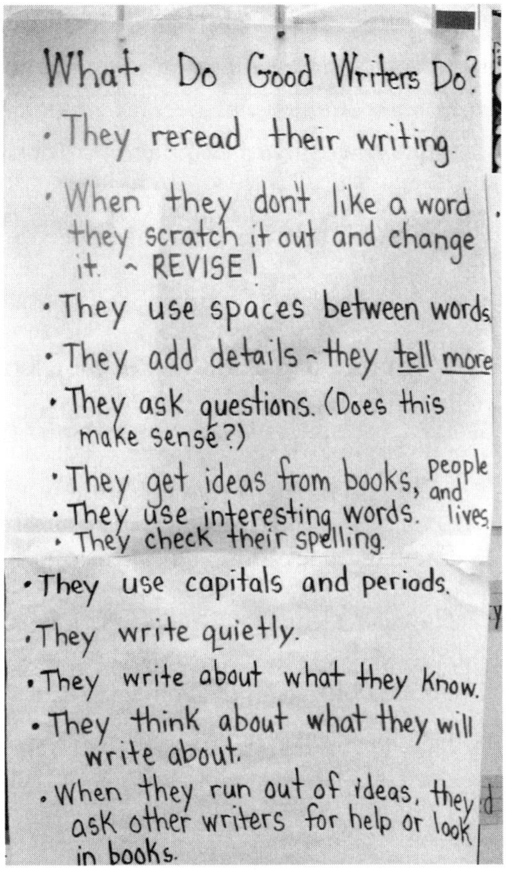

Figure 4.10 *Student-Generated List: "What Do Good Writers Do?"*

After students write facts, I continue, "The first thing we need to do is organize the information we have learned. I made a chart of empty boxes to help us as we record our information."

Students come up to the chart, reading their facts and placing their sticky notes in one of the boxes. We discuss our options, grouping similar types of facts into the same boxes. Then we title the different fact groups. For instance, we grouped these facts into one box, which we titled *Looks*:

They have white fur.
Males weigh 750 pounds.
Their paws are as wide as a ruler.

We grouped these facts with the title *How Polar Bears Move:*

They can swim 40 miles.
They run 30 mph.
They are athletic.

At the end of our fact-gathering and organizing lesson, students have several subtopics about polar bears with information about each (Figure 4.11).

Figure 4.11 *Student Chart of Sticky Note Facts About Polar Bears*

Days 3 Through 5: Drafting/Revising/Editing

Depending on students' attention level, I break this part up into one, two, or even three days, if necessary. I like to keep my minilessons short and this process can take some time. I use my judgment as to how long students will stay actively involved.

Students decide to turn our writing into a book. We will publish two copies; one will go to the library and one will stay in our classroom.

We decide to begin each page with a heading, a recently learned text feature. We start with a lead page.

I ask students, "How should we begin? Remember, we want to start with words that will grab our readers' attention."

Jordyn suggests, "*Have you ever wondered about polar bears?*"

"Great. I love starting with a question. Many authors do this. Is this a good lead?" Students agree.

I continue, "Okay. What else can we say?"

Nolan answers, "*Read this book and you'll find out a big amount of information.*"

Ryan suggests, "*Massive amount of information.*"

I make a revision. "Let's reread."

We recite what we have so far and Eleanor says, "We should add *It's all about polar bears.*"

"Good idea," I encourage. I write this last sentence and say, "Okay, we have a great first page."

> *Have you ever wondered about polar bears? Read this book and you will find out a massive amount of information. It's all about polar bears.*

"I think our readers will be anxious to read on. Let's start the second page: *How Polar Bears Look.* How should we begin? How about *Polar Bears . . .* "

Alex continues, "*Are big animals.*"

"All right. How big? How can we elaborate? What other information do we have?" I refer to our sticky notes, reading some of them aloud.

Laurelle says, "*In fact, male polar bears weigh 750 pounds.*"

I point out, "We just elaborated by giving a statistic. Remember, a statistic can be a number. In this case we tell how much the polar bear weighs—750 pounds."

Amber adds, "*Females are almost that big.*" I record Amber's idea.

Several students want to add, "*Their paws are as big as a ruler.*" As I record this last sentence, I suggest we add *(12 inches)* as a way to elaborate.

I then ask, "What color are polar bears?"

Ryan says, "*Polar bears have white fur.*"

Hanna adds, "And *underneath they have layers of blubber and black skin.*"

We reread our page. Kylie suggests we change the word *big* to *enormous*. Hanna suggests we change our subtitle to *Physical Characteristics*. I applaud both revision ideas.

Physical Characteristics

Polar bears are enormous animals. In fact, male polar bears weigh 750 pounds. Females are almost that big. Their paws are as big as a ruler (12 inches).

Polar bears have white fur and underneath they have layers of blubber and black skin.

I move students along. "I think we are ready for the third page: *Where Polar Bears Live.*"

Students work together to turn our notes into sentences that flow and make sense. We try to use content-specific vocabulary. We revise as we go.

Where Polar Bears Live

Polar bears live in the Arctic. The Arctic is at the top of the world. Most of the Arctic is ocean water. Lots of it is a frozen treeless land called a tundra.

We move onto the next two pages, writing about *What Polar Bears Eat* and *How Polar Bears Move*. Students enthusiastically share ideas about how to turn our notes into sentences. I guide the discussion and ask questions along the way, urging students to add definitions, examples, and statistics as ways to elaborate. Again, when twenty-three students share ideas, there are going to be disagreements, but they are mild. Students know this is a shared writing piece. When there are varying views, we negotiate what we record, but we don't belabor a disagreement. We keep the lesson moving.

What Polar Bears Eat

Polar bears are carnivores. That means they eat meat. Polar bears eat fish, walruses, seals, and small whales. Their favorite food is the ringed seal.

Polar bears hunt by sitting on the ice by a seal's breathing hole. They wait for the seal to come up for a breath and then they snatch them!

How Polar Bears Move

Polar bears are graceful and athletic animals. They can swim up to 40 miles. Their paws are webbed for swimming.

Polar bears can run 30 mph. Polar bears have fur on the bottom of their paws so they don't slip on the ice.

As we look at our chart of notes, I suggest we write a page titled *How Polar Bears Communicate.*

I say, "Our notes tell us a little about what polar bears do when they are angry. Can we write a page about how polar bears communicate? First of all, who do they communicate with?"

Jenny says, "They communicate with other animals."

Dylan adds, "Yeah, when they're angry they growl and hiss." I record both ideas.

"They also show their teeth," says Ryan.

"And put their heads down," adds Jordyn.

We work to add specific examples.

How Polar Bears Communicate

Polar bears communicate with other animals. When they are angry or upset they growl and hiss. They also show their teeth and put their heads down.

We move on to: *Having Babies.* Students describe, with interesting language, when polar bears are born. They elaborate by adding some statistics.

Having Babies

After polar bears mate, the female digs a den and waits for winter. For then is when the cubs shall come. The babies weigh only 1 pound. Their eyes are closed for 1 week after birth and they are deaf for 3 weeks.

Polar bear cubs stay with their moms until they are two years old.

Finally, we are ready for *Other Interesting Facts.* Students decide to title this page *Surprising Facts About Polar Bears.* We write a page, revising and editing as we go. I encourage students to end this page with a sentence that speaks right to our reader and lets them know our book is finished.

Surprising Polar Bear Facts

Did you know polar bears have been living for 100,000 years? Their biggest enemy is us (human beings).

If we don't take care of our earth, the ice will melt and polar bears will die.

Let's save these wonderful creatures for the future!

We are ready to reread our book from start to finish. Students decide to title our book *Polar Bears*. Hannah suggests we use our first page also as a blurb for the back. I am thrilled that students are connecting their learning in reading with their learning in writing.

We now look at our chart, "What Do Good Writers Do?" We review our list and I ask students to reflect on whether we did these things as we wrote our book about polar bears.

"Did we reread it to see if it made sense?"
"Did we use interesting words?"
"Did we elaborate?"
"Did we revise?"

We continue down our list and students agree we tried to do all of these things.

Over the next couple of days, I ask students for help typing our book. I use a large font and we type each page separately. We cut and paste our typed words onto twelve-by-eighteen-inch construction paper. Students pair up to illustrate each page, making sure their pictures match the text (Figures 4.12, 4.13, and 4.14).

We bind our book and read the published copy together. We place one copy in our classroom library and present one copy to our school library. This shared writing lesson becomes a wonderful springboard and model for students as they write their own individual animal books in the weeks to come.

Shared Writing—Get-Well Letter (Grades 1–2)

There are real opportunities to write every day. In today's lesson I want to teach students that writing is one of the ways we show appreciation and make people feel better. One of our parent helpers is having knee surgery and will miss a few weeks in the classroom. I decide to suggest we write Mr. Frost a get-well letter.

Figure 4.12 *Shared Writing Book Cover:* Polar Bears

The purpose of this lesson is to help students:

1. Write for a real purpose and audience.
2. Learn/practice letter-writing format.
3. Revise and edit (practice conventions of print).
4. Elaborate on ideas.

I begin by letting students know that Isabella's father will not be coming to help this week because he is having knee surgery. Before I make my suggestion, Adena says, "Why don't we make a get-well card or write a letter?"

"Great idea!" I reply. "I was thinking the same thing, Adena."

I gather students on the floor. Instead of choosing chart paper, this time I write on a piece of paper on the document camera or overhead projector and project it up on our screen.

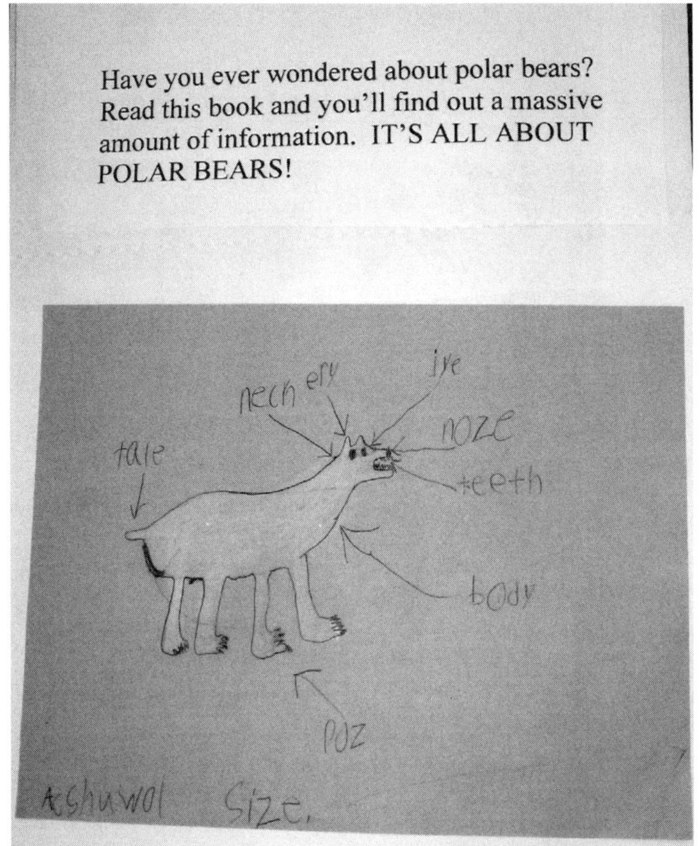
Have you ever wondered about polar bears? Read this book and you'll find out a massive amount of information. IT'S ALL ABOUT POLAR BEARS!

Figure 4.13 *Sample Page from Shared Writing Book:* Polar Bears

Isabella tells us a little about her father's surgery and how long he will be at home. Then we begin. I ask students, "Who remembers how we start a letter?"

Many hands go up and students say, "*Dear Mr. Frost, . . .* "

As I begin writing, Alex says, "Don't forget the comma."

I answer, "Oh yes. We always put a comma after the person's name when we write a letter. What does a comma tell us to do?"

Jessica remembers, "It tells us to pause."

I continue, "Okay. How should we begin?"

Reilly says, "*We are sorry you hurt your knee.*"

Miya says, "*We are very sorry.*"

"That's a good start," I say as I begin recording. "Anything we want to add to that?"

Jason says, "*We wish it never happened.*" I record this sentence.

I suggest the beginning of our next sentence. "How about we say, *Isabella tells us* . . . What did she tell us Mr. Frost will be having?"

What Polar Bears Eat

Polar bears are carnivores. That means they eat meat. Polar bears eat fish, walruses, seals, and small whales. Their favorite food is the ringed seal.

Polar bears hunt by sitting on the ice by a seal's breathing hole. They wait for the seal to come up for a breath and then they snatch them!

4

Figure 4.14 *Sample Page from Shared Writing Book:* Polar Bears

Many students share, "Knee surgery."

I write *Isabella tells us you are having knee surgery.* "Okay. What should we say next; maybe a good wish for Mr. Frost?"

Ricky suggests, "*We hope you get well soon.*"

I prod, "Is there anything else we could say to Mr. Frost to show how much we appreciate him?"

Miya says, "*Thank you for helping us.*"

Tatum adds, "*Thank you for helping us learn.*"

I revise, adding the word *learn.* "Okay. Should we tell Mr. Frost how much we will miss him?"

"*We will miss you while you're gone,*" suggests Jesse.

"Great. Now we are at the end of our letter. We need to skip a line. Then we need to write either *Sincerely,* or *Your friends*, or something before signing our names. What should we say?"

The class decides on *Sincerely.* Again, I take the time to talk about the use of a comma, and I sign: *Ms. Sloan's class.*

We reread our letter and Taylor wants to add a question: *How long will you be on crutches?* We find a good place for this and I ask for two students to work together to rewrite our letter on a nice sheet of paper. I remind them that when we publish our writing, our work must be neat and our spelling, capital letters, and punctuation must be correct.

Two students volunteer and we send the letter home with Isabella that day (Figure 4.15).

Modeled Writing—A Moment in Time (Grades 2–3)

When students write about camping trips, birthday parties, or baseball games, they often make a list of everything that happened. They want to tell you one sentence about every aspect of the trip, game, hike, or party. *We did this. Then we did this. Then this happened.* And so on.

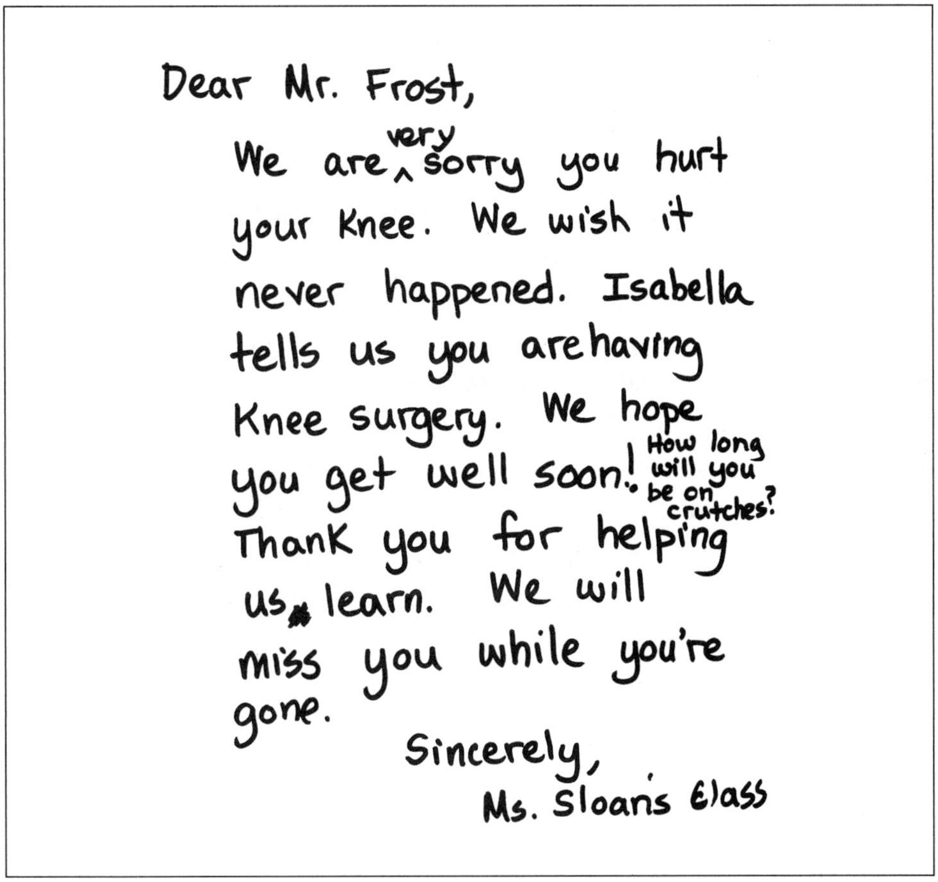

Dear Mr. Frost,

We are very sorry you hurt your Knee. We wish it never happened. Isabella tells us you are having Knee surgery. We hope you get well soon! How long will you be on crutches? Thank you for helping us learn. We will miss you while you're gone.

Sincerely,
Ms. Sloan's Class

Figure 4.15 *Shared Writing Letter to Mr. Frost*

I want students to write about moments (Calkins & Oxenhorn 2003; Flynn & McPhillips 2000). I want them to focus on one particular time, and slow down that time by telling what someone said or how they felt, or by using specific language like simile or metaphor. Calkins & Oxenhorn (2003) model teaching students to "catch small moments from their lives and stretch those moments out" (2). That's what I want to teach my students.

The purpose of this lesson is to help students:

1. Narrow their topics.
2. Focus on a moment in time.
3. Elaborate (slow the moment down) by telling what someone said or how they felt, or using specific language.

I begin my lesson by telling students that there are all kinds of moments: remembered moments, one-time moments, surprising moments, sad moments, exciting moments, and funny moments. The list goes on and on.

I explain, "Often we try to write about everything. We go on a trip and want to tell everything that happened. When we do this, it's like letting our readers only swim in the shallow end of the pool. They hardly get wet. We barely let our readers know anything before we tell something new. Our story becomes a list. If we want our stories to be great, we need to dive deep. Picture what it's like to swim to the bottom of the pool, eyes open, to retrieve an object. That's where we need to go with our memory; we need to bring the best details up to the surface. We need to decide on a moment. Maybe it lasts a half hour, maybe five minutes, maybe only thirty seconds. We need to tell about that moment and really slow it down so our readers know *why* it's memorable to us. Here's how we do it.

"First we need to decide on a moment. For instance, we just had winter break. I did a lot of things. Here is a list of some of the things I did."

- I decorated my tree.
- My niece came to visit.
- We had Christmas dinner with my family.
- We went Christmas caroling.

- I went shopping at the mall.
- My sister's dog got into lots of trouble.
- I read a good book.

"I could write about everything I did and everything that happened, but that might not make the most interesting story. I need to think about what is most memorable. I am going to pick just one thing to write about. I think I will write about my sister's dog. Now he got into a lot of trouble so I want to think about one moment—one thing he did and focus on that. I've got it. Bailey is my sister's dog's name. One night he got into a box of chocolate-covered cherries. I think I will write about that.

"I know good writers grab their reader with a good first sentence, so I want to think about how I should start my story."

I write:

Well, he did it again.

I ask students, "What do you think? Does that make you wonder and want to read on?"

Students say, "Yes."

I continue.

I'm talking about my sister's dog Bailey. He is a mischievous pet.

"I think I should tell why he is mischievous."

He gets into everything: garbage, toy boxes, and even toilet paper.

"Now I should focus on one particular moment and try to stretch it out. I will tell what I yelled, and how I felt. I'm even going to see if I can use a simile to try to slow this moment down."

One night, we were all sitting around. It was quiet and the fire was crackling. It was too quiet. All of a sudden, I asked, "Where's Bailey?" I heard a slight crinkling of plastic. I spun my head around, and there was Bailey—the resident thief—in my box of chocolate-covered cherries. "Bailey!" I yelled. "What are you doing?" I jumped up, quick as lightning, and ran to him. Chocolate cherries were scattered all over the floor like leaves in autumn. Bailey had one in his mouth. He was trying to grab another but I said, "No. Bad dog!" I grabbed his collar and led him outside for a time-out (something very familiar to him). I was disappointed to lose my cherries, but all of a sudden I began to laugh. My sister laughed too. What else could we do? That's our Bailey. He makes us mad sometimes, but you've got to love him.

As I write, I tell students what I'm thinking. I let them know I am trying to slow down this moment. I'm telling what I said *("Bailey," I yelled. "What are you doing?")*. I'm telling how I feel (*I was disappointed to lose my cherries*). I'm using similes to slow down the moment and describe (*I jumped up, quick as lightning; Chocolate cherries were scattered all over the floor like leaves in autumn*). I want students to know these are conscious decisions so I think aloud, "I can tell what I said here" or "I can tell how I'm feeling."

"Now it's your turn." I ask students to think about moments in their lives, perhaps moments from their winter break. Maybe they built a snowman. Maybe they watched their pet do something naughty, or cute. Maybe they snuggled with their mom or dad and enjoyed a good book.

When I ask students to write about a moment, I often say to them, "Write a lot about a little. Pick a small moment and stretch it out [Calkins & Oxenhorn 2003]. Slow it down." Ralph Fletcher and JoAnn Portalupi (1998) suggest, "Think about the time focus in this piece you are working on. Have you bitten off more than you can chew? If you are trying to cover too much time in one piece of writing, you might find yourself listing: we did this, then we did this. You might get better results by slowing down and focusing on one brief stretch of time" (60). I suggest that students slow down moments by including what someone said or what they felt, or using a simile. I ask students, "What kinds of moments can we write about?" Then we generate a list.

fun moments
embarrassing moments
exciting moments
sad moments
relaxing moments
once-in-a-lifetime moments
proud moments

I ask students to consider this list, think about a moment to write about, and then work on slowing it down. In Figure 4.16, Eleanor, a second grader, writes about a small moment.

Charting Elements of Good Writing (Grades 1–3)

I love piggybacking off one lesson by using a student piece as a model for good writing. I use this strategy for teaching beginning writing skills such as matching text to picture, using correct conventions, or adding one or two details, as well as for more advanced skills such as using simile or metaphor and elaborating by including anecdotes, examples, or statistics. For today's lesson, I focus on recent skills taught and ones students are practicing: writing lead and ending sentences, slowing down a moment, and staying on topic.

Students have been writing about moments. Jordyn wrote a piece about a brand new moment—one she had not experienced before. After conferring with Jordyn, I asked her if we could use her piece to talk about elements that make a good piece of writing. She agreed.

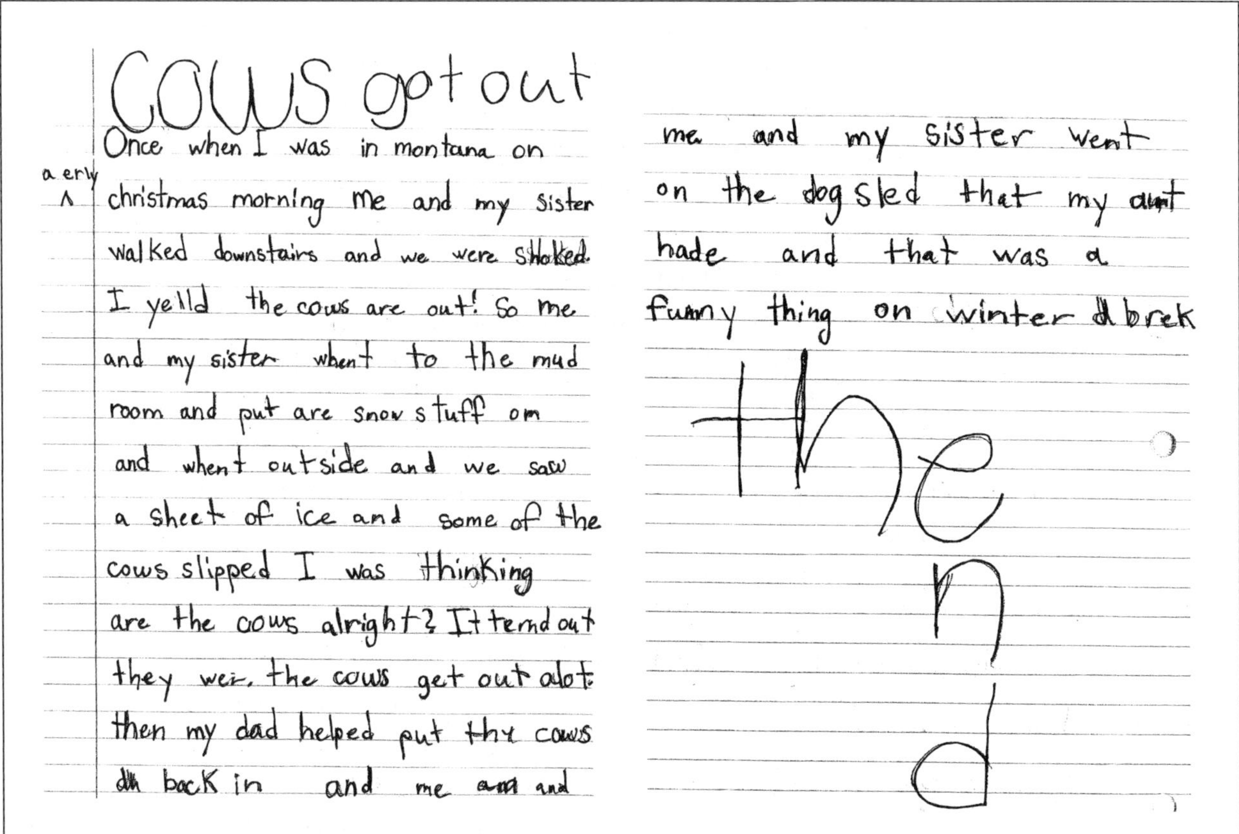
Cows got out
Once when I was in montana on
a erly ^ christmas morning me and my sister
walked downstairs and we were shoked.
I yelld the cows are out! So me
and my sister whent to the mud
room and put are snow stuff om
and whent outside and we saw
a sheet of ice and some of the
cows slipped I was thinking
are the cows alright? It ternd out
they wer, the cows get out alot.
then my dad helped put the cows
back in and me and
me and my sister went
on the dog sled that my aunt
hade and that was a
funny thing on winter brek
the end

Figure 4.16 *Eleanor Writes About a Small Moment*

The purpose of this lesson is to help students:

1. Read a classmate's writing with a positive, yet critical eye.
2. Identify elements from the piece that make it stand out as a good piece of writing and chart these elements.
3. Take what they have shared and heard during the discussion and apply it in their own writing.

I begin the lesson by telling students, "Today we are going to examine a personal story written by one of your classmates. Yesterday, Jordyn wrote about a brand-new moment for her: ice-skating. I would like us to take a close look at Jordyn's piece and share some of the things you think she does especially well." I project Jordyn's piece onto the screen so students can see—as well as hear—Jordyn's writing (Figure 4.17). "Jordyn, would you read your piece to us clearly and slowly so we can really pay attention to all of the positive things you did?"

Jordyn reads her piece to the class. I give students a moment to think. Then Jordyn reads the piece a second time. After the second reading, I ask students to tell a friend one thing they notice Jordyn does well in her writing. I prepare to record student ideas on a chart.

"Okay, what do you notice Jordyn does well? Think about what we know about good writing."

Adena says, "She has a good first sentence."

I prod Adena, "Tell me more about that."

"Well, she made me want to hear more when she said *You won't believe what I did.*"

I add, "I agree," as I write down Adena's words. "What else?"

Taylor says, "I like how she says *SMACK* in big letters. She said, *All of a sudden . . . SMACK!!!*"

"Yes, what does that do for the moment?" I ask.

Tatum answers, "It slows it down."

I chart Taylor and Tatum's words.

As I do, Dylan says, "She slows things down when she tells what she says and then what her mom says after her brother fell."

"Good. Writers slow down the moment by telling what someone says."

Josh adds, "She also slows the moment when she tells how nervous she was feeling."

Ice Skating

You will not beleve what I did over Christmas break! I went iceskating for the first time! first we got our skates. Now, you probley know how nervas I was feeling when I first got on the ice. I held on to my mom tight so I didn't fall. Once I got good and wasn't scared I let go to try by my self!

I was having so much fun that I forgot to pay atention. All of a sudden...SMACK!!!!! I fell on my bottem. But it didn't hurt to much so I just got right back up and tried agin. as I was skating I saw my brother crying. With the rest of my famly

he was siting out. I went and sat out to. Then I asked "what hapend?". My mom said "He fell!". Then they did the Zamboni thing. It makes the ice smooth. Afterwards we went agin. but before I new it..., We had to go home! I hope I ice Skating agin soon!

Figure 4.17 *Jordyn's Piece*

Miya adds, "And it's like she was talking to the reader because she says *Now, you probably know how nervous I was feeling*. I like that."

"So she really connects to her reader," I say as I add that to our chart. "What else?"

Amber says, "She adds lots of details." We go through Jordyn's story again and talk about some of the details like:

> *I fell on my bottom* but it didn't hurt too much.
> *I first got on the ice*. I held on to my mom tight so I didn't fall.

I direct students to Jordyn's ending. "What do you think? Does Jordyn tell us she is finished? Does she have a conclusion to her story?"

Students agree Jordyn lets her reader know she is finished with her story.

I finish recording and we review our chart of ideas (Figure 4.18).

I say, "Wow. Jordyn does a lot of things writers do when they write well. I notice many of these things in all of your writing too. You all are adding details and learning to begin with a strong first sentence and end with a mem-

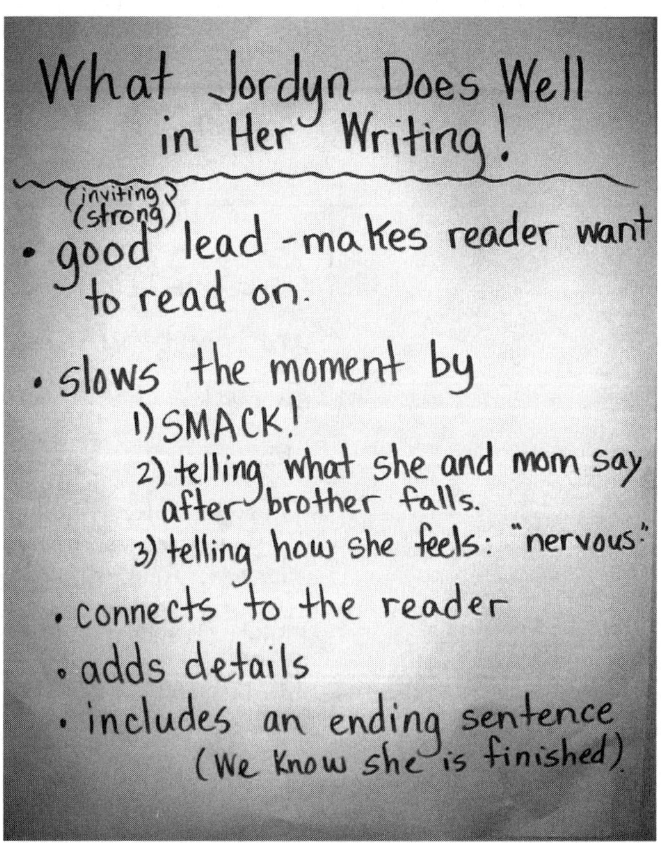

Figure 4.18 *Class List: What Jordyn Does Well in Her Writing*

orable ending sentence. You are slowing your moments down by telling how you feel and what someone says."

I continue, "Today when you write, think about this chart of things Jordyn does well. See if you can include these elements in your writing. Add details. Think of a first sentence that will grab your reader. Slow your moments down."

Students go off to write. The chart hangs as a reminder of what good writers do.

Student Modeling—Write About a Small Moment (Poetry) (Grades 1–3)

Day 1: Drafting the Small Moment

Today, I want students to have more practice writing about small moments (Calkins & Oxenhorn 2003). We have been out walking, observing the different colored leaves. We have noticed puffy white clouds in stormy skies. And we have watched older students playing double-dutch jump rope as we walk to P.E. class. We are constantly observing moments. I read to students from Valerie Worth's *All the Small Poems and Fourteen More* to show how an author or a poet can slow down a moment with words: observed moments such as a dog lying down for a nap, daisies growing along a lane, or crows flying low in the sky.

The purpose of this lesson is (again) to help students:

1. Choose a small moment to write about.
2. "Slow down the moment" by telling what you observe.
3. Use notes to record observations.
4. Use notes to write a personal narrative or poem.

I often have students help me teach, so I ask if there is someone who would like to help me with today's lesson. Katherine raises her hand.

I ask her, "Do you have any small moments that come to mind—something you would like to write about today?"

Katherine says, "Yes. I watched my cat go to sleep yesterday and I want to write about that."

"That's a great small moment," I say. "Tell me what you observed. I will write down your ideas on sticky notes so you will remember them."

Katherine begins, "Well, my cat jumped up on the bunk bed."

I write *jumps on bunk bed* on a sticky note. I ask, "Did she make it all the way up there on the first jump?"

Katherine answers, "No, first she jumped on the chair, then on the desk, then on the bunk bed." I stop and write on sticky notes. I number Katherine's ideas.

1. the chair

3. bunk bed

2. the desk

Katherine continues, "She makes a cave out of the blanket and crawls in." Again, I take notes.

4. makes cave from blankets, crawls in

I ask, "Does she go to sleep, or do something else?"

Katherine answers, "She goes to sleep and then wakes up and takes a bath by licking herself. Then she goes to sleep again."

I record Katherine's words to help her remember.

5. goes to sleep,
takes bath,
licks herself

I tell Katherine, "Take your sticky notes and use them as reminders of some of the words you want to use in your writing. I numbered them to show the order of the story you told. You may change the order if you like. Move things around and add some more ideas."

Katherine begins writing. I suggest to students, "Tell your small-moment stories to friends. Take some notes if it helps. Then write your story." Figure 4.19 shows Katherine's draft.

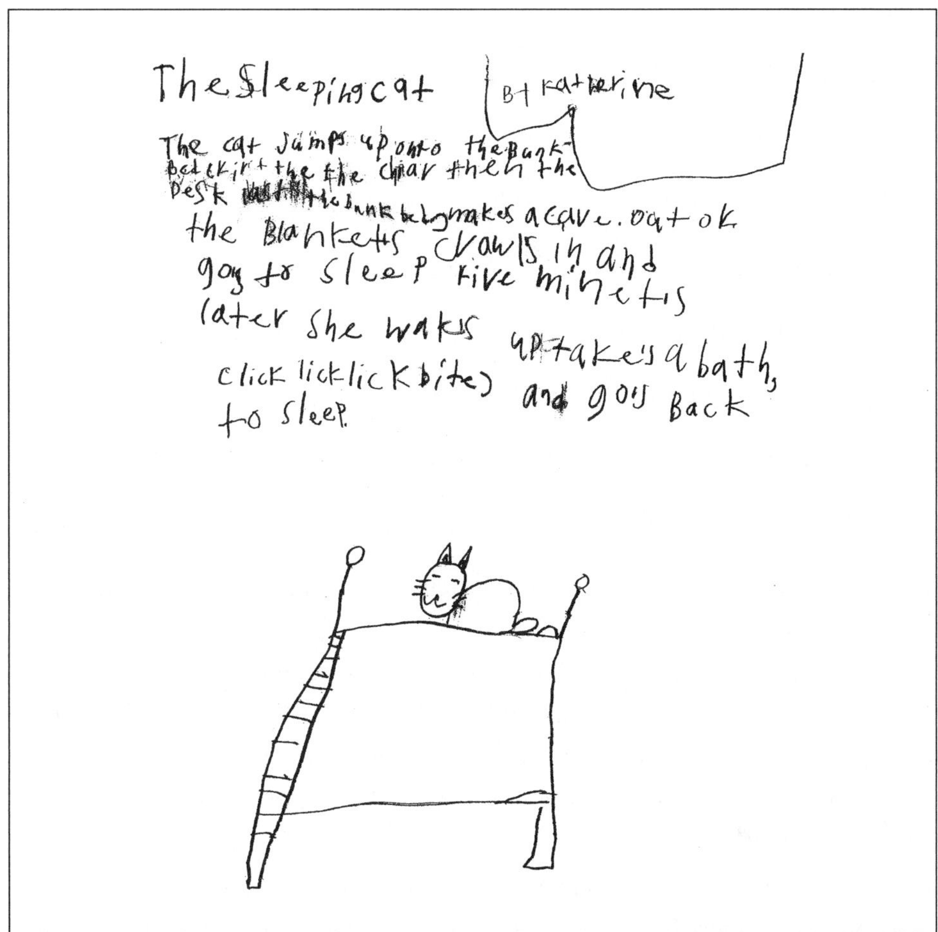

Figure 4.19 *Katherine's Draft*

Day 2: Revising, Editing, and Publishing Katherine's Small-Moment Piece

Now it is time to reread Katherine's draft and work toward publication. Right away, Katherine says, "I want to publish this as a poem."

I ask, "Why do you think it is a poem?"

Katherine answers, "It sounds like one."

Our conference becomes a minilesson for others who want to make their writing look like a poem. I ask Katherine to read her poem aloud, as we all listen. I tell her, "You are right. This does sound like a poem. You use some great language and make us anticipate what will happen next. Would you like to work to make this piece *look* like a poem?"

Katherine agrees and so we set to work, modeling for the class.

"Poetry is different than other genres. Let's make a list of things we notice about poems."

Here is what we notice about poems:

Poems

1. Often have a title.
2. Use words or phrases (don't have to use complete sentences).
3. Often begin with a word or line that grabs the reader.
4. Use interesting words and language.
5. Are filled with feeling.
6. Can be about anything.
7. Can be funny, sad, happy, or serious.
8. Use line breaks and white space (don't write to the end of the line).
9. Include an ending line/word that tells your reader the poem is finished.

We project Katherine's poem onto the screen. She reads it again and as she pauses, I make slashes to show where she might want to break lines. I remind students, "Poems are not written to the end of the page like stories. You need to decide when to go to the next line. When do you pause while reading your poem?"

Katherine reads her poem again, looking at the slash lines. Students comment on Katherine's language. Tatum says, "I like when you say *first, the chair, then the desk, then the bunk bed.* It makes me wait to find out what happens." Ricky adds, "I like the part where you say *(lick, lick, lick, bite).*" Katherine decides to have a publishing conference. In a publishing conference, I help students with the layout of their piece, as well as editing. In this case, I help Katherine with new ideas for line breaks for her poem.

The lesson continues

The next day Katherine comes to me and asks for a quick conference. She says, "If we already typed my poem, does that mean I can't change anything?"

I say, "You are welcome to make changes. Your poem is on the computer and we can revise it. If you think of something that will make your poem better, change it and we can retype that part."

Katherine makes some changes and we retype (Figure 4.20). Her revisions show an effort to include interesting language. Katherine shares her revising experience with students during our share/reflection time.

The Sleeping Cat

The cat jumps up
onto the bunkbed,
first, the chair,
then the desk,
last the bunkbed,
makes a cave
out of the blankets,
crawls in and
goes to sleep. drik t's ok to sleep
Five minutes
later
she wakes up
and takes a bath
(lick, lick, lick, bite)
and goes and driks
back to
sleep.

Figure 4.20 *Katherine's Revised Poem*

Using Student Writing as a Model—Write to a Prompt or Topic (Grade 2–3)

Sometimes I give students a topic or prompt. Today Hanna has come into class with special shoes. Amber has a special knit hat. Since I want students to focus on small topics, I suggest, "Everyone has some item of clothing they really like. Today, I would like us all to write about a special piece of clothing. This can include shoes, hats, and scarves too." I let students think and then turn to a friend and talk about special clothing items they own.

The purpose of this lesson is to help students:

1. Write to a topic/prompt.
2. Focus on something small.
3. Elaborate on ideas.
4. Include a lead and ending sentence.
5. Include interesting words.
6. Use correct conventions.

I begin my lesson by telling students, "We probably need some guidelines or a rubric for our writing. Should we make a list of ideas to include in our writing?"

We begin making a list together.

Favorite Clothing Writing

- Begin with a great lead sentence that grabs our reader.
- Choose interesting words.
- Describe your clothing item.
- Elaborate by telling
  - where and when you got it.
  - why it is special/why you like it.
  - where you wear it.
- Conclude with an ending sentence.

For younger writers, the list would be a bit shorter.

I ask Amber to help me teach the lesson today. She stands by our chart and tells us about her hat. I ask, "Do you have an idea for a first sentence that will tell your reader what you are writing about?"

Amber says, "*I have a fabulous hat.*"

"That's a great sentence," says Eleanor.

"I like the word *fabulous*," says Jason.

I record Amber's sentence. "Okay. Let's take some notes. I will write what you say on these sticky notes. How can you describe your hat?"

Amber pauses and Claire raises her hand. "It looks soft."

Amber nods, "It is."

As I write on a sticky note, I say, "That's a great description. What color is your hat?"

Amber says, "It is lots of colors, like orange and brown and yellow mixed in."

I write:

lots of colors like orange, brown, and yellow mixed in.

"Where did you get your hat?" asks Taylor.

Amber answers and I write,

It was a special gift from my mom.

We continue asking Amber questions and I take a few more notes. We are almost finished when I tell Amber, "You already have a great first sentence. You can bring your clipboard up here and copy your sentence right from the chart. I will also give you these sticky notes with some of your ideas. You may use them, but you might also like to elaborate with other ideas. Remember, you also need to make sure you have a great ending sentence that tells your reader you are done.

"For the rest of you, think about your favorite piece of clothing. What is it? Tell a classmate about it. Use our idea chart to think of details to write. Try to use at least one interesting word in your writing. If it helps to draw your clothing item first, you may do that."

Students begin writing and drawing. Here is Amber's finished piece.

My Special Hat

I have a fabulous hat. It's really soft like a kitten's fur. It has lots of colors like orange, brown, and yellow mixed in. It was a special gift from my mom. She gave it to me for my birthday. I love wearing my hat because I feel great when it is on my head. That's my hat.

Figures 4.21 through 4.23 show samples from first, second, and third graders.

Using Literature as a Model for Lovely Language (Grades 1–3)

Our best models of good writing are all around us: they live in the stories and poetry we read aloud, and in the books on our shelves that students read individually, in pairs, and in small book clubs. From Dr. Seuss to Kate DiCamillo, we stop to celebrate the language we see and hear.

Figure 4.21 *Joe's First-Grade Sample*

Michael
My favorite Clothing is
My Sweater and it is White.
MY MoM gave it for MY
birthday and I Love My mom

Figure 4.22 *Michael's Second-Grade Sample*

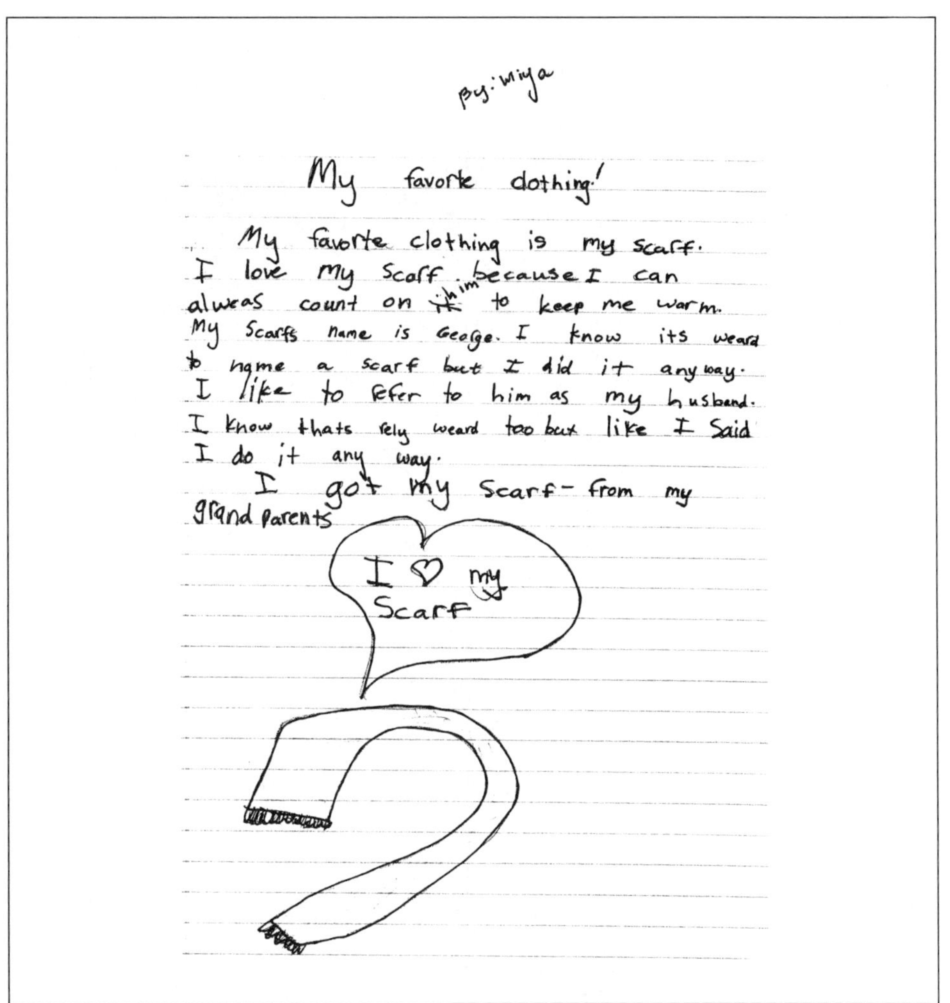

by: miya

My favorte clothing!

My favorte clothing is my scarf. I love my scarf because I can alweas count on ~~it~~ him to keep me warm. My Scarfs name is George. I know its weard to name a scarf but I did it anyway. I like to refer to him as my husband. I know thats rely weard too but like I Said I do it any way.

I got my scarf from my grand parents

Figure 4.23 *Miya's Third-Grade Sample*

We have been reading *Mrs. Frisby and the Rats of NIMH* by Robert C. O'Brien as a class. As we read, we note the interesting language the author uses. We keep track of some of these words, recording them on an Alphabox chart (Hoyt 1999). This is a chart broken up into about twenty boxes. Each box includes one to three letters from the alphabet. There is room in each box to display interesting or content-specific words that start with those particular letters (see Figure 4.24).

> The purpose of this lesson is to help students:
>
> 1. Notice interesting language in books.
> 2. Talk about interesting words and phrases in books.
> 3. Consider using interesting language in their writing.

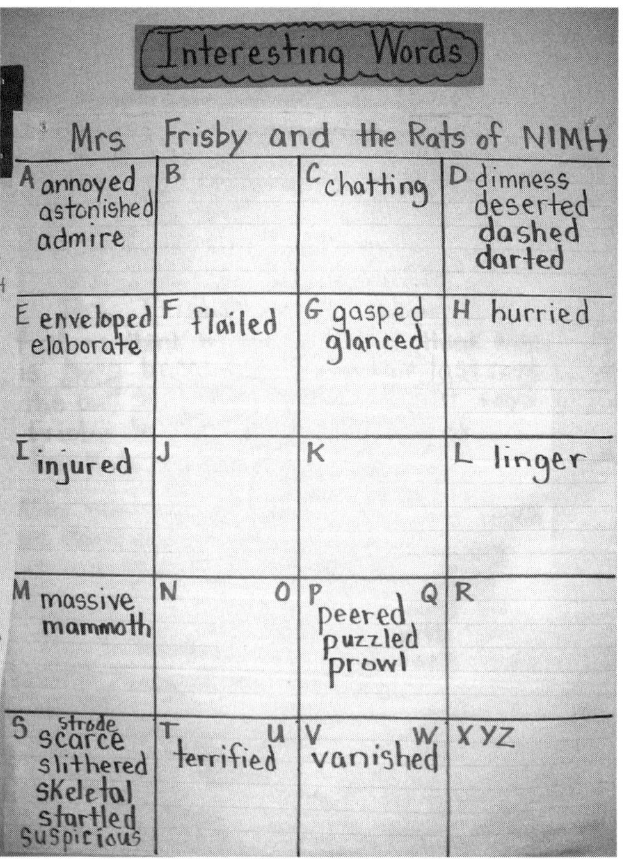

Figure 4.24 *Alphabox Chart of Interesting Words*

For today's minilesson I choose a picture book to read: *A Grand Old Tree* by Mary Newell DePalma. We read the book twice: once to hear and feel the flow, and a second time to stop and talk about the language. I ask students, "Are there interesting words you like? Do you notice a simile or metaphor? Is there any word, phrase, or sentence that you want to read aloud?"

Claire comments, "I like how it says *her arms reached high into the sky.*"

Rachel comes forward, turning the pages of the book. She explains, "I like the part where it says *and snow gently covered her*. It's peaceful."

"And it says *squirrels scurried*," Taylor adds. "I like the word *scurried.*"

I point to our chart, *What Do Good Writers Do?* "We know good writers use interesting words and phrases. Today, as you write, think about using interesting words, whether you are writing a nonfiction piece, a personal story, or a poem. Let's be inspired by *A Grand Old Tree.*" Figure 4.25 shows a third-grader's poem about her favorite season.

Miya

My farrotite Sesane

One of my farroite
sesans is Spring. It's nat
to hat and its nat
to cold.
The Spring breez feels
so good an my face. It
feels like the wind is wispering
a song to the trees.
I love to ride horses in
the spring because you dont have
to take of the fly mask and
you dont have to take of the
blanket. I lave the felling
of the real canter.

I ablsulutly lave spring.

Figure 4.25 *Miya's Poem About Spring*

On subsequent days, I choose to read other picture books with interesting language. *The Bee Tree* by Patricia Polacco includes many alternatives for *went* and *said*. We make a chart to remember all of these fantastic words (Figure 4.26).

Denise Fleming is a master at word choice. We read *Time to Sleep* and *Where Once There Was a Wood* to find and celebrate words like *slithered, rambled, unfurl, grumbled,* and *glittering* (just to name a few). We make a list of authors and poets who inspire us to use interesting words (Figure 4.27). I continue to encourage students to be inspired by the language of our favorite authors.

Shared Writing—Leads, Endings, and Elaboration (Grades 1–3)

I want students to write with a sense of beginning, middle, and end. I want to teach them that writers begin with an inviting lead. They fill the middle of their writing with details and interesting words and language. They end with

Figure 4.26 *Interesting Words from* The Bee Tree

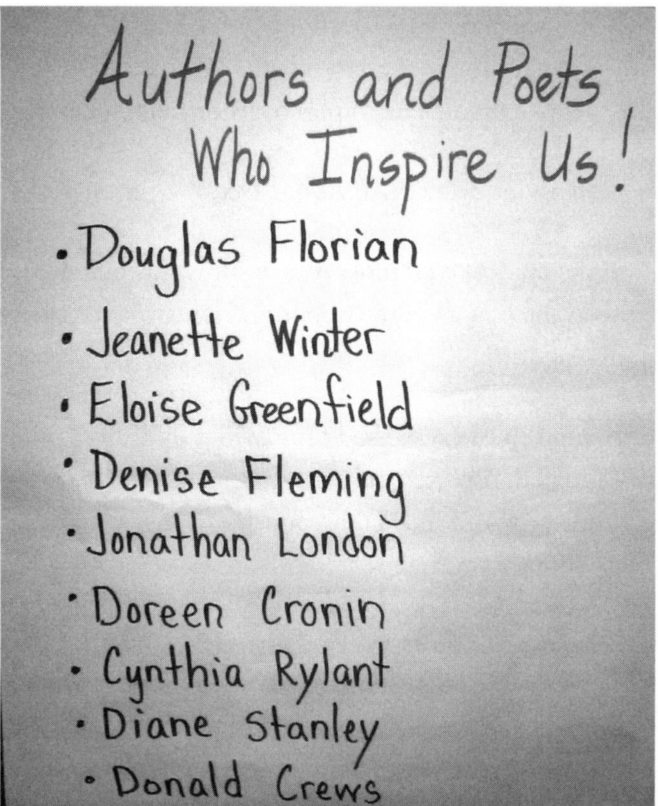

Figure 4.27 *Authors Who Inspire Us with Their Language*

a memorable ending sentence. This may seem a bit simplistic, but that is what I want—simple—so my primary writers will understand. I adapt this lesson as needed, simplifying the writing for younger writers and expanding for more experienced writers.

The purpose of this lesson is to help students:

1. Include an inviting lead.
2. Elaborate with details.
3. Use interesting language (including content-specific words).
4. Include a memorable or satisfying ending.

Whenever I can use a visual to help students understand a specific topic, I use one. Today I am teaching students about lead and ending sentences. I sometimes substitute the word *first* for *lead* for younger writers.

Over the past few weeks, we have talked about great lead sentences, paragraphs, and first pages in the books we have read. We ask, "Do they make us want to read on?" Here are some examples of leads from literature:

> "Have you ever wondered about deer?" (*All About Deer* by Jim Arnosky)

> "Two red wolves roam the coastal wetlands. A rare snow has fallen, and icicles glitter. . . . She-Wolf has a secret nobody knows." (*Red Wolf Country* by Jonathan London)

> "A thin crescent moon, high in the sky, shed faint white light over Dimwood Forest. Stars glowed. Breezes full of ripe summer fragrance floated over nearby meadow and hill. Dimwood itself, veiled in darkness, lay utterly still." (*Poppy* by Avi)

We discuss the different techniques authors use in their leads:

- Start with a question.
- Start with a quote from a character.
- Start with a bold statement.
- Start with a description of the scene.
- Start with a statement about how you are feeling.
- Start with a fact or statistic.

We have also stopped to consider the ending sentences, paragraphs, and pages of the books we have read. Do they leave us satisfied? Here are some examples of great endings from literature:

> "Good night, everyone, see you in the spring."
> (*Time to Sleep* by Denise Fleming)

> "They perched in silence for a long time.
> 'How can we be so different and feel so much alike?' mused Flitter.
> 'And how can we feel so different and be so much alike?' wondered Pip.
> 'I think this is quite a mystery,' Flap chirped.
> 'I agree,' said Stellaluna. 'But we're friends.
> And that's a fact.'"
> (*Stellaluna* by Janell Cannon)

"We can be sure of this:
It's a circle without end.
It's pumpkin seeds to pumpkins to pumpkin seeds again!"
(*Pumpkin Circle* by George Levenson)

"Brave Ramona, that's what they would think, just about the bravest girl in the first grade. And they would be right. This time Ramona was sure."
(*Ramona the Brave* by Beverly Cleary)

Finally, we begin to talk about applying first and last sentences in our writing. I draw a simple hamburger with a top bun, some meat in the middle, and a bottom bun (Figure 4.28).

I point to the top bun. I say, "This is your first sentence." I point to the meat and say, "This is your idea." Then I add some pickles and mustard and onions. I explain, "These are your details and interesting words and lovely language" (see Figure 4.29).

Then I point to the bottom bun. I tell students, "This is your last sentence. This is what holds your writing together. If you don't have a bottom bun your hamburger will fall all over the place. The same is true if you don't have an ending sentence. Your writing falls apart. It does not feel complete. Think of your ending sentence as the bottom bun of your hamburger."

I suggest that we write a piece together about recycling, a topic we have been reading and talking about in class. I guide students through a shared writing experience, asking questions, guiding discussion, and recording ideas.

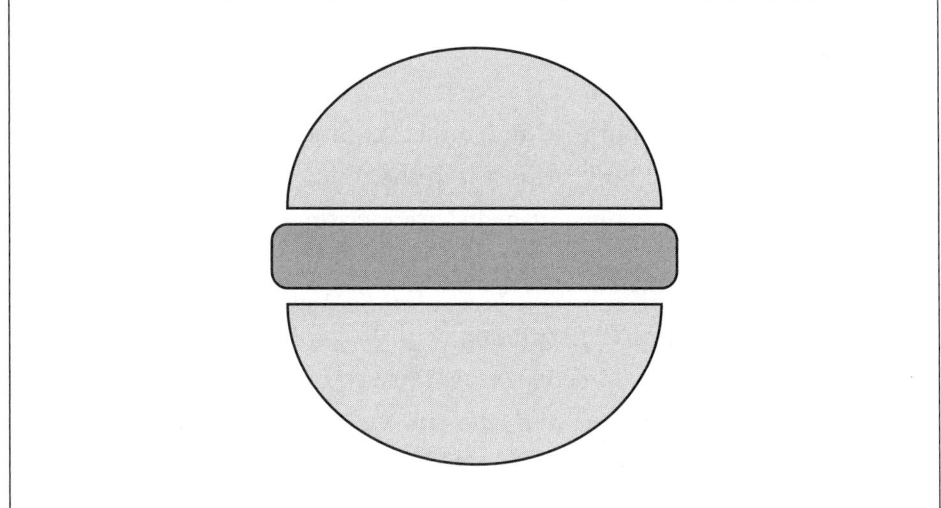

Figure 4.28 *Simple Hamburger*

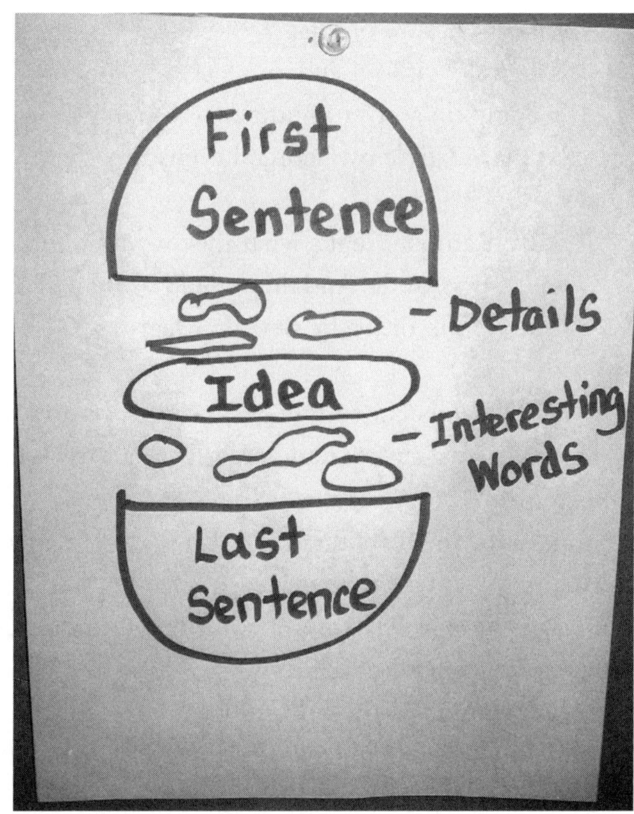

Figure 4.29 *Revised Hamburger*

I focus students on:

1. including a strong lead sentence,
2. adding details and interesting language (including content-specific vocabulary), and
3. including an ending sentence that will satisfy our reader and let them know we are finished.

We first discuss our purpose and audience. Students decide to write our piece for the school and hope to post it in the office to inform and persuade people to recycle. Here is our finished shared writing:

> *Recycling is an important thing to do. It is easy and can even be fun. You can recycle glass, plastic, paper, and cans. Just collect each in a container.*
>
> *Once you do that, someone brings them to be recycled. Paper becomes new paper. Glass, plastic, and cans are melted down and can be made into new products.*
>
> *If we don't recycle, it takes years for glass, paper, and cans to biodegrade. Biodegrade means a thing is eaten away by the sun, the rain, or wind*

and goes back into the earth. Plastic never biodegrades. These things take up room on our earth in garbage dumps called landfills. There's not enough room for all this garbage.

If we want to be responsible citizens, we need to take care of our earth. One way is to recycle. Everyone can do it and our earth will be a better place!

After drafting our piece we reread, revise, and edit. We ask ourselves, "Do we have a strong lead sentence?" (top bun). "Do we include details with some interesting words?" (meat, cheese, pickles). "Do we have an ending sentence that will satisfy our reader?" (bottom bun).

After publishing this piece on poster board, it becomes a "look to" chart in our classroom to remind students about good writing. In Figures 4.30

Figure 4.30 *Chase's Draft About Fall (First Grade)*

Figure 4.31 *Luca's Draft About Cheetahs (Second Grade)*

through 4.32, students include strong lead and ending sentences in their own writing.

Final Thoughts

- Students often write about different topics, and sometimes use different genres. Minilessons on word choice and use of language, elaboration, great leads and endings, sense of purpose and audience, or correct use of conventions are all pertinent, no matter the topic. Students can apply what they are learning in their individual writing.
- Modeled writing gives students a chance to see and hear the process a writer uses to connect with the reader, elaborate upon ideas, and work to write in a clear and organized way.

Name ________________ Date ________

Greetings from space
Mr. Carter,
Thank you for sharing
rockets with us. It was
great that you got
to share with us.
I was interested
with evrything and
it was strange when
you told us it
took about 5 years to
get to the moon.
from Cole. N

Figure 4.32 *Cole's Thank-You Letter to a Guest Speaker (Second Grade)*

- Shared writing of thank-you letters, nonfiction reports, personal narrative, and poetry can serve as models for students when they write in these genres and for these purposes.
- Interactive writing gives young writers a chance to participate in writing ideas, practicing the conventions they are learning every day.
- Minilessons need to be short. They must have a clear purpose and they should build upon each other. I like to ask, "What do my students need to learn about writing?" I start there.

CHAPTER 5

How Do I Balance Student Choice with Teacher-Directed Writing?

It's February. This morning I am teaching a unit on nonfiction writing. A few students need to finish writing their nonfiction books about topics they have researched—including rocks, the solar system, ballerinas, and (yes) a variety of animals such as frogs, wolves, and tigers.

We are just beginning our drafting time. As always, I suggest that students look in their writing workshop folders to see if they would like to work on something that is already in progress. I stress the importance of finishing their nonfiction books. I encourage others to begin, or continue to work on, topics of choice.

As students gather materials and settle into their spots, Kylie, a second grader, comes to me and says, "I'm not quite finished with my tiger book, but my hamster, Gus Gus, went to the vet today and he's really on my heart and mind. Could I write about him instead?"

I am overwhelmed with pride as I answer, "By all means, if Gus Gus is on your heart and mind, it sounds like he is the right topic for you today."

I smile as Kylie skips back to her spot. I am reminded of a quote by William Zinsser (2001): "If you follow your affections you will write well and engage your readers" (92). Kylie's nonfiction book about tigers can wait. What really matters is the topic she feels passionate about right now. This is what she will write well today, with voice and commitment. This is what her readers will enjoy reading. How can I steal that opportunity from her, even if she has something else to finish?

Writing for Real Reasons

The magic of writing workshop is choice (Figure 5.1). Students get excited when they have a chance to write about what matters to them. Young students write to make sense of the world. They write because it serves a purpose. I constantly see student-written signs around the room: *Join our reading club; Missing Eraser; Jump Roping at Recess. Join the fun.* Students write to communicate. They understand that sometimes writing is a better way to "tell something" than speaking it.

When Robbie lost his calculator, he posted the sign in Figure 5.2. Reilly created the sign in Figure 5.3 to announce a Teenage Mutant Ninja Turtle game. He let his classmates know what game was being played, when to meet, and where to meet.

Jordyn typed her own sign to communicate to her book club members (Figure 5.4).

Figure 5.1 *Student's Sentiment About Writing: "Write What You Want To"*

Figure 5.2 *Robbie's Sign Offering a Reward for a Missing Calculator*

Our kindergarten teacher, Mrs. Ask, shared the note in Figure 5.5 with me. Two of her students placed this flower-shaped sticky note on her desk to ask if she could walk them to their arts and crafts class after school.

We hope that children will bring these writing experiences home. Recently I visited my six- and eight-year-old nieces. Several signs hung on the wall. The one shown in Figure 5.6 communicated the menu they were having for dinner. It includes lists of food and drinks, pictures, and labels.

Katherine and Neil, two twins in my class, wrote the sign in Figure 5.7, which they placed on their bedroom door. Their mother said that every day the two would go into their room to read and write, imitating what we do at school. And Tyler's mom told me, "There are so many poems lying around the house, we need to get Tyler another notebook."

Lucy Calkins (1994) notes, "In the [writing] workshop children write about what is alive and vital and real for them" (19). This is what these students are doing with their signs and announcements. They are writing for a real purpose: to communicate to others about things they value.

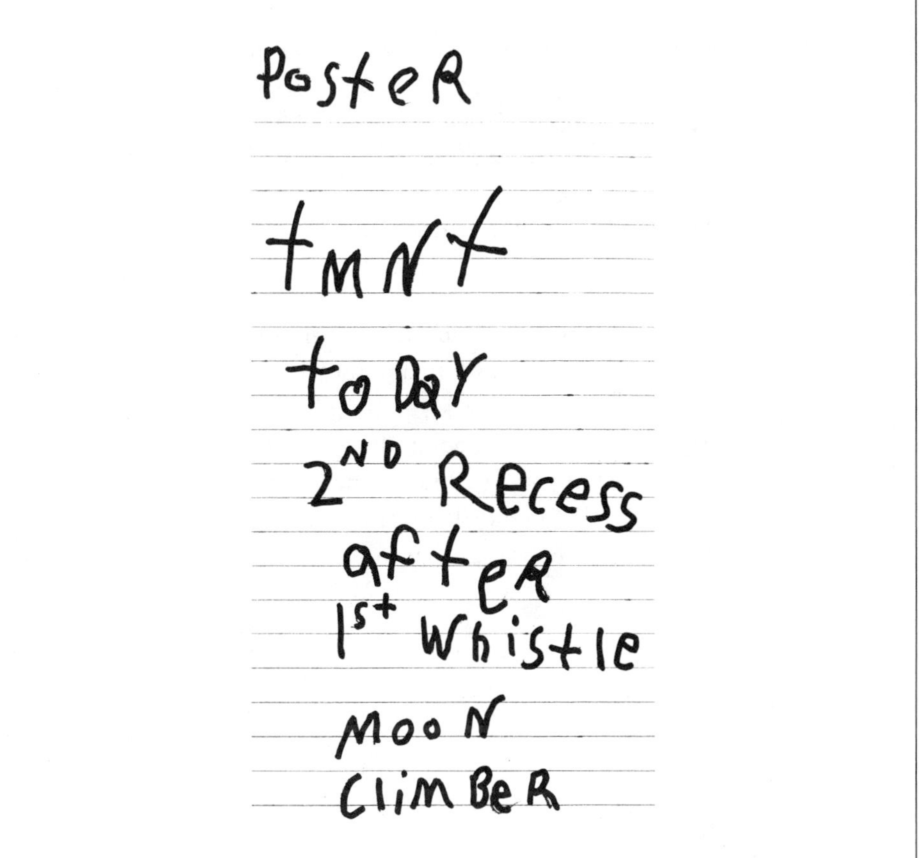

Figure 5.3 *Reilly's Game Announcement*

Vicki Spandel (2005) proposes that "Writing springs from who we are" (21). This is quite evident when I think about my students and what they choose to write about. For example, Eleanor is a thoughtful student. She knows about what is going on in the world and she is confident about expressing her feelings. One day during writing workshop she writes a letter to President Bush (see Figure 5.8).

It is clear that even through her individual choice of topic and genre, Eleanor is applying much of what she has learned about writing. She includes a lead and ending sentence. She elaborates. But most important, she writes with voice and commitment, and with a purpose and an audience in mind.

Another student, Rachel, adores dogs. (This is truly who she is.) In Figure 5.9, Rachel writes about them as her "passion."

Students are most interested in writing about what they love and what stirs their passions. I don't have to coax Rachel to write about dogs, or Eleanor to write about her objections to the war. It springs from them. I don't have

Book Club News

Dear Book Club Members,

Hi this is Jordyn your Club Leader and I have a special announcement for you. Book Club invites you to be in our finger puppet show in response to our recent book. We would appreciate it if you could join us because some of you said that Book Club wasn't very fun and we would like to change that. Anyway hope you can make it.

Figure 5.4 *Jordyn's Sign to Book Club Members*

Mrs. Ask can you walk me and Isabella to arts and Crafts?

Figure 5.5 *Note from Kindergarten Students*

Figure 5.6 *Dinner Sign*

Figure 5.7 *Reading and Writing Club Sign*

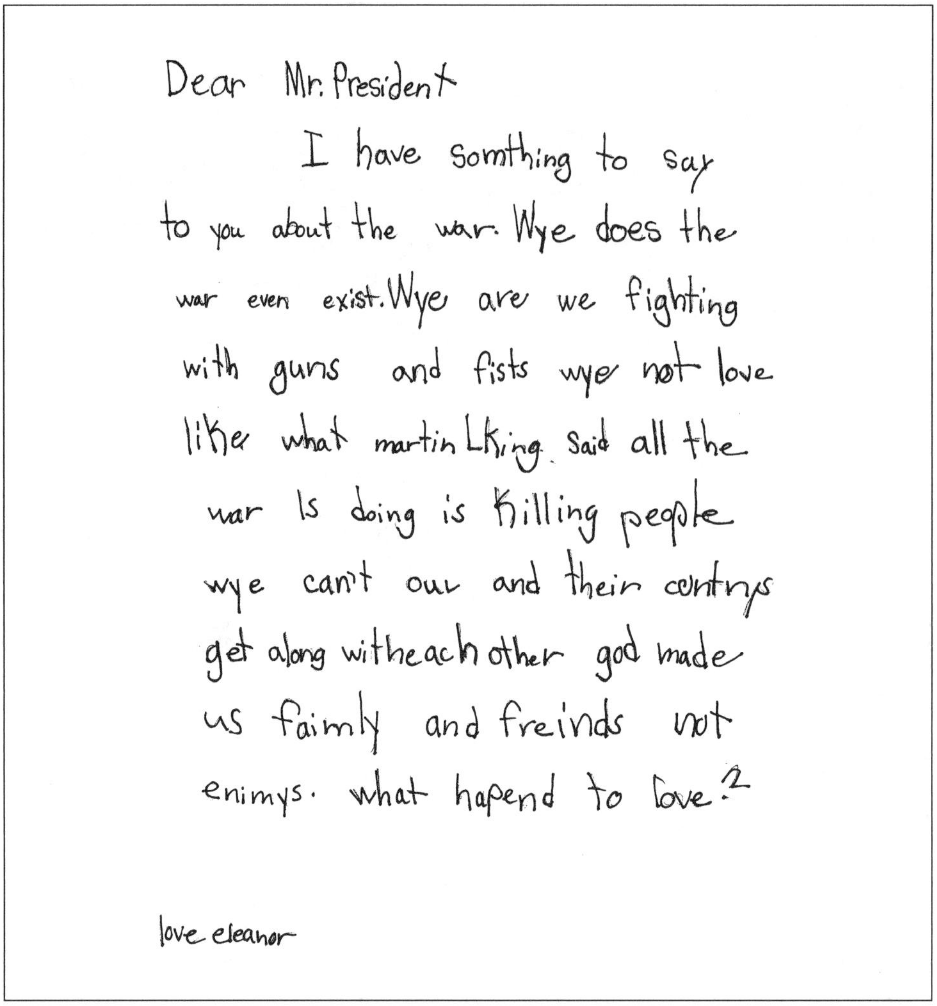

Dear Mr. President
I have somthing to say to you about the war. Wye does the war even exist. Wye are we fighting with guns and fists wye not love like what martin L King. Said all the war is doing is killing people wye can't our and their contrys get along witheach other god made us faimly and freinds not enimys. what hapend to love.?

love eleanor

Figure 5.8 *Eleanor's Letter to President Bush*

to coerce Reilly, Robbie, or Jordyn to write, when they get to pick a topic and genre that fits their interests and purposes. They just do it. It's natural. It makes sense.

Teaching the Traits

As I share in Chapter 4, I vary my minilessons. The topics spring from both a sensible writing progression and the current needs of my students. Many teachers focus a minilesson on one or two traits, such as ideas, organization, voice, fluency, word choice, or conventions. For example, during a minilesson I may concentrate on writing for real purposes and audiences, matching text to picture, using an inviting lead, or elaborating by adding examples and anecdotes. However, just because I have a specific focus for my lesson does

Figure 5.9 *Rachel Writes About Dogs*

not mean I teach only that one quality or writing trait. As I model my own piece to teach about elaboration, I still must begin with an inviting lead sentence and include a satisfying ending. I still need to ask, "Why am I writing this and who is my audience?" I may even stop to think about using an interesting word or to revise when I see that something is unclear.

As teachers we know we can't compartmentalize writing. While we often focus on a small moment in a piece, we still have to teach about the whole piece of writing. If I am teaching my third graders about opening with a scene as an effective kind of lead, I may only work with that part of the story today. However, I will still speak about word choices and conventions of print. I will still teach about effective ways to make the scene "grab the reader's attention."

The traits of writing are simply that: some characteristics of effective writing. They help us focus our teaching and our assessments, but they aren't the be-all and end-all. When they become too important in our minds, to the point where we worry if we are teaching them all the right way, then it's time to take a step back. Take a deep breath. Remember that real writers don't sit there with a checklist of traits; they write out of passion and curiosity, to share what they know, to peak their minds. Children are no different.

Do students still have choice when we're teaching the traits?

Whether I am focusing on one trait or teaching several, I often am asked, "Isn't the topic that students write about predetermined by your lesson?"

My answer is, "Not really." For instance, when I teach about opening with a scene, students can either study the same genre or choose to work on this skill with their own topic and own genre: fiction, nonfiction, biography, or personal narrative. If my lesson focuses on using interesting language, again the topic and genre are wide open. The same is true for elaborating on ideas. Any topic or genre will work.

Of course, there are times when a particular lesson lends itself to a specific genre. For example, I model how to take notes about a nonfiction topic, turn these notes into sentences, and elaborate upon the ideas. Although this lesson can transfer to other genres, students see clearly how it works with nonfiction. Then they can apply what they have learned with their own nonfiction topics.

When students participate in a shared writing as part of a minilesson, sometimes I suggest a topic and genre. For instance, we might write a fiction story about a turkey who is trying to avoid getting slaughtered for Thanksgiving. In this lesson, which might span a couple of days, students learn about story structure and share ideas for our class piece of writing.

I might also teach students about phrases as we write poems about the desert, a landform we study in social studies. After this lesson and teacher-directed writing, I provide students with opportunities to write poems on self-chosen topics. This work with phrases also affects the flow of narrative and nonfiction writing.

How do I fuse the "units of study" concept with student choice?

Other questions I am asked, and wrestle with myself, are "What do I teach and when do I teach it? Do I begin with fiction, nonfiction, narrative? How do I make sure students learn to write in all genres if I always give them choice? How do I stay true to the concept of writing workshop if I am directing what genres and topics students are using and writing about?

Let's revisit some definitions of writing workshop. Katie Wood Ray and Lisa B. Cleaveland (2004) talk about a writing workshop where "the focus is very much on the writers" (4). Included in her definition, Regie Routman (2005) lists "writing for purposes that the writer values and understands"; writing workshop is a place where students write about "mostly self-chosen topics" She also invites us to broaden our definition to include "the time in which everything that writers do to create a meaningful piece of writing for a reader takes place" (174). Can this be accomplished while teaching units of study?

In many classrooms teachers either teach using their own timeline for units of study or they follow published options such as the Units of Study for Primary Writing (Calkins et al. 2003), which provides a year-long curriculum. Ralph Fletcher (2006) praises units as "content-rich . . . help[ing] students gain a deeper understanding of various genres." But he warns that "these units of study whittle away at the student's choice" (45).

As I look at a "units of study" approach, I know I have a huge responsibility to lead students in a way that will keep purpose, audience, and choice authentic to the process. During the first ten weeks of the year, we explore our own following units: "Setting the Tone and Learning About Writing Workshop" and "Personal Narrative." To set the tone, I encourage a love for writing and focus on getting kids excited and comfortable with the process. This means I want them to write for real purposes: letters, signs, books, personal stories. Choice is essential.

I believe Lucy Calkins (2003) offers her units in a flexible order, knowing that classrooms vary and students' needs and interests are different. After "Launching the Writing Workshop," she begins with the unit "Small Moments: Personal Narrative Writing." I, too, want students to focus on the small things and experience the wonder of writing about moments that adults might not consider: a butterfly landing on a flower, playing in a pile of leaves, hearing the sound of rain, or even an elephant going to the bathroom (Figures 5.10 and 5.11).

After the first ten weeks, I am wide open for ideas on which kind of writing we study next. I let the students' needs lead me. I love to move students into poetry early because often my reluctant and struggling writers find success with poetry. Poems can be short. Students don't have to write complete sentences. Suddenly, children who don't think they are writers become writers. For the first time in their school lives, they are applauded for their work.

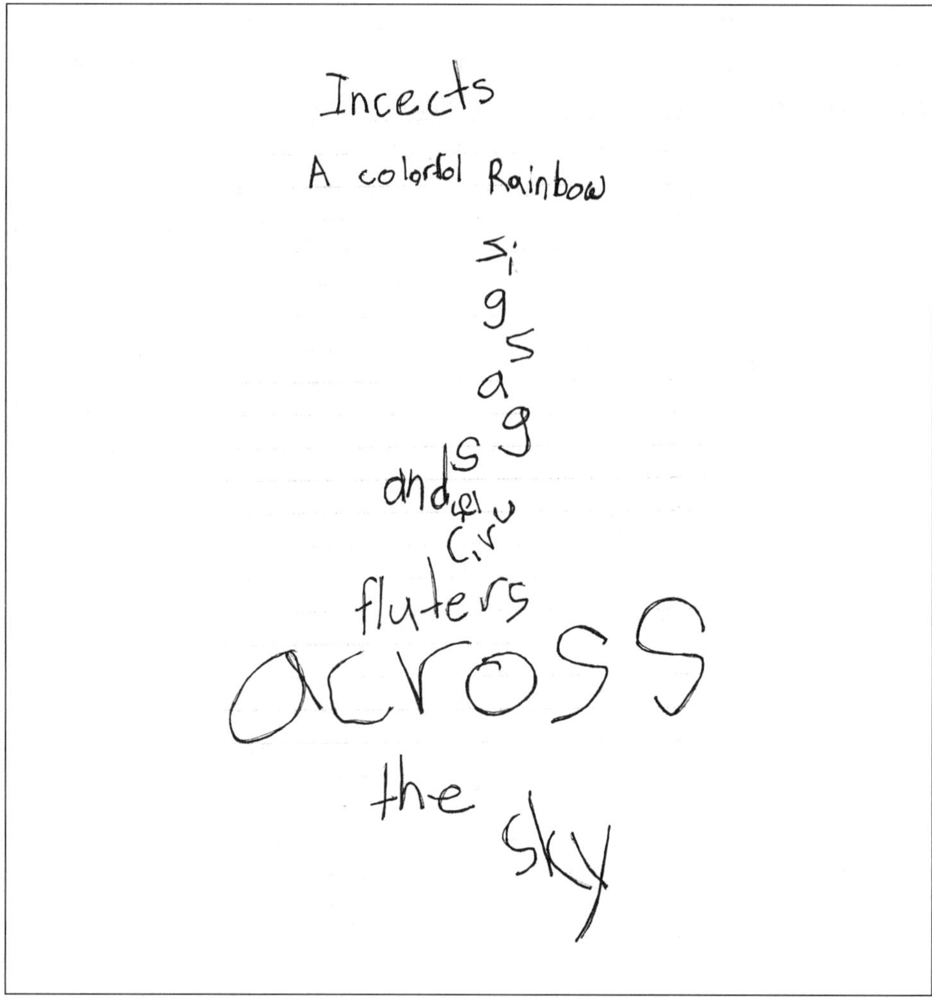

Figure 5.10 *Dylan Writes About a Butterfly*

An Argument for Starting with Poetry

Take Taylor. He struggled a bit with reading and writing. He didn't always have ideas and did not show much interest. Writing was hard for Taylor.

One day we all observed a fall tree. We charted what we noticed, including phrases rather than complete sentences. Bobby shared, "Almost bare." Alicia said, "Reddish-orange leaves." Emma added, "Dangling from the branches." Students remarked how the branches were "reaching for the sky" and the "dew sparkled like diamonds."

Back in the classroom, after hanging our chart of words and phrases, I invited students to write a poem about our fall tree. It was not a requirement, simply a suggestion. Students always have choice about what they write. I may require a genre at times, but the topic is theirs. Taylor took the challenge.

In an earlier lesson we had noticed how sometimes poets repeat lines or words if they really want their reader to notice them. Taylor remembered this and gave it a try.

Fall Tree

Leaves trying
To hold on the tree
For their lives.
Looking like
sparkly diamonds,
Hanging on the tree
Almost floating down
Almost fluttering down
Right now
Almost a
Winter tree.

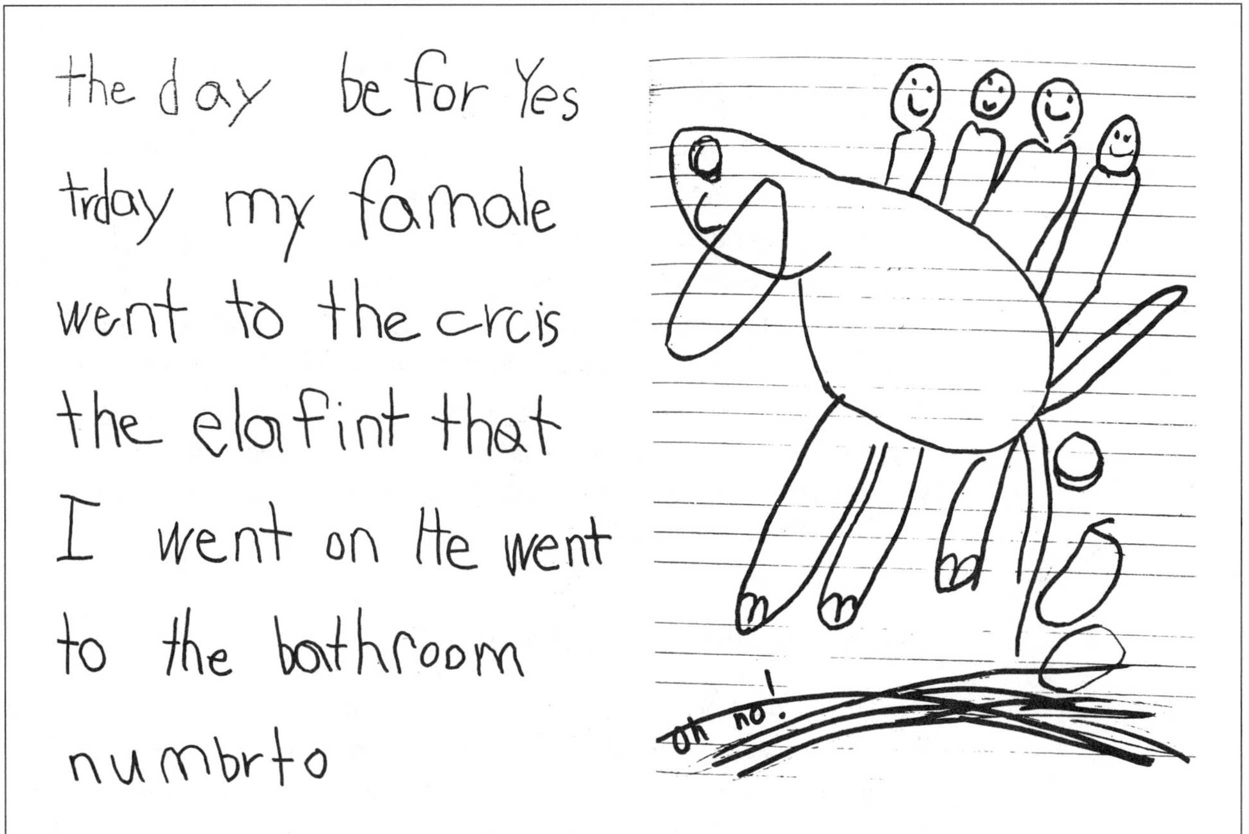

Figure 5.11 *Taylor's Trip to the Circus*

As I worked with Taylor to type his poem, I was in awe. I said, "Taylor, I love how you used the words *sparkly diamonds*. I love your descriptive words: *fluttering* and *floating*. I can picture this happening. But most of all, I love how you repeated the word *almost*. What was your reason for doing this?"

Taylor answered, "We learned poems repeat words sometimes when they are important."

I prodded, "Why was the word *almost* important?"

"Because it is *almost* a winter tree. It won't be fall much longer."

"Oh, I really understand and you really made me pay attention there. You know, I kept anticipating the next line. I leaned forward and wondered. Way to go."

Taylor read his poem to the class and students responded with what they noticed.

"I like *sparkly diamonds*. You used a simile," said Emma.

Serena added, "I like how you say the leaves try *to hold on the tree*, like they were holding on for life."

Several students commented, "I like *floating* and *fluttering*."

Bobby said, "That's what leaves do. They float and flutter."

Finally, Jessica said, "I like how you repeated the word *almost*. It really made me think about the tree and when you said *almost a winter tree* I could see winter coming."

I added, "Remember, repeating a word, line, or phrase can make the reader really pay attention to something important."

Our sharing time was finished but from that moment on Taylor was a writer, and a good writer, not only in the eyes of his classmates but also—even more important—in his own eyes. He believed he was a writer now and it made all the difference in the world, not just when he wrote poetry but when he wrote anything. And for the rest of the year, every time someone was working on a poem and wanted to repeat a word or line, students would say, "Oh, you should go ask Taylor for help. He really knows about repeating words in poems." Taylor was a star.

Organizing Units and Balancing Choice

As you've seen, I begin my year with "Setting the Tone and Learning About Writing Workshop." For the first six weeks of school, I teach students about writing and promise them, "This will become your favorite time of day." During this time, I model writing personal narrative because I want students to get to know me. I encourage them to tell and write their real stories. I teach students to write about what is on their hearts and minds. We practice writing for extended periods of time. We learn about choices for materials (paper, books, and so on), and about matching letters to sounds or looking to resources for spelling.

November–December

From there, I continue encouraging students to write personal narratives, and we dive deeper into writing about observed moments. I support this all year. I never want students to feel, "Well, I had a great story to tell about my dog, but we are finished with personal stories so I guess I can't write about that."

Our next unit explores poetry. (We will revisit this unit later in the year.) During our unit students write poems about all kinds of topics: fall, pets, holidays, animals, and more. Students still write personal narrative. Some write nonfiction and fiction (jumping ahead of what we are learning). I never require students to stick just to the genre we are focused on. It is too limiting. Students choose their topics and their genres all year long. What a shame it would be if, in March, a student had a great idea for a poem but I said, "We're not writing poetry anymore. We did that in November. Sorry." Similarly, if Grant could write adventure stories only during a six-week fiction unit, he would not evolve into the eager, enthusiastic, and talented writer he is.

January–April

This period is when I really see where the students' interests lie. I want them to continue writing for real reasons (notes, directions, recipes, personal stories, signs, and observations). I want them to continue to write about their lives and the stories that excite them. I also want to introduce students to lots of authors and let these authors serve as mentors. I gather tons of books and we concentrate on having authors teach us about writing.

We notice the language authors use, and students imitate. We write stories and poems inspired by the authors we read, such as Eloise Greenfield, Cynthia Rylant, Douglas Florian, and Mo Willem. Students write their own *"Dear Mrs. LaRue"* (Mark Teague) and *Diary of a Worm* (Doreen Cronin) stories. They explore many genres as they borrow the style, language, and organization of Denise Fleming, Avi, Dav Pilkey, and Patricia Polacco.

I would extend this unit with children in kindergarten. For students in first grade and beyond, I might focus on nonfiction or biography next. This is the time of year I introduce students to people of history such as Harriet Tubman, Ruby Bridges, Abraham Lincoln, and Chief Joseph. As we read about these people, students are inspired to write about them.

Students love to read nonfiction. I pair a nonfiction writing workshop unit with a nonfiction reading workshop unit. Students choose topics to read about and research. They write and create books, posters, pamphlets, or brochures about their topics. This is where I may take third-grade students a little more diligently though the writing process.

Again, I cannot stress more that I continue to allow students to write about other self-chosen topics and work with other genres. Yes, students are choosing their topics for this unit of study, but because I am directing the genre I want to make sure I leave time for students to work on their own writing projects. I may leave some days open for choice. Students also may work on their own writing workshop projects any time they are finished with other school work. And they do. Often students choose to write when other work is finished (Figure 5.12).

April–June

During the last part of the year I try to revisit poetry, and then I focus students on the genres they like to write. Maybe I introduce a simple definition of memoir. Maybe we revisit the way we write our personal stories. Perhaps some students want to extend their learning about nonfiction. I also encourage students to revise and edit a bit more; at this point, many are ready to do

Figure 5.12 *Adena Works on Her Own Topic*

so. I let my students lead me during this final part of the year. I want them to leave my classroom loving writing and feeling the true magic of writing workshop.

What about the test? What about prompts?

In this era, I know we are all worried about "the test," whether it is a state- or district-driven assessment of students' performance in writing. I was recently asked to come to a district to work with teachers on the Writing CBAs (Classroom Based Assessments) in Washington State. I understand that teachers are concerned. They want their students to practice the kinds of "writing" they will be asked to do on "the test."

It is true that students will have to write to a prompt for "the test." I am not against giving students prompts once in a while. Surely, this is a skill students will need in the future for interviews and college applications as well as for "the test." Prompts also help us assess students' writing in a specific genre. I administer about five prompts a year to see how students write to a predetermined topic and genre. It gives me different information about their writing. In addition to using writing prompts, I sometimes direct writing during reading, social studies, and science too.

However, I believe it is essential not to focus too heavily on prompts. Yes, prompts can give us a sense of control about what we are teaching students. They can make us feel we are keeping on track. And we have sometimes worked hard to write these prompts. However, as Vicki Spandel (2005) argues, "If we truly believe that writing is thinking, then we must let our writers go where their thinking leads them—as far as it will take them, even if that means leaving the best of our prompts far behind" (36).

I don't believe we need tons of prompts to prepare students for "the test." I think that by teaching them to write with purpose and voice, to elaborate on ideas, to use language that inspires, and to write in an organized way, we will prepare students for the test without even trying.

Final Thoughts

So, how do I balance student choice with teacher-directed writing? A lot of reflection goes into my decision. I want my students to feel in charge of their writing, choosing the topics and genres that excite them. This choice will move students forward as writers: Because they will *want* to write, they *will* write. As William Zinsser (2001) says, "You learn to write by writing" (49). Students will write if we give them choice.

However, I also need to consider what students need to learn. Which genres do students need to learn to write so they are well-rounded in their experiences and prepared for future assessments? Which genres might they learn to love, and show talent in, when taught and given the chance to write? It's always a dance, teaching in a way that honors the interests and needs of my students while moving them forward with direct instruction in the qualities and techniques that will help them become well-rounded writers.

Here is a summary of how I balance student choice and teacher-directed writing with my students.

1. I give about four to five formal prompts per year. Usually these are decided by a group of teachers at my grade level. We all give the prompt and we meet together to assess student writing (see Chapter 9).
2. I often offer suggestions for writing topics. For example, when I model writing about my grandfather, students are reminded of special people in their lives (grandfathers, grandmothers, uncles, sisters, moms, and so on). After I write, they have their own stories to tell. Mostly, I encourage students to write about what is on their hearts and minds, but I also suggest they write about one of these special people if they are inspired to do so. Some students try it, and some write down this topic idea for another day. I offer this as choice within a structure. For some less confident writers, the structure of a loose topic is reassuring.
3. I sometimes direct the genre during a unit of study. For instance, when we are learning about poetry, I have students write poems during some of our writing workshops. Most of the time they get to choose their topics. However, we do occasionally decide as a class to write some poems about shared topics such as "Autumn" or "What We Like About Ourselves." Even when the genre is directed, students almost always have a choice of topic.
4. During reading, writing, social studies, and science, I encourage students to write to think and to learn. There are times when I direct this writing: "Write what you observe during this science experiment" or "Write what you notice, feel, or wonder about what you read." However, there are often times when students have choice in their writing during reading and the content areas (see the chapter "Should I Be Teaching Writing During Science, Social Studies, and Math?" at books.heineman.com/sloan).

5. The bottom line is, most of the time students have choice about what they write. I want students to write what they are passionate about, what they love, what they can't get enough of. Regie Routman (2005) says, "Students need to be able to choose most of their writing topics if they are to take writing seriously, take pride in their work, and write with strong voice" (177). I believe this. And it is important for me to act on my beliefs.

CHAPTER 6

Have You Seen the Range I Teach?

Inspiring a Diverse Set of Learners

We receive class lists at the beginning of each year with the names of unknown children who will very shortly become our students. Sometimes there is a familiar name, a little brother or sister of a student taught a few years back, but for the most part these are just names without faces—yet.

During the first few weeks we get to know these children—their personalities and their academics. It does not take long before we realize that, although we may teach just one or two grade levels, the academic levels of our students span many years. Their experiences with reading and writing vary greatly. The range of capabilities is overwhelming at first. We ask ourselves, "How am I going to teach all of these students with such different strengths and needs?"

How do I teach writing to a diverse set of learners?

I remember that all of my students are writers. They come with different skills but they all have something to say. My first hurdle in getting over this seemingly insurmountable wall is believing that everyone can be taught to write, and write well. The question I ask is, "How do I teach writing well to all these different learners?"

Ralph Fletcher (2006) says, "We're not teaching writing—we're teaching writers" (167). We need to know our students. What motivates them to write? What are the topics that interest them? Once we have a sample of each student's writing, we will know our span and can begin there. There are some lessons every student will benefit from, regardless of their level.

Examples of Lessons That Benefit All Writers

- Writing for a set purpose and audience
- Choosing topics
- Writing about what's on your heart and mind
- Adding details or elaborating
- Rereading to see if your writing makes sense
- Revising (adding more, changing a word)
- Editing

While I teach these minilessons to all writers, my expectations for each writer remain high—but may differ. For instance, after a minilesson about adding details, I might expect some students to add more color to a picture, while I expect others to support an idea with several sentences. In between, there are students I urge to add one detail to the end of their piece, and students I push to add a few details.

While whole-group lessons are successful, I also need to teach to the small group or individual. This year I have students who cannot match letters to sounds and I have those who write fluently over several pages. I have students who cannot think of a writing topic and I have students who have a list of topics they can't wait to write about.

I identify students who will benefit from a specific focus lesson and pull them together during the beginning of drafting time. These lessons might concentrate on spacing words, using capitals to begin sentences, matching writing to a picture, adding an anecdote to elaborate, using more interesting language, editing, and more.

I also teach individuals during writing conferences. Here I can focus specifically on one student's needs. Does she need help using her spelling card, choosing a topic, adding details, or revising for clarity? Regardless of my students' writing abilities, I am able to meet every child at his or her own level.

I Can't Read What They Write. Now What Do I Do? Teaching Our Struggling Writers

Jimmy is a second grader. His literacy skills are very low, and it is clear that Jimmy is very aware that he cannot read or write like most of the other students. He knows most of his letter sounds, but not all. He sounds out small words like *it* and *is* with assistance. He can read with accuracy *the* and *I*, but his reading level is below a beginning first-grade level. Jimmy is unable to match some letters with sounds.

On the first day of school, he tells me quietly, "I don't know how to read or write."

I whisper back, "Don't worry. That's my job—to teach you." I quickly find some simple books with few words, sit down, and read with Jimmy. When I am sure he has memorized two or three simple stories, I leave him to reread these books on his own, telling him that readers also read the pictures. I want to boost Jimmy's confidence, as well as give him the chance to see high-frequency words over and over. As I walk away, I see Jimmy turning the pages with a look of pleasure on his face.

Now it is time for writing workshop. I ask all the students to draw a picture of anything they like, and then write about it. Jimmy draws a rainbow. This is a safe choice because he knows he can find color words on a chart in the room. I observe Jimmy as he writes one word by himself, asks the child next to him how to write a word, and then looks to the color word chart to spell the rest of the words in his sentence. Jimmy writes, *I sow a red yellow gra green blue* (Figure 6.1). Knowing that Jimmy struggles to read and write, I am pleased to see he *wants* to write, and finds a way to match some words to his picture.

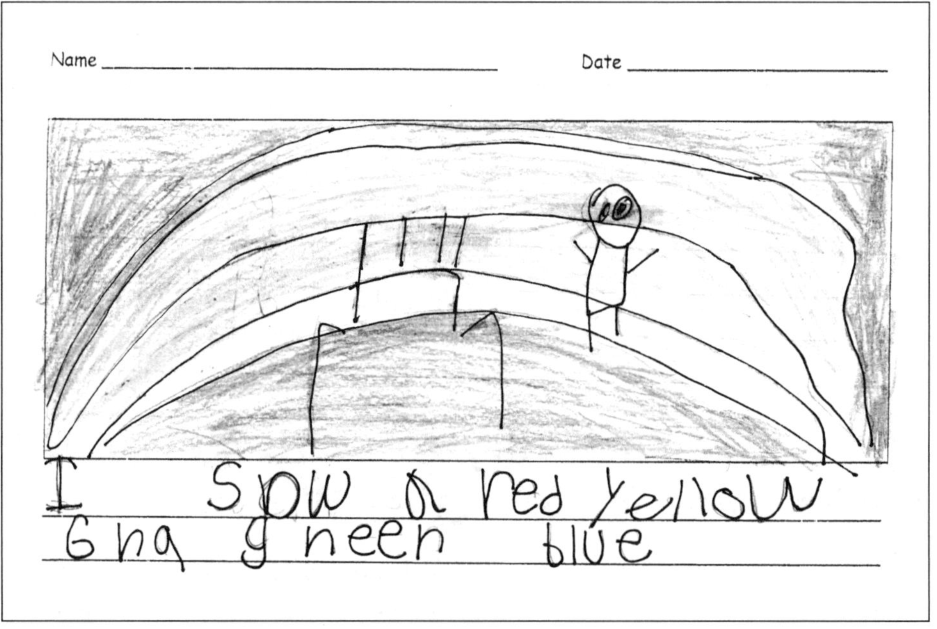

Figure 6.1 *Jimmy Writes About a Rainbow*

As I walk around the room, watching students as they draw and write, I think, "Second graders should be able to write something," but my mind knows that just because a child is a second or third grader does not mean that child meets the writing standards for these grade levels. Students come to us at varying levels, sometimes struggling to meet the standards we have set for them. Jimmy is such a student.

The rest of the week I meet with Jimmy briefly during each writing workshop. I ask about his picture, I praise his ideas, and I have him tell me what he wants to write. I suggest he say each word aloud, stretching the sounds to see if he hears certain letters, then write those letters down. I remind Jimmy to put a space between each word. I help Jimmy, supporting him as he learns to match letters to the sounds he hears.

It is now the second week of school and Jimmy is writing. After a lesson about topic choice, Jimmy decides to draw a picture of something he likes to do. He draws a picture of himself kicking a football. He writes about his picture but only a few words are recognizable. Even with the picture, I cannot read the message Jimmy has written (Figure 6.2).

I ask Jimmy to read his piece to me. As he does, I can see some letters that match a few sounds, but most don't. I scribe Jimmy's message on a sticky note

Figure 6.2 *Jimmy Writes About What He Likes to Do*

and ask if I can place this on his paper. I tell Jimmy, "I am so proud of you. You spelled some words just the way they are spelled, like *I, it, is,* and *to.* You thought about the other words you wanted to write and you sounded out each one. You chose to write something important." Jimmy smiles and I know he feels proud of himself too because he has been able to write what he really wanted to write. His choice of topic did not depend on words he could find in the room. I then tell Jimmy, "Your goal is going to be to continue stretching out the sounds in words. I am going to find out which sounds you already know and which ones are difficult. Then we are going to work on those letter sounds together."

This child, along with others, does not know all his letter sounds. This is evident in his writing. I am thrilled to have him writing letters on the page, even if I can't read what he has written, but what do I do to help him? How do I move students like Jimmy from writing messages that are unrecognizable to ones I can read? Here is my plan.

1. Keep encouraging him to write. Praise his ideas. Make sure he knows he *is* a writer by telling him. Ralph Fletcher (1993) says, "Our words will literally define the ways [students] perceive themselves as writers"(19).

2. Have him use his "best-guess" spelling. I want him to be independent, rather than asking me to spell every word he wants to write. And he likes to write. Keep that enthusiasm going!

3. Get to him quickly during or after he has written so I can scribe his message. I don't want him to forget. Write it on a sticky note and place it on the page, or write his message on the page, away from his writing and picture. That way he won't lose his message. Always ask to do this. I find students almost always agree.

4. Begin individual or small-group lessons. Teach Jimmy to use his spelling card or word wall to find high-frequency words. After assessing which letter, digraph, or blend sounds he does not know, begin teaching these in my reading lessons, but also model writing sentences with these sounds in writing minilessons. Interactive writing lessons are beneficial for students like Jimmy. Have him "share the pen" with me and other students with similar needs, as I practice writing words with challenging sounds. Students like Jimmy will not miraculously start writing with correct or even phonetic spelling. They need focused and intentional teaching. This teaching can come in lots of five-minute

lessons to small groups of students, as well as short individual writing conferences focused on this goal.

5. Keep the faith and watch for progress. If I teach intentional lessons and confer with students individually, they will begin applying what is taught. In this case, I will see Jimmy begin to match letters to sounds and his writing will become recognizable, then readable (with phonetic spelling), and then close to spelling-perfect.

Shouldn't students learn to read before they learn to write?

The question that begs to be asked is, "Shouldn't students learn to read before they learn to write?" If students can't read words, how can they write words? Well, let's revisit Jimmy. He can read only a short list of words. Besides a few specific ones, he cannot write words. Does that mean he has no stories to tell? Just because students lack knowledge of sound-symbol correspondence and correct spelling does not mean they are not writers with important and entertaining messages.

Another student, Nicole, knows several consonant sounds but she does not read any words (except *mom*). She reads pictures and can remember stories read to her. She also loves to tell stories: all kinds of stories about her family, her dog, and what she likes to do. We could ask, "Why doesn't Nicole dictate these stories until she learns to read?" She could. Dictating is a fine strategy for students before they know letters and sounds. It can be coupled with "best-guess" spelling as a teacher works to help students add more to their writing. However, if we limit nonreaders to dictating, we do not see on paper what they are learning about letters and sounds. This strategy also prevents students from moving toward independence.

In addition, I want to teach students to connect letters and words to their messages. At some point, I need to help nonreaders learn about stretching out sounds and matching these sounds to letters. I need to encourage them to hear the messages they want to write and think about the letters that make those sounds. I need to teach students about concepts of print, such as spacing and working from left to right. I also want to help build these students' sight word vocabularies, teaching them to look around the room for the words they want to spell.

Teaching reading and writing goes hand in hand. If we separate the two, we lose many opportunities for teaching and learning. When I teach writing, I am also teaching reading. When I sit with a student, or a group of students, asking them to stretch out a sound and identify the letter as they write, I am learning whether they can match that letter with its sound. If they can't, I stop and focus on that letter sound again, perhaps bringing in a book that will help.

A student's writing is a great assessment of his reading. If I cannot make heads or tails of a piece of writing—meaning I don't have any idea what the student wrote—I know he either needs more instruction on letter sounds and sight words, or he needs instruction on slowing down as he writes, stretching the sounds and matching letters to what he hears.

The bottom line is that I don't want to keep students from writing their stories because they can't read yet. Who is to say these students aren't better writers than those who can read? They may have the ideas, the language, and the organization. They just don't have the conventions . . . yet.

How do we teach writing to our ELL students?

Edgar is a delightful second grader. He is new to our classroom, joining us two weeks into the school year. He is quiet and I am not sure about his knowledge of English. I notice right away that during "Read to Self" time, Edgar picks up a tub full of small easy-to-read books with patterns in language.

During his first writing workshop, I notice that Edgar is reluctant to begin. I encourage Edgar by saying, "Start with your picture. I will come back and help you with the writing." Edgar is satisfied with this answer and begins drawing a stick figure on his paper. I walk around the room, checking on Edgar's progress from afar. I hope to gather clues about Edgar and his abilities.

Finally, Edgar raises his hand and shows me his drawing.

"Tell me about your picture, Edgar."

"That's me," he says.

"Who are these people?" I ask.

Edgar responds, "My family. This is my sister and this is my brother and this is my baby."

I continue, "And who are these people?"

"That is my mom and that is my dad."

"Well, this is a beautiful picture of your family. Tell me about these colors." I point to each person in the picture.

Edgar responds, "I just made them different colors."

"Oh, well, that's a good idea. That way we can tell who each person is in your family. You made them all different. How would you like me to help you today?"

Edgar says, "I want to tell who they are."

I ask, "Would you like to label each person in your family?"

Edgar nods.

"Okay. How about we start with your dad?" I want to know if Edgar knows how to write important sight words. Right away, Edgar is able to write *Dad* under the first person in his picture. "And this is your mom, right?" I point to the tallest girl figure. Edgar nods. I ask, "Can you write *Mom*?" Edgar writes the word *Mom* under the tall girl figure.

Next, I ask about the smallest figure. "What do you want to write here?"

Edgar answers, "*Baby*."

"Okay, let's say that together." I stretch out the word *baby*, saying each sound slowly. Then I invite Edgar to say the word with me again as he begins writing. He writes *Beb*. We move to his sister, stretching out the sounds. Edgar writes *setr*. We do the same for his brother, and Edgar gets some help from a friend as he writes *bruther*. Last, Edgar writes *me* under the picture of himself.

I ask Edgar, "Now that you are finished, would you read me your writing?"

Edgar points to each picture, reading their names. "Is there anything else you would like to add?"

Edgar says, "*This is my family*."

"May I add that to your writing?" I ask.

"Sure," Edgar says. I write Edgar's sentence at the bottom of his page.

Knowing that the other students in our class are anxious to learn more about Edgar, I ask, "Would you read this to the class during our sharing time?" At first Edgar is reluctant, but then he agrees. After our drafting time, Edgar reads his piece, and students ask questions that I hope will prompt Edgar to add some details the next time he writes about his family:

Where do you live?
How old is your baby?
Is the baby a girl or boy?
What is your brother's name?
How old is he?

With Edgar answering these questions, I get to observe a little more about Edgar's knowledge of English and oral language skills in general.

Edgar is just beginning his journey with writing. It is clear by his next few pieces that Edgar feels comfortable writing about his family, so I encourage this. Every day Edgar draws pictures of his family and labels them. He is practicing what he has learned about stretching sounds. He no longer needs me by his side.

Figure 6.3 *Edgar Writes About His Family*

One day I teach a lesson about topic selection. I suggest that students write about what they like to do. I model a piece about something I love to do: dance. I draw a picture first and think aloud for students as I write my piece.

> *I love to dance. It makes me feel alive. I glide around the floor as I listen to the music. My partner swings me and twirls me. My heart beats fast as I keep to the step. I feel happy.*

I intentionally keep my piece short, telling students that I am trying to capture a moment. I explain that I might add to my writing later. I encourage all students to think about what they like to do. Is it swimming, sewing, reading, or maybe dancing like me? I say, "If you don't have a topic today, you might consider writing about something you enjoy or like to do."

This lesson is for all students. I am teaching about topic choice, but also about elaborating on one idea. I encourage students to *tell* more: "Tell how you feel." Many students, including Edgar, benefit because I am nudging them to consider a new topic for writing. Edgar draws a picture of himself playing soccer and tells me that he is playing soccer with his friends. I ask, "What would you like to write?"

Edgar answers, "*We play soccer.*"

"That is a great sentence and it matches your picture. Say your first word again: *w-e*. What do you hear?"

Edgar writes *w-e-t.*

I encourage him. "Okay, what is next? We play . . . "

Edgar says, "*p-a*" as he writes these letters.

Edgar continues writing his sentence, using the letters *s-k-r* for *soccer*. I ask Edgar to reread his sentence. Then I ask, "How do you feel about playing soccer?"

Edgar answers, "It is fun."

"Oh." I ask, "Would you like to add that detail to your writing?"

Edgar nods and he begins to write independently. He does not look to me to help him sound out the words but mimics what I have been doing with him up to this point, stretching the words as he says them. He writes *ti fun* for *It is fun* (see Figure 6.4).

Edgar is beginning to branch out. He is moving from drawing pictures of his family, with labels, to writing about what he likes to do, with two sentences. Like most ELL students, as well as other struggling writers, Edgar needs lessons in idea development and conventions. Interactive writing is a great strategy because it involves discussion about ideas as well as conventions of print such as spelling, spacing, and directionality. It actively involves students in a nonthreatening and focused way as it puts the pen in students' hands. Interactive writing offers the support of the teacher, who guides the lesson, and other students as they participate.

Figure 6.4 *Edgar Writes About Soccer*

When students' English is limited, I encourage the development of ideas by asking them to talk about and add to their pictures. In addition, when students tell their stories before they write, as well as afterward, they develop elaboration skills and practice speaking English. ELL students must have lots of one-to-one conversations about their writing, as well as many opportunities in small-group writing situations.

What about reluctant writers?

They can write, but they don't want to. These students might be the most frustrating challenge we have. They have the ability to write, and perhaps write well, but for a myriad of reasons they choose not to write. Are they disinterested? Do they lack confidence? Is writing a new experience for them?

I believe it might be a little of each. Take two boys in my class: Tommy and Joshua. They are both third graders, but they are on opposite ends of the continuum as far as academics. Both are smart, but Tommy struggles to produce work and qualifies for special education in math and written language. He had previously qualified in reading, as well. At third grade, he does not believe he has anything worth writing about.

Joshua is a good reader and mathematician. However, he does not like to write and is disinterested in writing workshop. He rushes through assignments, writing the minimum. Joshua does not see the worth in writing workshop. He often sits, reluctant to write.

Two different boys: both reluctant to write, each owning a set of different issues. So what is a teacher to do? My answer comes from an experience I had many years ago with a first-grade student named Phillip. This child taught me a lesson for teaching all students, but especially those reluctant to write.

During writing workshop, Phillip stared at a nearly blank journal every day. One of his typical entries appears in Figure 6.5.

As much as I tried, I could not encourage nor inspire Phillip to write more than one short sentence. Then one afternoon in April, Phillip came in from recess, desperately asking, "Mrs. Sloan—Can I write?"

I tried to downplay my excitement. I said, "Of course."

While other students participated in a short choice time, Phillip worked studiously on his writing. He was writing a note to our vice principal, intervening for a friend who found himself in a bit of trouble on the playground. Figure 6.6 shows Phillip's note.

Figure 6.5 *Phillip's Journal Entry*

After that day, Phillip began to write on a regular basis. Figure 6.7 shows a piece Phillip wrote to describe a camping trip. While this writing still has obvious areas for improvement, it is certainly a far cry from "I lik skool."

Why the sudden change? I believe Phillip finally found purpose and power in writing. Even though his note to the vice principal did little to alter his friend's fate, Phillip felt he had a reason to write. In reflection, I realized I had never taught him this. That day after recess, Phillip discovered that people write for a purpose, and with an audience in mind. Once he figured this out, the flood gates opened. Phillip finally found a voice to write about all kinds of things.

So, how can I help my reluctant writers like Tommy and Joshua find their voices? Ralph Fletcher (2006) urges us to find out what kids care about and encourage them to write about that. I need to discover what matters to Tommy and Joshua and let them know they can write about anything. I must encourage them to write for real purposes: a thank-you note to a guest speaker, a handbook for new students, a note to a friend who moved away, or a letter persuading the principal to let them sell popcorn at recess. Teachers need to

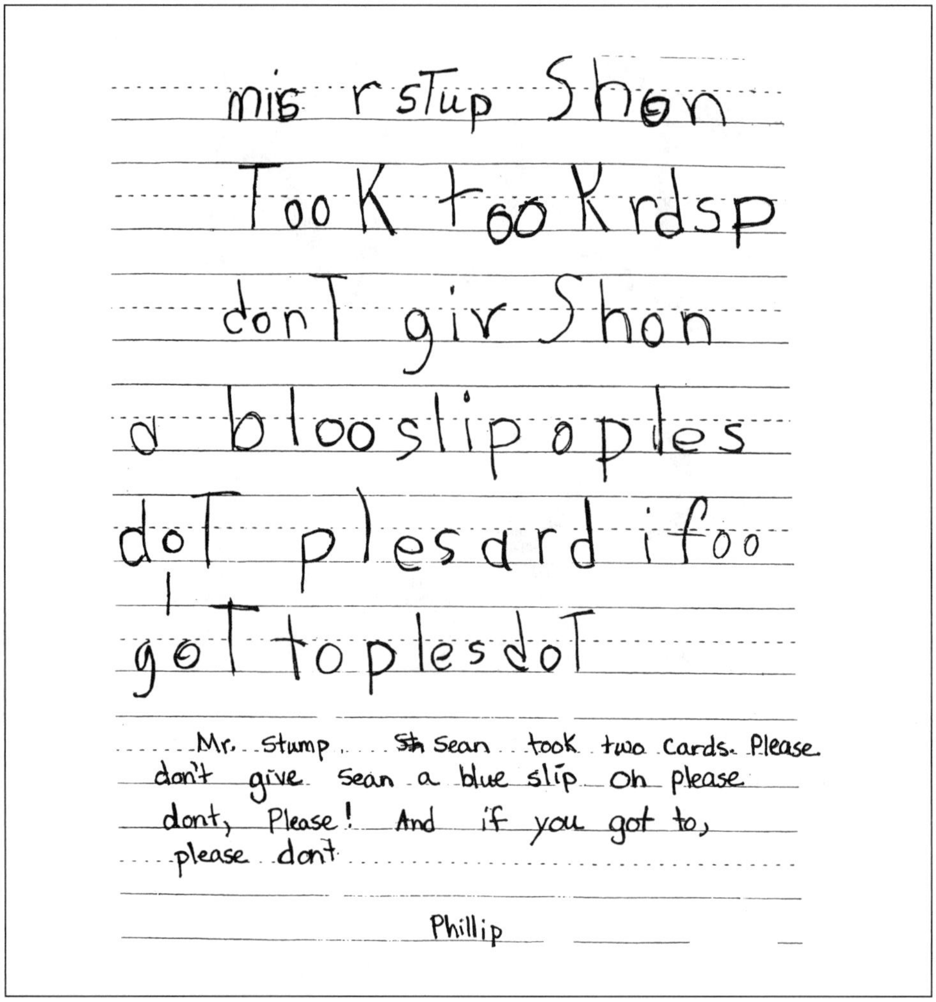

mis r sTup Shon
TooK too Krdsp
donT gir Shon
a bloo slip oples
doT plesard ifoo
goT toples doT

Mr. Stump Sean took two cards. Please don't give Sean a blue slip Oh please dont, Please! And if you got to, please dont

Phillip

Figure 6.6 *Phillip's Note to Mr. Stump*

find out what reluctant writers want to write and for whom they want to write. Talk these things up. Model these kinds of writing.

For Tommy, video games are important. He begins writing directions for his friends on how to play these games. Because Tommy also struggles with writing, I provide support, and my expectations fit an appropriate level of success. Video games are not my idea of a great writing topic, but I have to open my mind. For Tommy, a video game is the perfect topic. I start there, encouraging Tommy to expand his topics as the year progresses.

Joshua loves Star Wars, so I take that passion and help him create stories with a clear beginning, middle, and end. He works hard on this and learns a lot about fiction writing. Joshua also has a cat he adores. I encourage him to

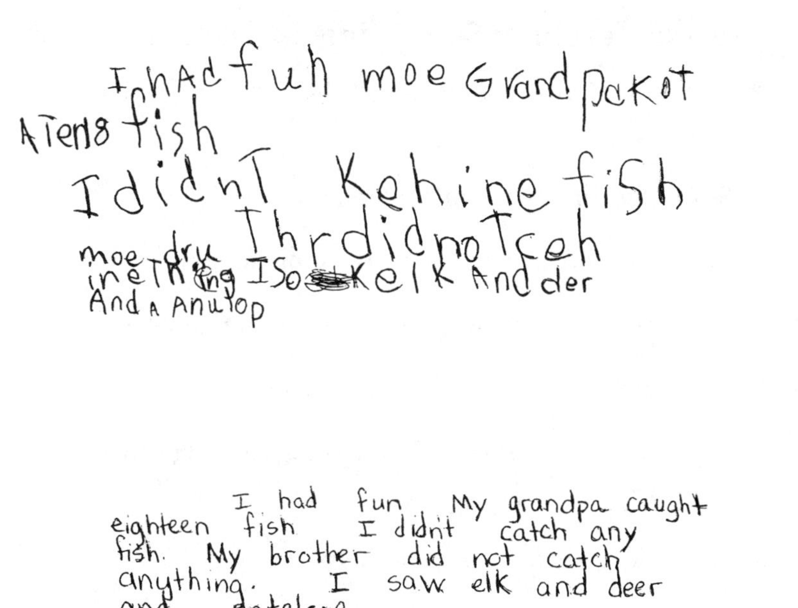

Figure 6.7 *Phillip Writes About a Camping Trip*

tell stories about his pet. It takes some time, but after listening to other students' stories and poems about their pets, Joshua finally begins writing about Jed, his big white cat.

Joshua also starts writing in his journal day after day. Some of his writing is repetitive, but he is writing and that is all I can ask at this point. I stay away for awhile, wanting him to feel safe, giving him a chance to develop some writing fluency—just continuous writing. After a while, Joshua begins expanding his topics and varying his sentences. Writing day after day does a lot to prove to Joshua that writing can be useful and fun.

Our reluctant writers need to develop confidence. They often do not believe they are writers with something to say—maybe because everyone has always told them what they should write about and how it should look. These students need opportunities to explore writing that is meaningful to them. They need to see that writing is an important skill that helps them tell their stories, express their opinions, and explore their interests. Unless they experience this kind of writing, these reluctant writers cannot start moving toward being active, confident writers.

Tips for Teaching Struggling and Reluctant Writers

- Spend time with students to get them started (even a few minutes).
- Be excited about students' ideas.
- Make students believe they have something to say.
- Have students write for real purposes and audiences.
- Celebrate the smallest of achievements.
- Type students' writing. (Handwriting can bog some students down.)
- Let students dictate some of their writing.
- Give students a writing buddy.

What about my boy writers?

Oh—the boys! I just shared my thoughts about three boys who are reluctant writers: Joshua, Tommy, and Phillip. Sometimes, boys don't want to write. Of course, this is not the case with all boy writers. Many are very motivated with lots of topics they can't wait to write about. This year I have Alex, who writes about everything from the day he got sick to poetry about the seasons. Demetry writes book after book about different animals. And Ryan loves to write about his family experiences.

However, some of the boys who like to write are focused on less traditional topics and genres. Grant loves to write comic books (Figure 6.8). Reilly writes almost exclusively about Teenage Mutant Ninja Turtles. Dylan's recent book is called *The Adventures of the Talking Snake and the Flying Cat.* Like many teachers, I have not always valued these genres and topics. They don't fit neatly into our mold of what good writing looks like. As Tom Newkirk (2002) has demonstrated in his research on boys' literacy, teachers don't always make room for the kinds of genres boys prefer.

So, what is good writing? Doesn't it happen when writers find their voices and write with conviction? These boys have a great deal of commitment. Dylan is very determined as he staples papers together to make his book. He has a clear story in his head. Grant reads his comics to me with a sense of pride,

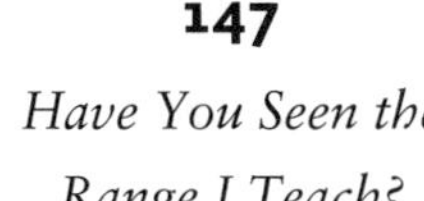

Figure 6.8 *Grant's Comic Book*

and if I misinterpret the story, he is eager to set me right. And Reilly is utterly enthusiastic as he tells what will happen on the next page in his story.

The quickest way to shut down these boy writers is to disallow their fantasies, making them comply with traditional topics. Vicki Spandel (2005) argues, "Writers write best what they know. Writers write best what they love" (82). These boys know comics, battles, and imaginary creatures. They know sports, cars, and big machinery. Newkirk (2002) adds, "And as many boys claim, when they are writing these adventures, they feel themselves physically inside the stories. Rather than denying the physical needs of boys, writing can employ that energy—if we can keep the space open for their play" (178). The question becomes: How can I use their topics to teach them to write well?

If boys want to write about topics that are less than genteel, I administer a few rules, such as no crude violence. But I don't disallow all violence. According to Newkirk, "Any categorical banning of violence would effectively preclude their attempting their favorite genres, removing one of the few motivations boys have to attempt writing" (175). Many boys like to include shooting and battles and war in their stories. Without them, they may feel there is no story. I have a boy obsessed with World War II. That's a worthy writing topic, but also one that can include violence. My rule is that you can't have violence without a reason. The story has to be clear. I explain to students that it is not okay to make a book filled with a "shoot 'em up" mentality instead of a story:

> First page: *There was a battle.*
> Next page: *He stabbed him.*
> Next page: *AAH. He blew him up.*
> Next page: *AAAH!*
> Next page: *I'm shot.*
> Next page: *Blood spurted everywhere.*
> Last page: *The End*

Instead, I often ask my students to start with a plan. Who is the main character? What is going to be the problem? Is there an enemy? Why are they enemies? If there is a battle coming, make sure it makes sense. Explain to your reader what is happening so they are not confused. Limit your "AAAHs" and violent incidents. It is more effective to include just a few.

If my boys want to write about these topics, I often take the time to engage them in shared writing experiences. I teach them about writing a comic by bringing in a real example. What are the essential elements? I teach them to write a story about a video character that makes sense and is suspenseful. Through their topics and genres, I teach about elaborating on ideas, using interesting language, creating leads and endings, and following conventions. We write some of these "boy stories" together so students have models to follow.

Of course, we need to help boys write about traditional topics too. They will be tested on these in state, district, and schoolwide writing assessments. They will also be expected to write for social studies and science more and more as they progress in grade levels. I recently had all students consider autumn. We observed fall trees and I encouraged them to express their observations in a poem, which traditionally could be considered quite a "girly" assignment. However, even the real "boy's boy" writers found pleasure and success with this.

Our boy writers need us to understand their interests. They are not completely unable, nor disinterested, in writing about traditional topics, as long as they know they will also have opportunities to write about what is important to them, even if these are topics I don't at first prefer. Ultimately, I honor their topics and genres, and I teach about good writing through them.

At the same time, I also need to honor the boys' need to draw. During writing workshop, the boys love to draw: cars, spaceships, sports pictures, aliens. The list goes on and on. I sometimes find myself wanting to say, "This is not drawing workshop. This is writing workshop." However, I also need to consider why some students, predominantly boys, draw. Ralph Fletcher (2006) reminds us that boys need to draw. This is the way they process ideas. I believe girls do this too; they just draw different types of pictures. I understand this need and try very hard to embrace it. I let all of the students draw and then I expect them to write.

In my classroom, I also consider boys' learning styles. I allow all students (not just boys) to find comfortable places to write: lying on the ground, sitting against a pillow, lounging with feet perched on another chair. Some students' bodies need to be grounded in space. Some may need a lap weight; others simply find that a student chair is the least productive place to write. I even see students writing all cramped up in a big plastic tub (Figure 6.9). I set rules, but I'm flexible about where in the classroom students write.

Figure 6.9 *Claire Writes in a Big Plastic Tub*

Tips for Teaching Boy Writers

- Embrace boys' topics and learn to love their writing.
- Teach writing skills and strategies within the topics that interest your boys.
- Encourage boys to write about what matters to them.
- Honor boys' writing. Choose boys to share their writing with the class.
- Type students' writing. Let them see it in fancy print. (Handwriting can be a problem for some boys, which turns them off to writing.)
- Allow students to be comfortable: let them write on the floor, at a table, or with a clipboard.

How do I challenge my exemplary writers?

In the midst of our classrooms, there are usually a few students who really shine as writers. They come to us with skills far above our expectations, making us feel both delighted and afraid. Of course, we love reading their stories and poems. We know they will be creative and self-motivated. They won't need us right by their sides to write. However, we also question whether we will be able to challenge these talented writers. How will we push them to become better writers while we deal with the many writers in our class who require more of our time and support?

Two Students: Annie and Tatum

I love how writing workshop allows me to teach a range of learners quite successfully. Even if all students participate in the same minilesson, my expectations for each student's writing may vary greatly. For instance, today I am teaching a lesson on *telling more* by *giving examples*. We discuss some of the facts we've learned about pumpkins from our reading on a previous day. A few students decide to write their own pumpkin fact books. One is Annie, a beginning writer, and one is Tatum, a very capable writer. Annie begins writing by drawing her pictures. She has a four-page book. On the first page she writes, in phonetic spelling, *There are lots of pumpkins.* On the second page she writes: *There's the Jack-Be-Nimble.* On the third page she writes: *There's Red October.* And on her last page Annie writes: *Some are small and some are big.*

Tatum writes on the same topic. The beginning of her book looks like this:

> *Pumpkins are all around in October.*
>
> *There are lots of varieties like Red October, Trick-or-Treat, and Sugar Pie.*
>
> *I've seen a Red October pumpkin at the pumpkin patch. This kind of pumpkin is not the largest pumpkin but it does have some interesting bumps.*
>
> *We carve our pumpkins but they don't all look the same.*

Clearly, Tatum is able to write much more capably than Annie. And my expectations reflect my knowledge of this fact. I ooh and aah over Annie's book. I tell her, "I am so proud you have a different sentence on each page, and I love that your picture matches your writing." I add, "You give some examples of different kinds of pumpkins when you mention the Red October and the Jack-Be-Nimble. Way to go!" I do not worry about spelling because I see that Annie has sounded out the words she has written, using all the skills she has at this time. She is just beginning to do this, so I don't want to make her self-conscious by focusing on misspelled words. Instead, I encourage her with talk about the content of her writing. I nudge Annie to write about one more kind of pumpkin and add it to her book.

When I confer with Tatum, I praise her for starting with a great lead sentence. Focusing on her third page, I say, "Wow. I love how you told more about the Red October pumpkin here. You gave some interesting details." As we revisit the fourth page, I encourage Tatum to add more by asking a question. "You say your pumpkins don't all look the same. Can you give some examples of how they are different? Remember that writers elaborate by giving examples." Tatum then works to revise page four:

> *We carve our pumpkins but they don't all look the same. For example, my dad carves a happy face for Nolan, a scary face for me, and a surprised face for Emma.*

I know Tatum is capable and I can push her to apply strategies taught in my lessons. I remind her to start her sentences with capitals, and I help her find the word *they* on her spelling card.

Two students at either ends of the continuum, both inspired to write about pumpkins, both practicing *telling more* by *giving examples*. I add some editing practice to Tatum's conference because I want to hold her accountable for words I know she can spell and for starting sentences with capital letters.

Varying Assignments for Exemplary Writers

I also challenge these writers by giving them longer and more complex assignments. Maybe they move to writing biographies far before others in the class. Maybe I expect them to elaborate with more detail about the science experiments we conduct. Perhaps they edit student pieces before publication. I also stretch these students to experiment with different genres, and I prod them to consider using elements of language such as metaphor and simile in their descriptions.

Tips for Teaching Exemplary Writers

- Raise expectations for students' writing within the lesson taught to the entire class.
- Stretch students to try new things: new language, new genres, new topics. Don't underestimate their abilities.
- Give students important writing jobs: editor for publication, revising expert.
- Let students help teach a minilesson: use their writing as a model.

Final Thoughts

All of these students are writers. They come to us with different strengths and varying needs. Writing workshop is one of the places I feel I can reach all of these children. I teach a short lesson or two and then students practice applying strategies at their own pace and ability. Because one-to-one conferences are so important to the writing workshop (see Chapter 9), I can tailor my talk during these times to meet the needs of each individual. I prod, teach, practice, celebrate, and encourage children in small groups and in one-to-one conversations about their work. I plan lessons that make sense for the bulk of my class and pull those students with specific needs into small groups for additional teaching and practice. Most of all, I value all students, celebrating their individual interests, strengths, and (yes) even their challenges as writers.

CHAPTER 7

How Do I Teach Writing During Reading?

One day in class I read aloud *Fox* by Margaret Wild. Students love this book! As I turn each page, they are in awe of the language. Eduardo, who is a struggling reader and writer, keeps saying, "That's a simile," as he often does when we come across a simile in our reading. When I read, "saplings are springing up everywhere," Claire comments, "I love that description."

Students are disappointed in the ending—not in a negative way, but in a way that shows they are invested in the story and the characters. They do not like that Magpie is left far away from home and has to find her way back by herself. Our discussion is very rich, and I know that if I ask students to write, I will extend this great discussion to another level of thinking. It will also give me a chance to teach students writing during reading.

I encourage students to continue to talk in pairs. When they are ready, I say, "Please respond to this story in writing. What are you feeling? What did you notice the writer did? Was there anything special you noticed about the language, or the pictures, or the story line, or the characters? Do you have any connections?" I record these questions on chart paper to cement their importance.

I ask students to elaborate. "Tell how, why, or who. Add some reasons for the way you feel. Use interesting language in your writing—words that will wow us. Make sure you use your spelling card when you need to spell those everyday words." Then students take out their reading journals, notebooks used specifically for responses to reading.

In Figure 7.1, Laurelle comes up with her own word to describe how Magpie must have felt (*heartbroken*). She also notices some lovely language. In Figure 7.2, Ryan chooses to ask questions. It is clear he thinks deeply as

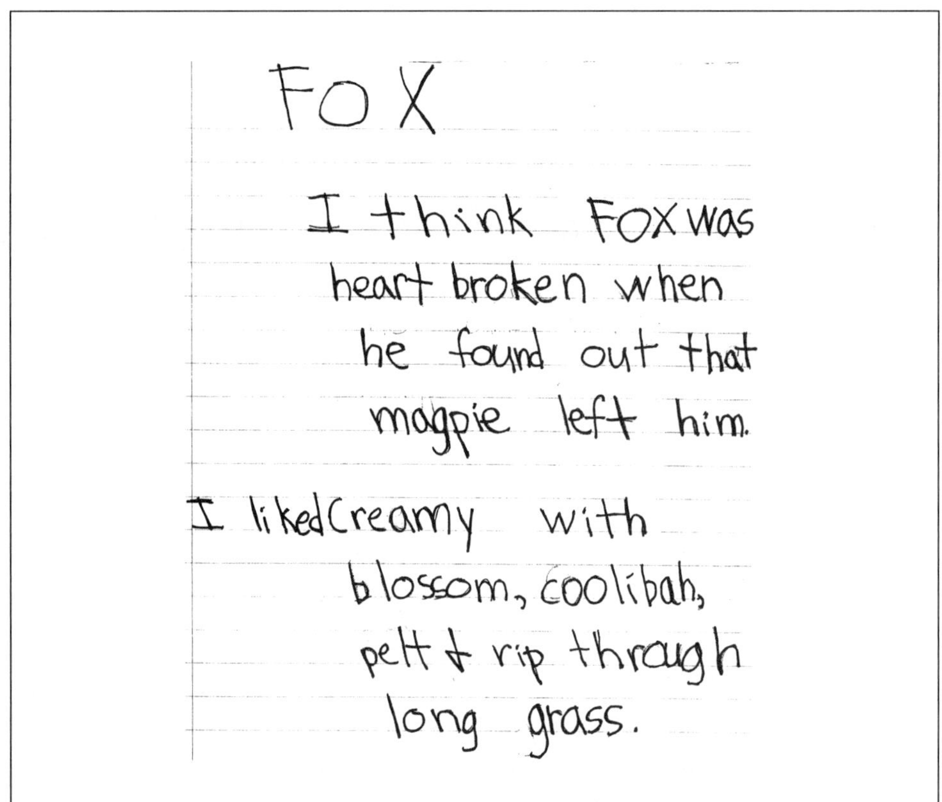

Figure 7.1 *Laurelle's Response to* Fox

he writes. Like Laurelle, he also notices some language (a simile), which indicates that he is looking at the text like a writer.

What a rich opportunity for "writing to learn." Students share their journal entries with others, and of course this sparks more discussion about the story, and more writing.

During reading instruction, when teachers ask students to reflect upon a text in writing—how it relates to their own lives and what they notice, think, feel, or predict—we not only extend them an opportunity to think more deeply, but we also give ourselves another opportunity to teach writing. We can model and teach students to elaborate, support their points with specific examples, use interesting language, incorporate the use of text features such as bullets and labels, and use correct conventions, perhaps teaching students to use spelling cards to edit their reading journal entries.

Several years ago, I had a schedule that made it difficult for me to make time for writing workshop on Tuesdays. Try as I might, I could not fit writing workshop into my day. I began looking for ways to teach writing within the

Figure 7.2 *Ryan's Response to* Fox

other subject areas so I would know I was still teaching writing five days a week.

I looked to my reading workshop schedule and decided that instead of giving students a choice to write in their reading journals, on Tuesdays I would require a written reflection about what they had read. And during my reading instruction I would also teach writing.

In our already busy days, it is imperative that we think of ways to infuse writing into our other subject areas, including reading. Writing is thinking. When we ask students to write, we ask them to think. The more they think, the more they will learn. In addition, by infusing writing into our reading instruction, we capture more time to teach writing in a meaningful setting. As a teacher, I know the big question always is, "Where's the time?" We just found some.

Teaching Writing During Reading

Students are gathered on the carpet. We have just finished reading *The Librarian of Basra* by Jeanette Winter. Our conversation ranges from the courage of Alia Mohammed, the librarian who saves many of the books amidst war, to the vibrant colors used by Jeanette Winter in the illustrations.

Students make text-to-self connections relating to Alia's love for books, and text-to-world connections recognizing this war is still going on (Keene & Zimmermann 1997). I invite students to respond orally using the leads shown in Figure 7.3.

Eleanor says, "Alia's library is like a book club. They come there to talk about books."

Amber adds, "I love books just like Alia does."

"I think Alia must be scared, but she shows a lot of courage," says Nolan.

Alex agrees, "Yeah, I wonder if I would have that much courage."

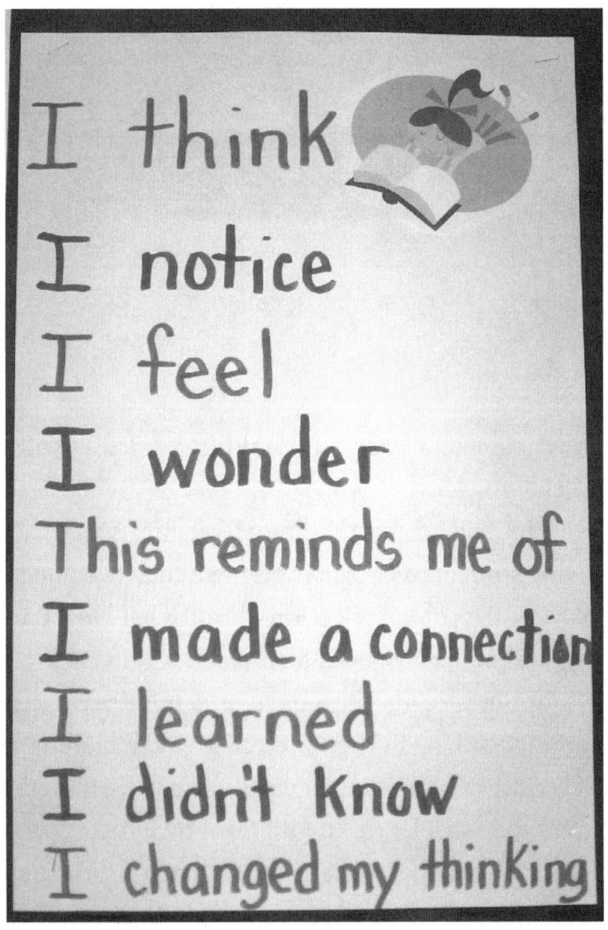

Figure 7.3 *Chart of Leads for Class Discussion*

Modeling for Students

After students share all together and with turn-and-talk partners, I model writing a response in my own reading journal:

> *Alia Mohammed reminds me of my mom.*

I stop and say, "Let me see if my sentence makes sense." I am now teaching reading *and* writing. I continue, "This does not say too much. I need to elaborate. I bet you are wondering why Alia reminds me of my mom. I should *tell why*." I continue writing.

> *Alia has such a passion for books. She was willing to risk her life for them. My mom loves books too. She is getting ready to move to a smaller apartment. The first thing she said was, "I won't be able to take all of my books with me." It made me feel sad. I figure that's how Alia felt when she thought she might lose her books. I bet my mom and Alia would really get along.*

Again, I model rereading my writing to see if it makes sense.

Inviting Students to Respond

It is now time for students to give it a try. I say, "You now will have a chance to write a response." Here, I have a choice: I can engage students in a shared writing experience about the book or, if I feel I've given enough support, I can invite students to write individual responses. Today, I believe they are ready to write on their own. I tell them, "Remember to write about something you are thinking or feeling. Make sure you elaborate: tell more by telling how, telling why, or telling how you feel. I try to do that in my writing. I *tell why* Alia reminds me of my mom (they both love books). I also *tell how I feel* (very sad) when my mom says she can't bring all of her books."

I remind students to use capitals and periods and that I expect them to use spelling cards to spell high-frequency words. First graders look to our word wall for help with spelling.

While this is primarily a reading lesson focused on comprehension, it includes many writing skills and strategies. This is a perfect situation for weaving reading and writing lessons together. We want students to practice writing about their understanding of books they have read. We teach them to infer, ask questions, synthesize, and make connections, expressing themselves orally and in writing. When we teach and expect students to write for a purpose, elaborate upon ideas, include interesting language, and use age-appropriate conventions in written responses, we teach both the qualities and process of writing.

Writing Taught During This Reading Lesson

- Write with purpose.
- Elaborate on an idea by telling how and why.
- Elaborate on an idea by telling how you feel.
- Reread your writing to see if it makes sense.
- Use capitals to begin sentences.
- Use periods to end sentences.
- Use your spelling card and the word wall to spell simple words.

Figures 7.4, 7.5, and 7.6 contain three students' reading journal entries responding to *The Librarian of Basra*. Each student elaborates with a different degree of detail. Alex adds one idea that connects to his original idea. Tatum quotes a simile straight from the book: *She cared about the books more than mountains of gold.* Claire uses interesting language when she says, "she has a ton of courage." Both Tatum and Claire include endings that tell us they are finished.

Extending Writing Instruction: Students Write About Their Independent Reading

After students have had many opportunities to respond in writing to books I have read aloud, I encourage this same response to books they have read independently or in literature circles. Again, I model for students, this time writing about a book familiar to many of them.

Modeling for Students

I begin by saying, "During my read-to-self time yesterday, I was reading *Amber on the Mountain* by Tony Johnston." Students smile as I show them the book.

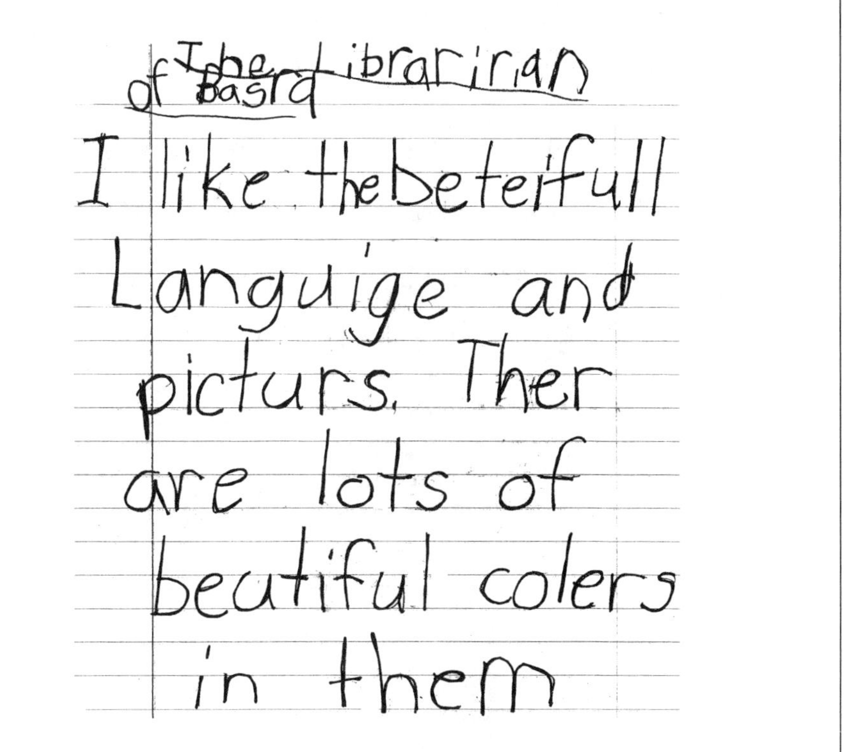

Figure 7.4 *Alex's Response*

"As I was reading, I was doing a lot of thinking, and I decided to write in my reading journal." I share my writing:

> *I think Amber is a very determined girl. She worked really hard to learn to read. It reminds me of when I learned to ride a bike. I was in first grade and I practiced on my driveway. I fell sometimes but I kept on trying and I finally learned. I had to work really hard, just like Amber. I think Amber can do anything she sets her mind to do. Determination is the key to success.*

I ask students, "What do you think of my writing?"

Allison answers, "You make a text-to-self connection."

Ryan adds, "You elaborate, too. You didn't stop after telling it reminded you of learning to ride your bike. You added details."

I respond, "Yes, I tried to elaborate."

"I like the word *determination*. That's an interesting word," says Jordyn.

Hunter adds, "And your last sentence really tells us you are done. You said, *Determination is the key to success*. That's a good last sentence."

"Well, thank you Hunter."

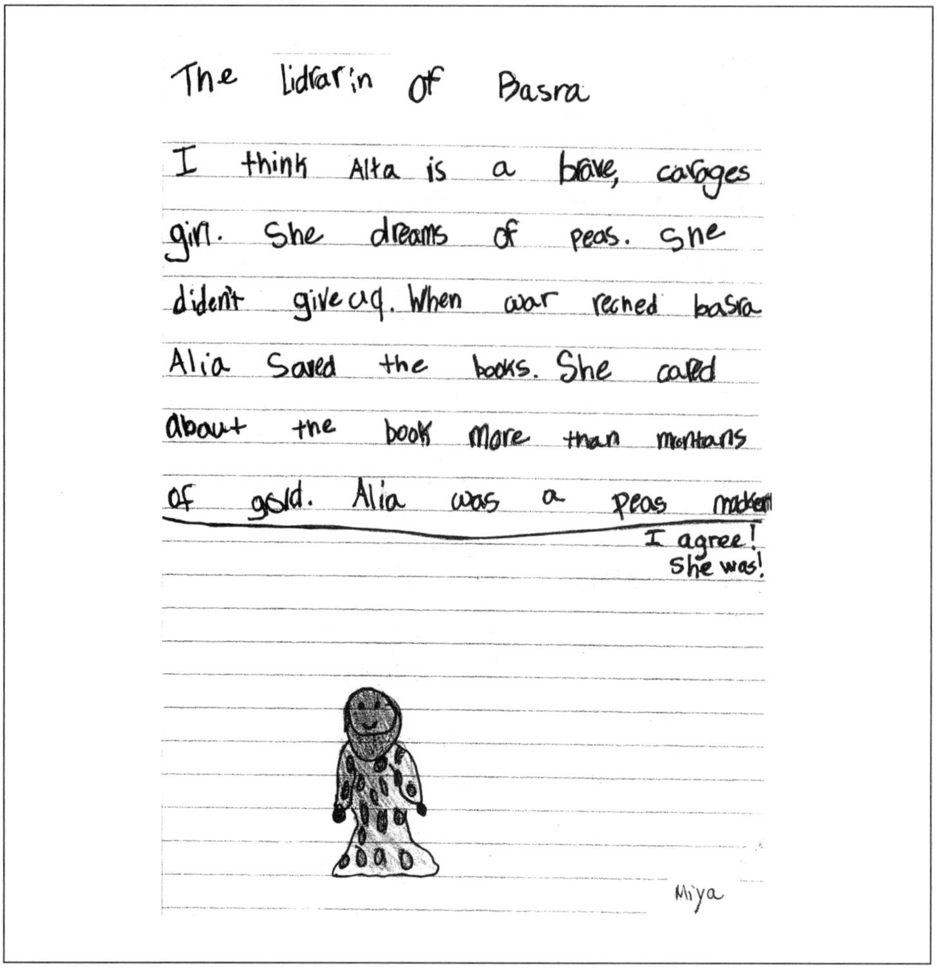

The lidrarin of Basra

I think Alta is a brave, caroges girl. She dreams of peas. She diden't give uq. When war reched basra Alia Saved the books. She cared about the book more than mantans of gold. Alia was a peas maker

I agree! She was!

Miya

Figure 7.5 *Tatum's Response*

Inviting Students to a Shared Response

I tell students, "Today we are going to write a response to the chapter book we are reading, *Mrs. Frisby and the Rats of NIMH*. How do we want to begin our writing?"

Josh raises his hand and says, "*Mrs. Frisby and the Rats of NIMH* is the best book."

I ask students if this sounds like a good beginning sentence. They nod yes, so I write the sentence on our chart. "Okay, let's elaborate. Why is it the best book? What are some reasons?"

Miya answers, "It has really interesting characters like Nicodemus and Jeremy."

I begin to write, saying, "I like how you are giving specific names."

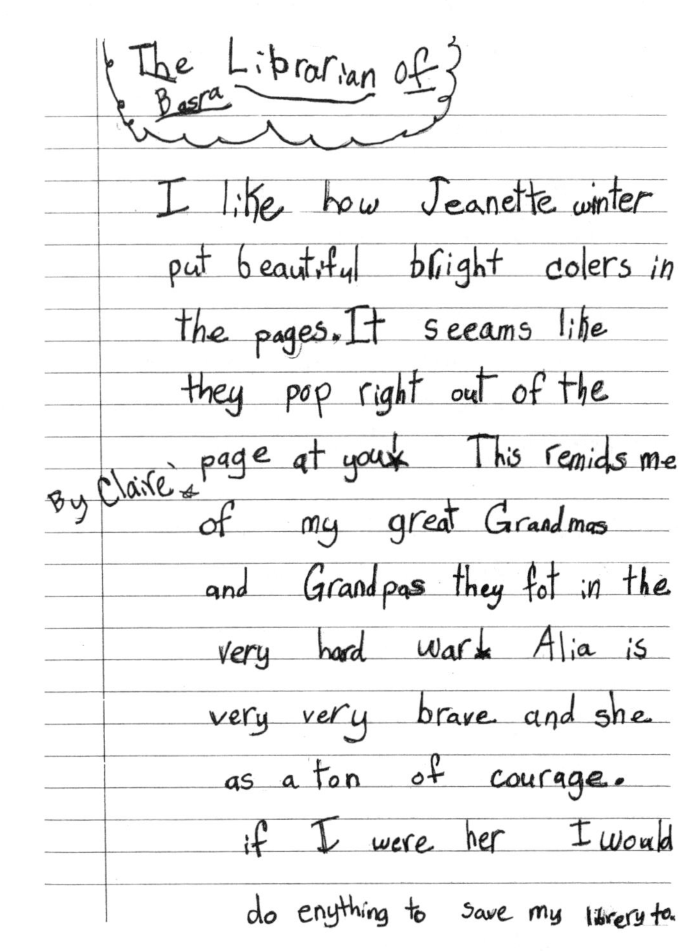

The Librarian of Basra

I like how Jeanette winter put 6eautiful bright colers in the pages. It seeams like they pop right out of the page at you. This remids me of my great Grandmas and Grandpas they fot in the very hard war. Alia is very very brave and she as a ton of courage. if I were her I would do enything to save my librery to.

By Claire

Figure 7.6 *Claire's Response*

Bobby says, "But these two are very different. Nicodemus seems wise and Jeremy is kind of silly and still acts like a kid."

I move things along. "Okay, why else is the book interesting?"

Joey says, "It has lots of things we don't know yet . . . like *What is NIMH?* and *What is the plan?*"

"So you still have lots of questions. How can we say that? Could we say, 'As we read, we have a lot of questions, like *What is NIMH?* and *What is the plan?*' "

Students agree to my wording, and I record Joey's idea. Because I want to keep this lesson short, I suggest we reread what we have to see if it makes sense. As we reread, students find places that need some revision. I ask questions such as, "How can we make that sound better?" "Will this be clear for the reader?" "Is there anything else we want to say right here?" We write a strong ending sentence and our piece is complete:

> ***Mrs. Frisby and the Rats of NIMH***
>
> *Mrs. Frisby and the Rats of NIMH is the best book. It has interesting characters like Nicodemus and Jeremy. These two characters are very different. Nicodemus is wise and Jeremy is kind of silly and still acts like a kid, maybe because he is a kid bird.*
>
> *As we read, we have lots of questions like "What is NIMH?" and "What is the plan?" Maybe the author wants us to have these questions. We can't wait to read to find out more!*

On the next day, we discuss our shared writing about *Mrs. Frisby and the Rats of NIMH.* We review the elements of our response:

- We had a lead sentence and an ending sentence.
- We elaborated, giving examples from the text.
- We tried to include something interesting.
- We said how we felt about the book.

Inviting Individual Response

I tell students, "Today, all of you will have a chance to write in your reading journals. I would like you to write about a book you are reading now, either on your own or with a friend. You will get to share your responses with a small group of classmates."

"Here are some things to remember as you write about what you are thinking."

1. If you like, you may start with one of the starter phrases on our poster. Tell how you feel, what you are thinking, or what you notice. Or you can use a beginning sentence of your own.
2. Remember to elaborate. Include details that tell more (tell why, how, when, where, and who).
3. Try to use some interesting words.
4. Remember to sound out big words you don't know, and use your spelling card to spell everyday words.

5. Use capitals to begin sentences, periods to end sentences, and question marks for questions.

6. End with a sentence that tells the reader you are finished.

Students find places in the room to read and write in their reading journals. Robbie, in response to *Jack and the Beanstalk,* writes from the heart: "Isn't Jack kind of bad because he stole?" (Figure 7.7).

Miya chooses to write in response to *Appelemando's Dream* by Patricia Polacco (Figure 7.8). Miya elaborates and uses a simile to describe what she notices. She thinks beyond the story and reaches out to connect to it with her wondering.

As these students write, I meet with Amber (Figure 7.9). She is reading a Dr. Seuss book and then picks up Mo Willem's *The Pigeon Wants a Puppy.* Amber shares, "I think I have a lot to say about this book."

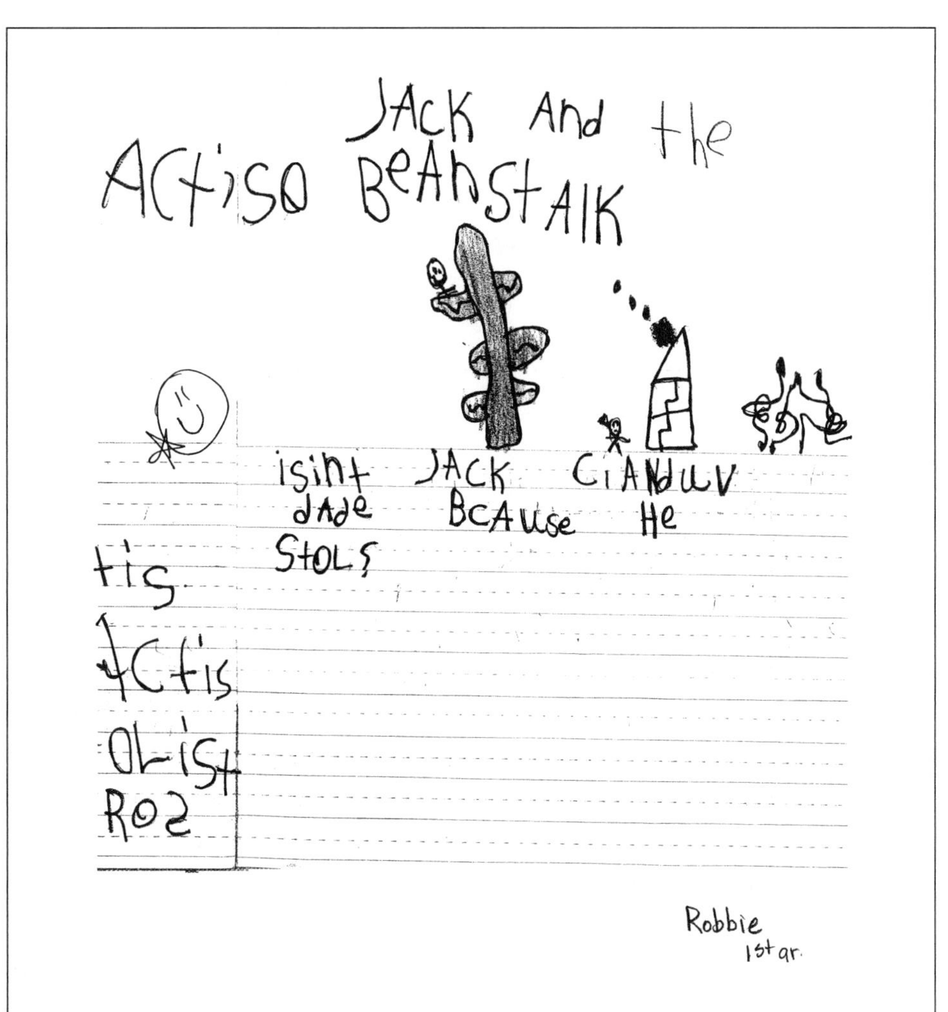

Figure 7.7 *Robbie's Journal Entry*

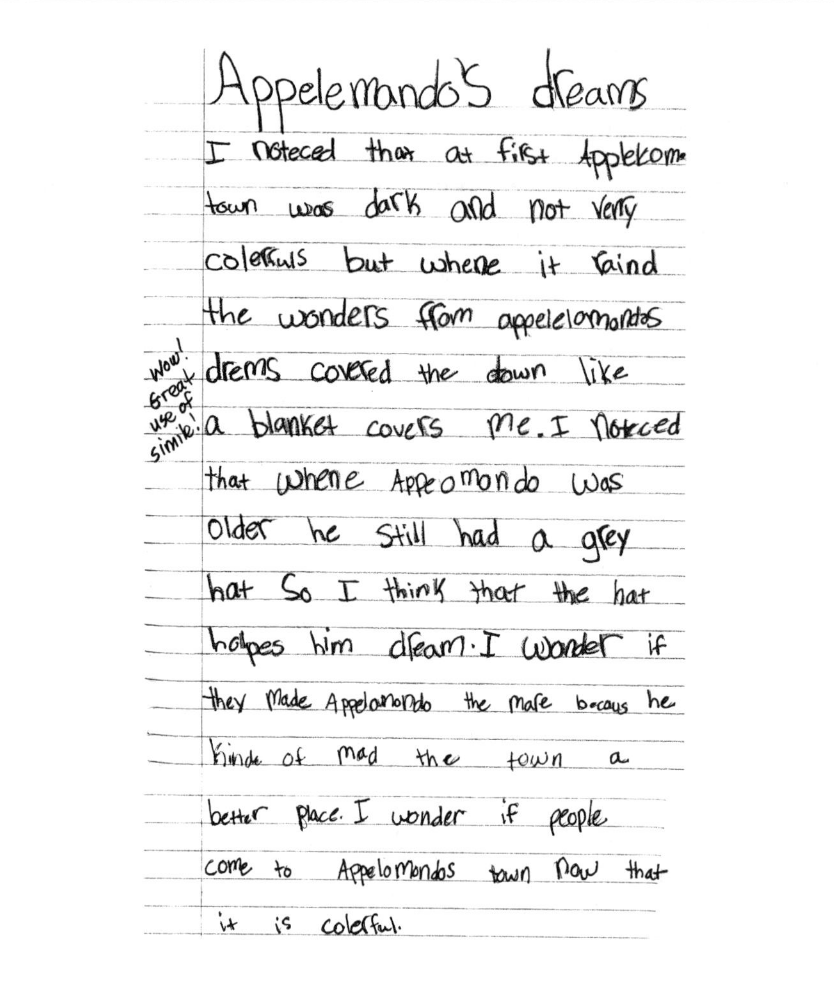

Appelemando's dreams

I noteced that at first Applekom-
town was dark and not verry
colerfuls but whene it raind
the wonders from appelelomandos
drems covered the down like
a blanket covers me. I noticed
that whene Appeomondo was
older he still had a grey
hat So I think that the hat
holpes him dream. I wonder if
they made Appelamondo the mare becaus he
kinde of mad the town a
better place. I wonder if people
come to Appelomondos town now that
it is colerful.

Wow! Great use of simile!

Figure 7.8 *Miya's Journal Entry*

"Like what?" I ask.

"This pigeon is crazy," she answers.

"What do you mean?" I ask.

"He's just crazy."

I suggest Amber write down her thinking and see if she can answer this question: "What from the story shows he is crazy?" I leave Amber. I watch her go to the basket containing the other books from the series. She lays them out on the floor with her reading journal. About fifteen minutes later, she reads her journal entry to me:

> *The pigeon, in all the classic pigeon stories, has some issues to work out like anger and crazy. The crazy is the pigeon wanting a puppy and the anger is him wanting to drive the bus.*

Figure 7.9 *Amber's Reading Conference*

Inviting Different Kinds of Writing as Response to Reading

I never cease to be amazed by my young students. They surprise me each year with their original and creative writing ideas for responding to reading. Of course, there are the obvious writing responses I get each year, such as takeoffs on *Don't Let the Pigeon Ride the Bus* by Mo Willem. Students wrote *Don't Let the Pigeon Baby-Sit* and *Don't Let the Pigeon Drive the Airplane* just this year.

Students are also inspired by Doreen Cronin's "*Diary of . . .* " series (*Diary of a Worm, Diary of a Spider).* Hannah, who up to this point was not interested in being an independent writer, soared when she was inspired by Cronin and started writing her own *Diary of a Ladybug* series of books (Figure 7.10).

Response to a read-aloud

After I read aloud Sharon Creech's *Love That Dog*, Joelle wrote the poem in Figure 7.11.

Response to individual reading

Kylie has done some research on cheetahs in the past, but she is still inspired by this topic. One day during reading workshop, she couples *Cheetah Cubs* by

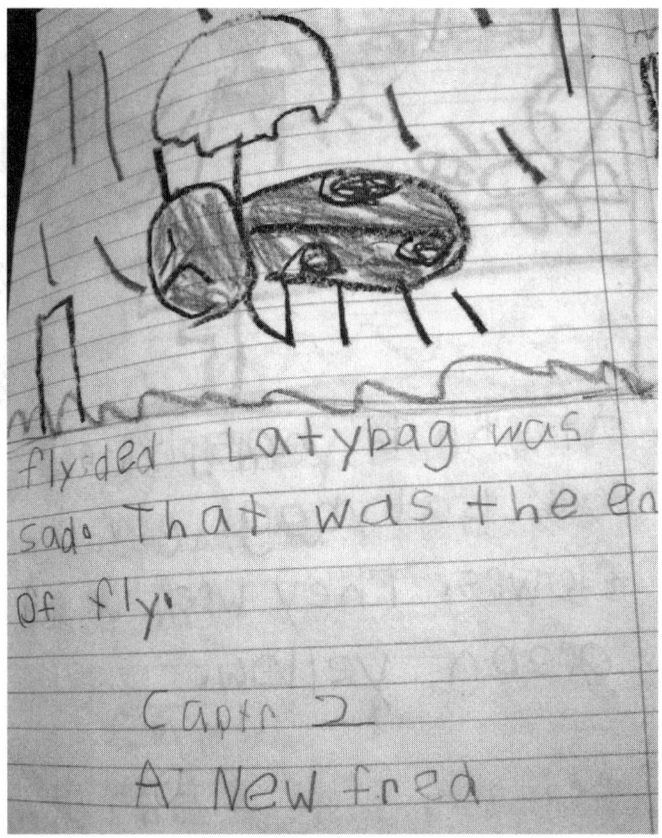

Figure 7.10 *Hannah Writes* Diary of a Ladybug

Ginjer L. Clarke with the poetry books *Color Me a Rhyme* by Jane Yolen, and *Haiku Hike* by the fourth-grade students of St. Mary's Catholic School in Mansfield, Massachusetts. Kylie takes out all three books and flips through each. She decides she wants to write a poem. She begins to write her poem and, as I come over to confer, she has a brilliant idea. She turns to me and says, "I would like to write my poem on this side of the paper and then write a fact on this side, like they do in *Haiku Hike.*" She opens the book and shows me. "Then my book can be a poem book and a nonfiction book too." Kylie begins scanning the book about cheetahs and finds a fact she wants to write: *Cheetahs can run up to 70 mph.*

I ask, "So, is this just the beginning of your book? You plan to write other poems and facts like this one?"

Kylie answers, "Yes. But now I will have to get some information about some other animals."

"Well, how will you do that?" I ask.

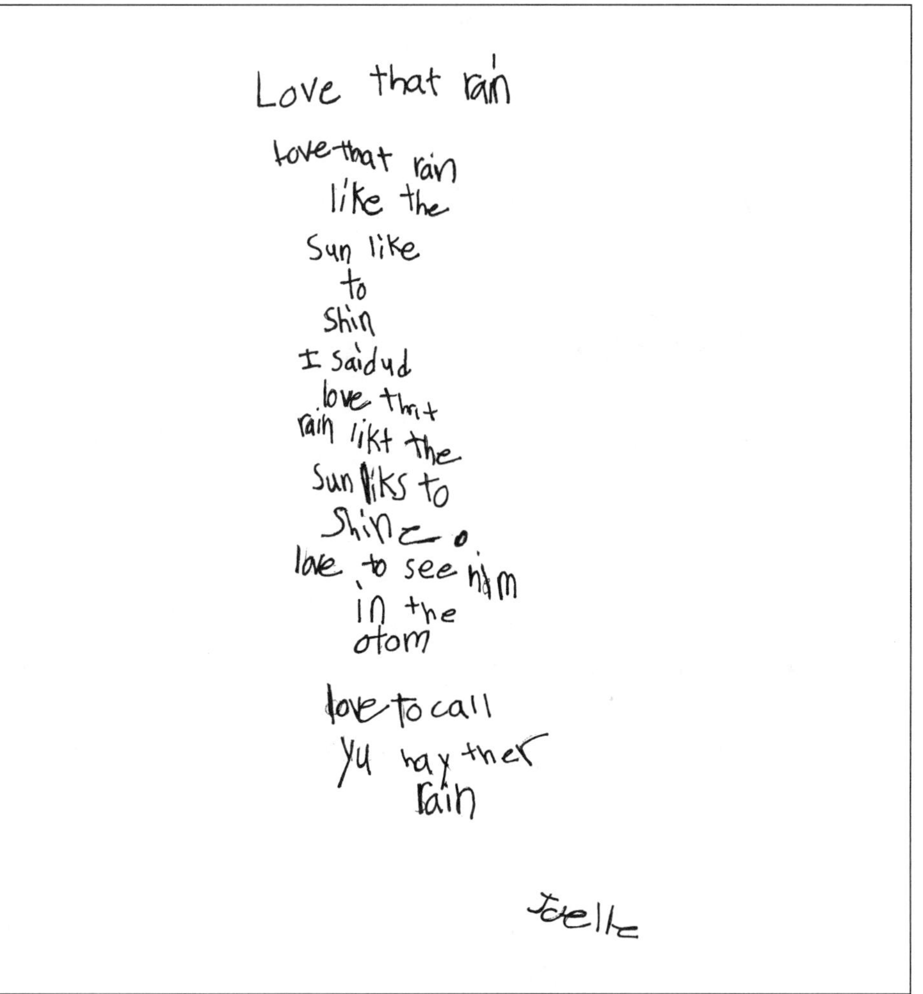

Love that rain

love that rain
like the
Sun like
to
Shin
I saidud
love tht
rain likt the
Sun liks to
Shine.
lave to see him
in the
otom

love to call
yu hay ther
rain

Joelle

Figure 7.11 *Joelle's Poem, Inspired by* Love That Dog

"I think when I am finished with this one, I will find another animal book and see if I am inspired to write a poem. Then I will find a fun fact."

I encourage Kylie, "It sounds like you are on your way. Is there anything I can do to help?"

Kylie says, "Maybe later, if I get stuck."

"Okay," I say. I leave Kylie to her work (Figures 7.12 and 7.13).

Writing and literature circles

Jordyn is part of a literature circle that is reading *Emily Dickinson's Letters to the World* by Jeanette Winter (Figure 7.14). As the students talk through the book, their discussion delights me. They are amazed that some of Dickinson's poems were found in a drawer after she died. They love that Jeanette Winter

Figure 7.12 *Kylie's Poem About Cheetahs*

includes snippets of Dickenson's poems in the book. Jordyn likes this one in particular:

Snowflakes

I counted till they danced so
Their slippers leaped the town,
And then I took a pencil
To note the rebels down . . .

As a response, Jordyn writes her own poem. She is inspired by Dickinson's notion of the snowflakes dancing; she even borrows the word *slippers* as she writes:

The Snow Ballet

The wind blows,
The snow falls
I walk out
and watch the
snow ballet,
beautiful
silver slippers
swirling, twirling,
dancing in the wind.

Figure 7.13 *Kylie Works on Her Book of Poems*

Figure 7.14 *Students in a Literature Circle*

Reading with Writers' Eyes

In reading workshop, as we focus on comprehension, vocabulary, fluency, and even accuracy, students are inspired by ideas from books. After a read-aloud, literature circle, or individual reading, students want to respond with their own stories, poems, and thinking. Students' skills grow stronger when experiences are extended into a reading/writing workshop. What a shame it would be if I planned for them to answer preconceived questions or fill in a worksheet to assess learning. Imagine what would be missed!

How do I teach students to read with writers' eyes?

If we expect students to write the way authors write, we need to provide opportunities for them to see books through writers' eyes. Rather than always focusing on the "reading" aspects of the text, we must also consider the writer's craft: How does this author elaborate? Does he give examples, tell anecdotes, or include statistics? What kinds of word choices does the author make? Does he use simile or metaphor to draw us in? Why does the author choose to use an ellipses, and what kind of effect does it have on us as readers?

Using literature as models

I share books as models for what writers do to make a good story, poem, or nonfiction piece of work. Today we are reading *The Pilgrim's First Thanksgiving* by Ann McGovern. Several pages into the book, McGovern writes:

> Day by day, things got worse. Storms came. The wind blew hard. The waves tossed the ship about. . . . The rain soaked the ship. The rain poured on the Pilgrims.

I stop to point out how the author is elaborating. "Look, Ann McGovern tells us *Day by day, things got worse.* Then she elaborates by telling what happened that was worse: *Storms came. The wind blew hard. The waves tossed the ship about.* Authors often make a statement and then *tell more.*"

Later in the book we notice McGovern elaborates by *telling more* again.

> The Pilgrim children learned to work hard—just as hard as the grown-ups. They had to watch the cornfield and shoo away birds and animals. They had to make big roasts and turkeys.

I note, "Here the author elaborates again. She tells us that the *children learned to work hard*, and then she tells us the jobs they did: *They had to watch the cornfield and shoo away birds and animals. They had to make big roasts and turkeys.*"

The next day we revisit Mary Newell DePalma's *A Grand Old Tree*. While we enjoy the story, we also look through the lens of a writer to notice the writer's craft—the way the story tumbles out onto the pages with a certain flow, the interesting word choices, and the clear sense of beginning, middle, and end:

> *She was home to many creatures. Birds nested among her branches, squirrels scurried through her leaves . . .*
>
> *The grand old tree lived a long, long time. She basked in the sun, bathed in the rain, swayed in the breeze, and danced in the wind.*

Similarly, we celebrate the author's language while we read George Levenson's *Pumpkin Circle*, noticing his use of simile, metaphor, and alliteration:

> *Twisty tendrils grasp like hands stretching out to cling.*
> *Velvet petals open brilliant sunlit bowls . . .*
> *Now comes the harvest. Pluck treasures from the vine.*
> *Sleeping seeds.*
> *The walls are lined with teardrop seeds, each one a slippery jewel.*

I suggest we record these wonderful phrases on a chart to remind us to use interesting language when we write.

And as we read *Hello Ocean* by Pam Munoz Ryan, we stop to consider the first sentence—*Hello, ocean, my old best friend*—deciding if it makes readers want to read more. We also take time to pause at the last page, asking ourselves if the author left us with a satisfying ending. Does the writer tell us she is finished? We do the same with Lois Ehlert's *Snowballs*. We consider her first page and notice she begins with a question: *Do you think birds know when it's going to snow?* This offers a wonderful springboard for discussion about different kinds of leads and becomes a model for students as they experiment with starting their own stories with a question. We admire the last page: *So long, snowball.* Jenna responds for all of us when she says, "That is a perfect ending."

Recognizing elements of good writing

Once we open the door for students to read with a writer's eye, they find elements of good writing on their own, at such a rapid pace we can hardly keep up with them. Right after we read a book about idioms, Hanna says, "Look Ms. Sloan, there's an idiom in my Horrible Harry book: *roll with the punches.*"

"Do you know what that means, Hanna?"

She answers, using context clues, "I think it means to go along with it."

Linnae begins reading workshop with the book *Pumpkin Eye* by Denise Fleming. She writes in her journal, "I like how Denise uses alliteration. . . . I like how she really thinks about writing" (Figure 7.15).

Jackson begins to notice interesting words in the book he is reading. He writes them on small sticky notes and puts them on the inside cover of his reading journal (Figure 7.16). Later he says to the class, "I'm collecting these words to keep track of all of the interesting words I read, but also because I might want to use some of these words when I write."

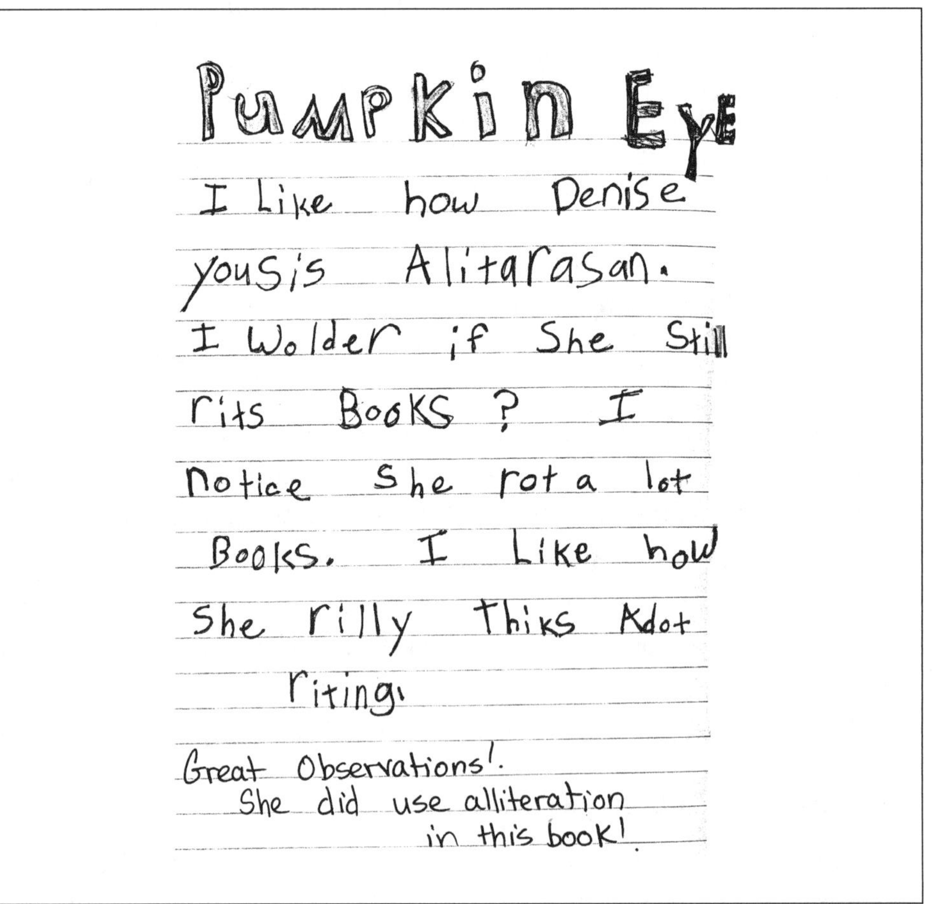

Pumpkin Eye
I Like how Denise
yousis Alitarasan.
I Wolder if She Still
rits Books? I
notice She rot a lot
Books. I Like how
She rilly thiks Adot
riting.

Great Observations!
She did use alliteration
in this book!

Figure 7.15 *Linnae's Journal Entry*

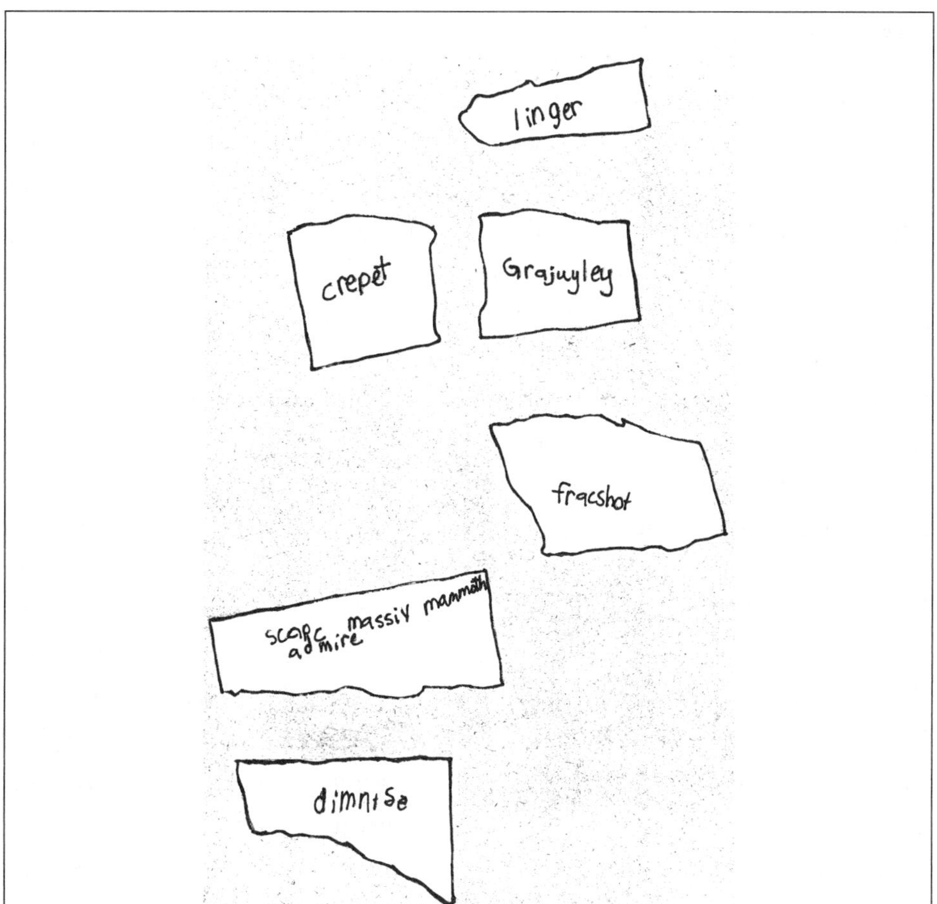

Figure 7.16 *Jackson's List of Interesting Words*

And as Mackenzie finishes reading *The Great Barrier Reef: An Undersea Adventure* by Susan Ring, she tells me, "I like this ending: *I didn't find his watch, but I think I discovered the real treasure.* It really lets you know the book is done, and it kind of tells you that there are lots of neat treasures to see under the water."

On the other hand, Ricky notices an ending in his book about crabs and says, "This isn't a good ending. I didn't think the book was over. I turned the page and it was done."

When we talk about "the writing" as we read books to and with students, they begin to notice these qualities—elaboration through examples or anecdotes, metaphor, simile, alliteration, great leads, interesting word choices, and satisfying endings. And when students notice these qualities of good writing, they take the first step to experimenting with them in their own writing.

Final Thoughts

There is a great deal of emphasis on teaching reading, as well there should be. We want our students to be proficient readers who question and think deeply about the text they read. At the same time, I can't imagine teaching reading without teaching writing right alongside. I know that when I teach writing during reading, my students become better readers. When I encourage them to write down their thinking, they think more deeply. And when students share their writing during literature circles and partner reading, they engage in an exchange of ideas that would not exist without the writing that preceded these discussions.

Learning to write well requires constant reading. When authors write, they must read and reread what they've written. In the same way, I truly believe that writing can improve students' reading abilities. When my students respond to books in writing, they pore over these texts to find support for their thinking, to enjoy the language and write it down, to find that one part that will inspire their own original writing. Jordyn, for example, makes a deep connection with both Emily Dickinson and Jeanette Winter as she writes her own poem inspired by Dickinson's words. She reads *Emily Dickinson's Letters to the World* over and over, enjoying Winter's story and Dickinson's words.

Similarly, it is clear that Jackson is building his vocabulary when he takes time to record interesting words he finds in a book. And the class does the same as we record favorite words and phrases from *Pumpkin Circle* and other read-aloud books.

And when Kylie decides to write a poetry/nonfiction book about cheetahs, she reads and rereads, collecting the facts she finds interesting. She takes notes, and she makes sure the words in her poems are accurate.

When students read books not just with a reader's eye but also with a writer's eye, they read with more attention. They learn to appreciate, understand, and enjoy story, plot, language, organization, mystery, detail, and character. When students look at text features, noting the reasons authors use bullets, headings, labels, bold print, and captions, they better use these features as they read to understand and learn.

Because I weave writing into my reading lessons, my students really *know* the books they read. Through writing, my students learn, reflect, predict, change their thinking, and make connections. They inspire classmates with their writing, which makes them all better thinkers. I know in my heart that writing has made my students better readers.

CHAPTER 8

Do I Really Have to Run a Mini–Random House?

Bringing Balance to Revising, Editing, and Publishing

Years ago I attended a meeting in which teachers shared and discussed the methods we used to teach writing in our primary classrooms. A couple of teachers from one school district shared beautifully published student work (mostly books, which students had handwritten and illustrated). The teachers explained that in their classrooms, students went through the entire writing process: drafting, revising, editing, and rewriting for publication. I was very impressed and asked, "How often do your students publish their work like this?"

Their answer made my jaw drop to the floor. "About once a week," one of them said.

My first thought was, "How on earth do they do this?"

The teachers continued, "We all prewrite on Monday; we do our first draft the next day; then we revise and edit together before students rewrite their books at the end of the week."

My next thought was, "I must not be doing enough."

I went home and reflected. I pored over Lucy Calkins, Donald Graves, and Donald Murray, searching for direction. Maybe I wasn't doing enough. Maybe I needed to have students bring every piece to publication, keeping them together in the process. However, this did not resonate with my own philosophy about teaching writing. I believe that primary students need lots of drafting time, followed by small segments of practice with revision and editing. They need to work in their own way, spending lots of time writing about different topics. I believe older primary students should pick the pieces they feel the most passionate about, the ones they revisit most in their writing, to revise, edit, and publish.

However, what these teachers had accomplished with their students was impressive, and I felt twinges of self-doubt. Maybe I needed to rethink how I was teaching writing and implementing the writing process.

Again, I went back to the experts to find some answers. In *The Art of Teaching Writing,* Lucy Calkins (1994) describes the process as follows: "Most of us follow a cycle in our writing: rehearsal, drafting, revision, and editing." No matter the genre or topic, "we often move through these same stages. Some of us spend longer on rehearsal, others on revision. Some revisions fit between the lines of a draft, others require a sequence of drafts" (22).

In *A Fresh Look at Writing,* Donald Graves (1994) says "The writing process is an untidy business." After reviewing the stages, he states, "Although this suggests a general order, in fact many of these steps occur simultaneously. For some writers a new topic may emerge while they are in the midst of writing about another." Graves goes on to observe, "I've found that some teachers have misunderstood the writing process. They deliberately take children through [the] phases. . . . Of course, these processes do exist, but each child uses them differently. We simply cannot legislate their precise timing" (82).

My continued reading of the experts cemented my view that each writer has her own individual process. We all are different in the way we write. Some writers jot down ideas first. Some begin writing and then revise, and some do more thinking before they write.

As I thought about my own writing, I realized that I do things in my own unique way. I don't follow a predetermined sequence. I don't "rehearse," gathering ideas on Monday; "draft" on Tuesday; "revise" on Wednesday; "edit" on Thursday; and "publish" on Friday. I'm not sure I know anyone who truly writes this way.

Instead, I rehearse, gathering ideas for a while, making notes about observations or experiences. Then I begin to draft, taking my notes and observations and putting them down in a first piece of writing. As I write, I reread, which is when I begin to revise and edit. I go back to more drafting, then back to more revising and editing. Then I may even gather more ideas before I draft again. The process circles over and over each stage, bringing me to another until the piece is finished. I sometimes even abandon my writing for a while to gather ideas for another piece of writing. I would not do well on a schedule that directed me to rehearse, draft, revise, and edit on particular days.

Ralph Fletcher and JoAnn Portalupi (2001) say that the writing process is "messy and nonlinear" (62). This fits with what I believe and what I teach my students. I also know from personal experience that writers don't take every idea through the entire writing process. We sometimes let ideas, notes, observations, and even stories sit in our notebooks untouched. They never get "finished," and that's okay. Bringing pieces to publication doesn't ensure improved writing for a lifetime.

Maybe, during the elementary school years, drafting many, many pieces is best. Perhaps revision, if overemphasized with primary and intermediate students, can make writing seem too arduous. We have to trust our instincts about what is developmentally appropriate for our students, and keep questioning and wondering with our colleagues throughout the grades.

Ultimately, after the meeting, I decided that although I was impressed with my colleagues' efforts, I would stick to my gut feeling about what works best for my students. I breathed easier and had a new sense of confidence for my plan in teaching my young writers.

What About the Writing Process?

Earlier I shared a definition of the writing process as a series of stages that writers work through in a cyclical rather than linear manner: rehearsal (prewriting), drafting (composing), revising, editing, and publishing. Writers revisit the phases as they overlap one another. They move in and out of these stages to meet their needs. For example, a student works on a first draft of a nonfiction piece about elephants. She realizes she needs more information, so she goes back to do some additional research, gathering ideas to plug into her piece. The next day, the same student begins her writing session by rereading her piece. She notices a place where her writing is unclear. She revises for clarity, adding some sentences. Afterward she continues drafting, picking up where she left off.

Students do not move through the writing process in a sequential line. As Fletcher says, it's messy. As we take students through the writing process, we must be flexible and allow individuals to move through the stages at a pace, rate, and order that works best for them.

How do we teach the writing process?

In my early years, I was guilty of saying, "I teach the writing process to my students." Now I recognize that we are all individuals, with various approaches to writing. So, how can we teach our students *the* writing process? I agree with Ralph Fletcher (Fletcher & Portalupi 2001), who argues, "We don't want to teach our students *the* writing process; rather, we want each one of them to find *a* process that works for him or her. This process will inevitably differ from student to student" (62). So instead of teaching the writing process, we must make ourselves knowledgeable about how the writing process works, share this with students, and teach them to find a process that will best meet their needs as writers.

I always remind myself that I teach children, not writing. Sometimes we forget the latest techniques, strategies, or curriculums are just vehicles to help our students better understand and learn what we are trying to teach them. Does it help to have knowledge about writing? Absolutely. I believe that to teach writing effectively, we must study and understand writing: what good writers do, how they come up with ideas, and which strategies they use to affect their readers. But while our knowledge about writing is essential, we must couple that knowledge with what we know about students and what we know about teaching.

The Writing Process and Young Writers

In my classroom, young writers do not bring everything they write through all stages of the writing process. Not even close to everything. It depends on their developmental writing level, their purpose for writing, and the other writing projects they are working on. Most beginning writers rehearse and draft. They may play with revision and editing, but their first draft is often their only draft.

Nicole—rehearsal, drafting, and revising

Take Nicole. She begins by drawing a picture of herself with her friend. They are holding hands. Nicole includes lots of color in her picture. She is just beginning to match letters with sounds. I sit down next to Nicole and prompt, "Tell me about your picture."

She says, "This is me and this is Katie."

I ask, "What are you doing?"

"We're playing."

"What are you playing?"

"We're dancing," she says.

I ask Nicole, "What would you like to write?"

She answers, "*I like playing with my friend.*"

I help Nicole as she connects letters with the sounds she hears as she repeats her sentence over and over.

After she is finished, I ask Nicole to reread her sentence. I ask, "Would you like to add anything else, maybe a detail about what you are playing? What did you say you are doing?"

"We are dancing," says Nicole. She stops to color in eyelashes and brighten the lips with pink crayon. "We're having fun."

"Could I add those details here at the bottom of your page?"

Nicole agrees and I praise her for her picture and her writing (Figure 8.1).

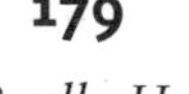

Figure 8.1 *Nicole's Writing*

So what part of the writing process does Nicole work through? She certainly does some rehearsal (prewriting) as she thinks about her friend and draws a picture about her idea. Drawing is a wonderful rehearsal for young writers. Nicole also tells me about her picture.

Nicole drafts when she writes her idea in a sentence. It does not matter that the words are not spelled correctly and that she has no capital to begin or period to end. This is where she is as a writer right now. Later, she will learn and practice the conventions of spelling and punctuation.

When I ask Nicole to tell me more about her picture, she says, "We are dancing. We're having fun." This is a moment of revision. She adds two details. Even though I record these for Nicole, they are her ideas, and she agrees she would like to add them to her writing. Recording is a great way to teach beginning writers about revision without making it a chore. When the teacher plays "secretary," students are much more inclined to revise by adding details. Nicole also revises her picture, adding more color.

I choose not to work with Nicole on editing, because I know she has already pushed herself with conventions by sounding out the words. As far as publishing, Nicole does not rewrite her message, nor do I type this for her. She does, however, share her piece with the class. For me, this is a form of publishing, because it involves a public sharing of her work. I don't believe in this situation that her work needs to be edited to perfection. Nicole is a first grader who writes about something from her experience (rehearsal), revises by adding details to her text and picture, and shares her piece publicly.

Chloe—rehearsal and drafting

Let's also look at the case of Chloe, the kindergarten student who wrote the note to her teacher shown in Chapter 5: *Mrs. Ask, Can you walk me and Isabella to arts and crafts?* (Figure 8.2). Chloe clearly rehearsed in a quick and simple way by thinking about her purpose and audience. Her arts and crafts class was on her mind. She drafted her piece and set the note on her teacher's desk. It does not appear that she reread her note to make any changes or do any editing. Is this okay? Yes. Chloe wrote for a real purpose: to convey a message to someone. This was not a piece of writing she hoped to save; it was functional writing. When I leave a short note for a family member, I rarely revise and edit the note. And usually, after reading the note, the recipient throws it away. In the case of Chloe's note, her teacher delighted in her writing and saved it for that reason alone.

Figure 8.2 *Chloe's Note to Her Teacher*

Joelle—rehearsal, drafting, revising, and editing

Joelle begins writing workshop by telling a friend about her experience when school was cancelled because of snow. I listen in.

"It was like a snowstorm at my house. The snow was coming down really hard. My brother and I wanted to go out and play. We made a snowman but then it got so cold we had to come in, and my mom made us some hot cocoa."

I suggest that Joelle might like to write about her experience in the form of a personal narrative or a poem. Joelle sets off and finds a spot to work. She begins to write and then walks to a shelf to find Jane Yolen's book of poetry *Color Me a Rhyme.* Joelle flips to the page with words for *white.* She continues writing. I watch Joelle from a few feet away, observing her process. She looks to the book. She writes. Then she rereads her writing. At times Joelle stops and appears to be thinking, looking up into the air. Joelle squeezes some writing in between two lines, apparently revising by adding something new. Joelle comes to me and reads her poem (Figure 8.3).

I ask Joelle, "Where did you get your idea for this poem?"

She replies, "Well, this happened yesterday when we were home because of the snow."

"Real experiences give us the best ideas," I encourage. I focus on the poem now. "Wow. I love the word *chalky* to describe the snow. Did you get that from the word *chalk* in Jane Yolen's book?" Joelle nods, and smiles. "I love how you change the word a little bit. Good writers do that. They tweak words to make them work for them in their writing, just like you did."

I continue, "Tell me what you did here." I point to where Joelle added *ten minutes later.*

Joelle answers, "Well, I wanted to show some time has gone by."

"That's a great idea." I continue, "I notice you erased some words, like here under the word *storming.*"

Joelle answers, "Yes. I wrote *falling* but then I wanted to write a better word and I remembered it was like a snowstorm."

"Another great idea." I continue to praise Joelle for her word choices: *storming* and *peers.* I also praise her use of white space and line breaks to ensure that this *looks* like a poem.

Then I ask, "Tell me, would you like to publish this by typing it?"

Joelle answers, "Yes. I want to put it in our student poetry basket."

"Okay," I say. "Let's publish it."

In Joelle's case, she visited all stages of the writing process. She engaged in rehearsal when she talked about her experience with a friend. She also

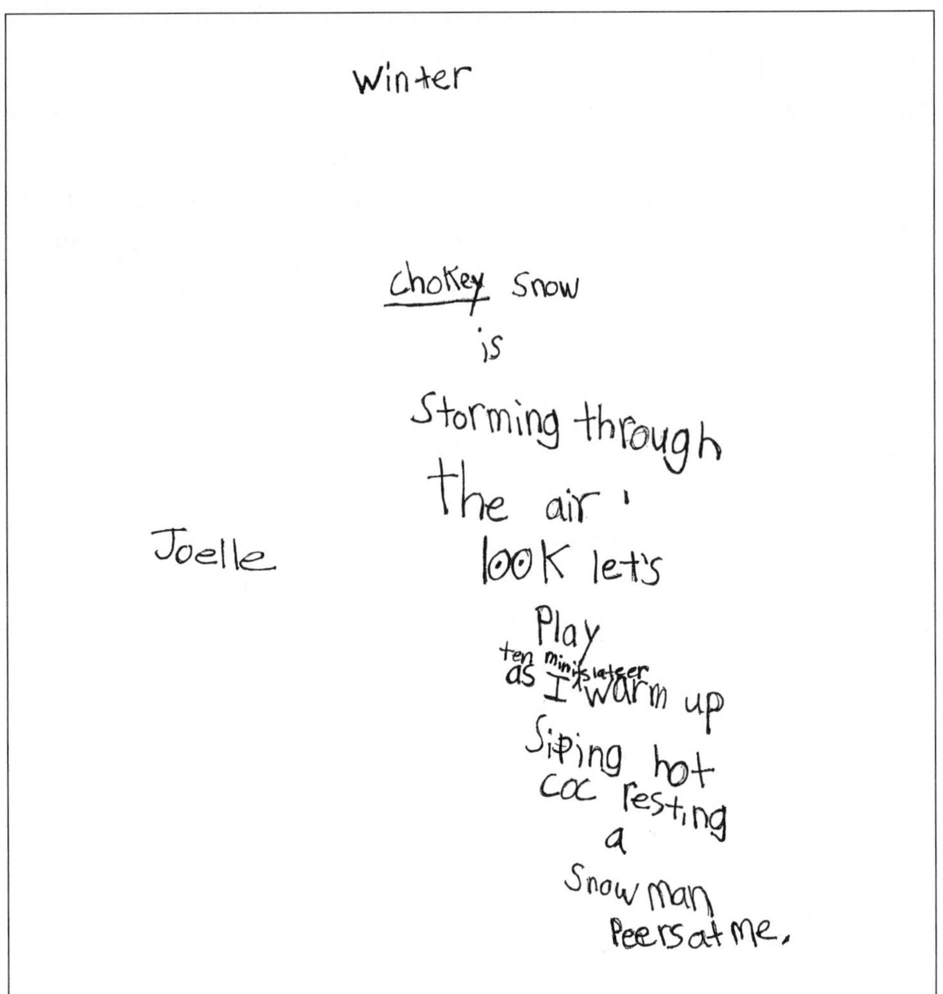

Figure 8.3 *Joelle's Poem About Winter*

gathered words in Yolen's *Color Me a Rhyme*. Joelle drafted her poem and revised as she changed words and squeezed in another phrase. She reread several times to make sure she was satisfied with her poem. Joelle edited a few words after I suggested she look for them on her spelling card. And last, Joelle decided to publish this piece. In a later section in this chapter (Publishing Joelle's Poem on page 184) I will talk about her role during this publishing stage.

How much work should be published in the primary grades?

This is a very tough question. And it probably gets many answers. My definition of publishing includes the notion that a poem, book, story, or other piece of writing is shared publicly. This could mean either:

1. The author orally shares the piece with the class, another class, or an individual at the school.

2. The teacher provides a place for student pieces in book baskets or on the walls in the school office or hallways for others to read. Students also publish when they send their work to other classrooms or to outside audiences.

At my school, students publish in these ways on a regular basis. And, like Katie Wood Ray and Lisa B. Cleaveland (2004), I find that "it is OK for [published pieces] to look like the work of children who are *learning how to write*" (79).

The more traditional definition of publishing, which my students practice less frequently, includes editing a piece to perfection and then rewriting or typing it. However, I find that young writers do so much creating as they write, it would be unfair to ask them to rewrite it. On their very first pass, they often staple a book together, decorate a cover, and illustrate and write a story, poem, or piece of nonfiction. They don't want to rewrite, and even if I offer to type the book, they usually don't want to redraw the pictures. Moreover, some of the charm of these young writers' creations is the developmental level of the writing: the spelling, grammar, and punctuation.

Of course, this does not mean I don't work on editing with these students. I do. However, I narrow the focus of editing to small elements, such as a few words they can respell or punctuation they can add to the end of a sentence. Sometimes we edit just for a capital letter to begin a name.

My young writers learn to like editing because I help them pick and choose the elements to fix, rather than having them correct their entire piece, which usually causes a lot of destruction. When students decide to publish a piece as a typed copy, I let them do a little editing, and I cover the rest. Often we hang these "perfectly published" pieces, just as we hang the beginners' "unpublished" writing (Figure 8.4).

What is the student's role in publishing?

Publishing, by rewriting or typing, usually occurs after some revising and editing. Most of the time my students choose which pieces they would like to publish in this way. They usually select stories and poems they have revised and edited after taking ample time to draft. Of course, how much revising and editing takes place depends on the student's level. As I mentioned earlier, I very rarely have emergent or beginning writers rewrite their pieces. They usually

Figure 8.4 *Typed Poems Hanging in a Window*

don't want to, and editing, typing, and redrawing illustrations uses up precious time they could spend to gather ideas and draft something new. If emergent writers want to publish a piece such as Nicole's (*I like playing with my friend. We are dancing. We're having fun.*), then I usually let them guide me as I type the piece so they are pleased with the final appearance. I make most of the editing changes and then encourage students to draw a picture to go with the writing.

As students gain more skills with writing, I help them publish pieces after they show some effort with revising and editing. Students don't have to fix all of the spelling and punctuation, but I want them to make an effort. Then I will edit the rest. Again, the amount of work I require depends completely on each child's developmental level.

Publishing Joelle's Poem

Okay, let's revisit Joelle. She wants to publish her poem *Winter*. In this case, she has shown some effort with regard to revising and editing. Joelle is a second grader, so I expect more from her than I expect from Nicole. I have three choices: I can help Joelle edit the rest of the spelling and then she can rewrite the poem; I can help Joelle edit the rest of the spelling and then she can type the poem; or, I can get input from Joelle, who will work with me as I type the poem.

I choose the third option for a few reasons. Poems are short and we can get this piece published quickly if I type it myself. Also, I have only one computer in the room. If students always do their own typing, it is difficult to get everyone on the computer to publish. And last, this poem will look polished and professional if it is typed instead of rewritten.

Joelle sits right next to me as I type. She has done a great job making this look like a poem. I first ask, "Which font should we use?" I show her a few examples and she chooses. We then decide on font size. Next, Joelle reads as I also look at her poem. I type and she makes sure everything is right. I ask questions such as, "Do you want a punctuation mark here?" I make a suggestion to use an exclamation mark in one spot. I also suggest some periods and commas. Joelle likes my ideas, but of course she has the final word. Joelle also looks for mistakes in spelling and spacing, which often occur when I type quickly. We look at the poem when it is finished, and Joelle decides if she is pleased with its appearance. Do we need to make any changes to the content, spelling, punctuation, or spacing?

Joelle is happy with her poem. She makes an illustration to match, and mounts it on construction paper. We laminate her poem and place it into our student poetry basket for others to read all year.

How do I encourage students to revise their work?

How much revision should young students engage in as they work through their daily writing? I ask myself this quite often. Of course, I have high expectations for my students. I know they are capable and I want them to meet lofty standards. However, I also know they are young children at a variety of developmental levels in their writing. I need to honor this and find a balance when it comes to revision.

As I have mentioned, in my classroom young writers usually do not continue beyond one draft. They draw; they write; they finish. They do little revision and no rewriting. Donald Graves (1994) notes, "I seldom encourage very young writers (kindergarten, first grade) to revise. I want them to write extensively and to experience the flow of writing" (235). Similarly, Katie Wood Ray and Lisa B. Cleaveland (2004) explain, "We simply do not push our youngest writers to do lots of revision work, particularly rewriting" (71). I couldn't agree more. Young writers are just beginning to put their ideas down on paper. We need to encourage them to write, and write a lot. They are not ready for lots of revision, and certainly not much, if any, rewriting. Ask any six-year-old, "Would you like to copy that over?" I'm sure you can guess the response.

Teaching revision through shared and modeled writing

Shared and modeled writing offer two great ways to teach young writers of all levels about revision without pressuring them to work on their own piece. In Chapter 4 I share several examples in which I model moments of revision in my own writing, or students engage in revision while we write a shared piece. During these times, students learn about the importance of revision (adding details, changing words, shortening sentences), as well as editing, especially if the piece will be published. Is this a thank-you letter we are sending to someone? A nonfiction book we will publish for our classroom library? If so, we need to make sure we revise and edit. Shared and modeled writing also teaches students that revision and editing do not follow in an automatic sequence behind rehearsal and drafting. Rather, these two stages intertwine with drafting, as we work to create a published piece.

When do I push students to revise their work?

As students approach the end of second grade or move into third grade, some are ready to be "nudged" a little more firmly to revise their work independently. At this point, they have watched me revise my own writing many times, and we have also spent months working on revision together through shared writing. This gives them the know-how, experience, and confidence to try revising on their own. For example, when Joelle worked independently to revise her poem *Winter,* she made some small but important changes to her writing.

Students begin slowly. During their first attempts at independent revision, they add a detail or change one word. Soon, they build enough confidence to scratch out whole lines and squeeze in phrases when they think it will improve their piece (Figure 8.5). They reread with a sense of purpose, to make their writing the best it can be.

Generally speaking, primary age students won't engage in full revision. Instead, they will find spots to revise: places in their writing where a different word will be more specific, a few details will add clarity, or an ending sentence will tell readers that the piece is finished (see Figure 8.6 on page 188). We need to honor and build upon these places where students revise—accepting students, and their writing, as they become more proficient in this stage of the writing process.

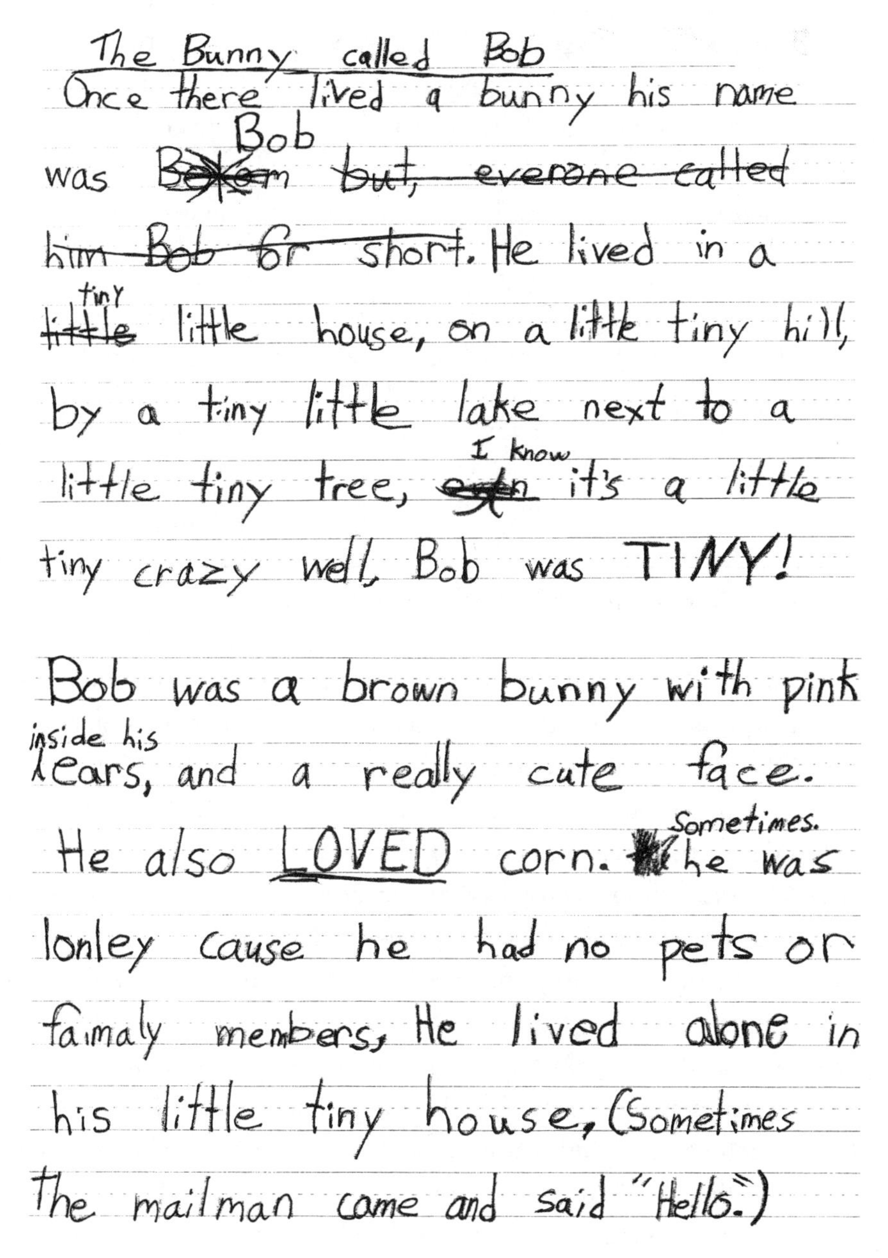

The Bunny called Bob
Once there lived a bunny his name
was ~~Bokem~~ Bob ~~but, everone called~~
~~him Bob for short~~. He lived in a
~~little~~ tiny little house, on a little tiny hill,
by a tiny little lake next to a
little tiny tree, ~~even~~ I know it's a little
tiny crazy well, Bob was TINY!

Bob was a brown bunny with pink
inside his ears, and a really cute face.
He also LOVED corn. Sometimes. he was
lonley cause he had no pets or
faimaly members, He lived alone in
his little tiny house, (Sometimes
the mailman came and said "Hello.")

Figure 8.5 *Tatum's Independent Revision (Third Grade)*

Final Thoughts

Although the suggestion of running a mini–Random House in the classroom is a bit tongue-in-cheek, the sentiment and concern are very real. It is tempting to push our young writers to publish all of the writing they do. However, as I think about my students, I also consider what I know about writing and what I know about teaching. In the end, I recognize that all writers do not follow

Revision: What to Expect of Primary Writers

Beginning of Year	Middle of Year	End of Year
Students: • Watch teacher add details, change words, cross out words. • Participate in simple revision as part of shared writing.	Students: • Begin to add a detail or two. • Add beginning and ending sentences with help. • Begin to focus their topics.	Students: • Add details with help and on their own. • Focus their topics. • Cross out words and add new ones. • Add leads and ending sentences with help and on their own.

Figure 8.6 *Revision: What to Expect of Primary Writers*

one path. We work through a writing process in individual ways, and we write for different purposes and audiences. Some writing requires revision and editing; some does not. And some publishing requires editing to perfection.

Young students mostly need time to rehearse and draft. They need lots of opportunities to put their ideas onto paper. Students need to develop as independent writers, choosing topics that engage them and make them want to write. Young writers are individuals. Some students are ready to revise and edit small pieces of their work; some need to be nudged to revise and edit; and some need us to celebrate their first (and only) draft, delighting in the perfect imperfections of the early writer. We also need to allow students to revise a particular piece without taking the additional steps to publish it.

Good teaching starts with knowing our students and knowing our topic. It involves modeling for children and showing them the way with a kind and encouraging heart. Good teaching means having high standards for our students and guiding them to meet their potential. It also means that sometimes we need to let go of perfection and let the process be, as Graves says, "untidy."

Young writers can't publish everything they write. If they did, teachers would go crazy. We would be so busy publishing work, we wouldn't have sufficient time to teach students to write—to discover topics, experiment with ideas, and put those ideas down on paper. Every so often, my beginning writers select pieces they would like to publish. They complete some revision and editing through their own processes, and then we usually type their pieces together. But when I consider how much publishing will occur in my classroom, I recognize that young writers' time is best spent *writing*.

CHAPTER 9

How Do I Keep Assessment Easy?

Observations, Conferences, and Looking at Student Work

Years ago I participated in several trainings led by assessment expert Rick Stiggins, who taught us to determine our purpose for assessment first. Are we evaluating existing curriculum? Are we qualifying students for a remedial program? Do we want to know if students are making progress? Or meeting standards? Are we using an assessment to drive future instruction?

These different purposes lead to different methods for assessment. As a classroom teacher, my most important reasons for student assessment are to:

1. See if students are making progress (and what kind of progress).
2. Communicate that progress.
3. See if students are meeting standards.
4. Determine what I will teach next (as well as how, and to whom).

I use a variety of methods to help me determine how students are doing and what I need to teach next: student writing samples; observations; and one-on-one conferences. Because each method gives me different information, I am thoughtful about the kinds of assessment I choose for each purpose.

As a teacher, I need to think very clearly about what I want to know about my students. Then, I must consider each method for assessment. Will the information from this assessment help me understand my students better? Will the information help me direct meaningful instruction to challenge and meet the needs of my students? Will this assessment provide information that will help me communicate my students' progress to parents and other parties? As

Vicki Spandel (2005) explains, "Good assessment does not come about by accident. It is the result of clear vision and thoughtful planning" (97).

What Does This Child Know About Writing? Looking at Student Work

One of the reasons I assess is to determine whether students are meeting standards. In Washington State we have performance expectations at each grade level for every subject, including writing. One of my jobs is to teach and evaluate students based on these standards, which define what students should know and be able to do by the end of first, second, and third grade (Figure 9.1). My colleagues and I pore over our performance expectations to help us determine the skills we will teach.

However, I don't assess just to see if a student meets the standards. When I assess, I really want to know what a student knows about writing. What are the strengths? What are the struggles? What do I need to teach next?

Assessing Summer's Writing (Second Grade)

Let's look at the work of a second-grade student, Summer. Figure 9.2 contains her story about a lion. Summer's piece reveals a lot about what she knows about writing:

- She understands story structure. She has two characters and she includes a problem.
- While her plot does not have lots of detail, she has a clear beginning, middle, and end to her story.
- She makes great word choices: *brownish-gold, lionesses, attractive, shy, hovered.*
- She includes some detail: *All of the lionesses hovered over John . . . He tried everything to get her to marry him. But she always said "No" to flower and candies.*
- She understands about writing an ending that will let her reader know she is finished.
- She uses age-appropriate spelling, capitals, and periods. She even tries a recently taught spelling convention (change the *y* to *i* and add *ed*) when she spells *marryied.* Even though she forgot to delete the *y*, I applaud her attempt.

Kindergarten	First Grade	Second Grade	Third Grade
• Uses drawing, drama, or objects to discover and plan writing. • Draws and labels pictures. • Uses words or simple sentences to express ideas. • Tells stories. • Draws details rather than always writing details. • Spells some high-frequency words. • Uses beginning and ending sounds to write words. • Participates in shared and interactive writing. • Begins to discover favorite books and authors.	• Talks and/or draws to generate ideas. • Begins to write for a sustained period of time. • Begins to discover a variety of genres (lists, letters, stories, books). • Writes for self, friends, family, and teacher. • Develops ideas from a list of topics. • Elaborates on ideas with a few details and specific word choices. • Adds details through drawing. • Makes very simple revisions and edits. • Begins to use a variety of sentence type and length. • Participates in shared and interactive writing. • Begins to reread writing. • Spells first-grade high-frequency words, and uses grade-level spelling patterns. • Blends using beginning, middle, and ending sounds. • Begins to use spelling resources (spelling cards, word walls).	• Writes with a sense of purpose and audience. • Writes in a variety of forms and genres (journals, fictional stories, personal narratives, rhymes, poetry, nonfiction, letters, procedural writing). • Writes for a sustained period of time. • Maintains focus on a topic. • Elaborates on ideas and includes supporting information. • Uses simple transitions. • Writes with a sense of organization, experimenting with lead and ending sentences. • Uses word choice to elaborate or be more specific. • Learns to write a variety of sentence beginnings, types, and structures. • Learns to use more sophisticated spelling patterns and spelling rules. • Rereads writing and revises for detail, word choices. • Edits for simple spelling, capitalization, and punctuation. • Uses spelling resources (spelling cards, word walls).	• Writes with a sense of purpose and for a variety of audiences. • Writes in a variety of forms and genres (journal writing, personal narrative, nonfiction, fictional stories, poetry, letters, procedural writing). • Talks and uses a variety of rehearsal strategies to plan writing. • Writes for a sustained period of time. • Elaborates on ideas using a variety of strategies (including anecdotes, examples, statistics). • Writes with a sense of organization (clear beginning, middle, and end; including clear lead and ending sentences). • Uses a variety of word choices and begins to explore using simile and metaphor. • Uses a variety of sentence beginnings, types, and structures. • Rereads writing and revises for detail, word choices, and sentence variety and structure. • Participates in shared writing. • Uses grade-level spelling. • Edits for spelling, capitalization, and punctuation. • Uses spelling resources (spelling cards, student dictionaries).

Figure 9.1 *General Writing Standards, K–3*

Summer

Onse there. was a lion that had brownish gold fer. He was very atraktive. All of the lioneses huvered over John! John espeily liked Jessie. One of the girls he had a crush on She was a very shy lion. He always dremed of them being maryied. He tryed every thing to get her to mary him. But she always said no to flowers & candys. John kept trying but his dreams never came true. poor John.

Figure 9.2 *Summer's Story About a Lion*

It is clear that Summer knows a lot about writing. I am both delighted and impressed. She definitely "meets the standard" for a second-grade writer. However, I also want to use the assessment to ask questions: How can I nudge her forward? What can I do to help Summer improve her writing, especially if she chooses to publish this story?

First, I decide to help Summer use elaboration to make her writing more complete. I suggest adding a sentence or two to explain why "all the lionesses hovered over John." What made him so popular? I also suggest explaining why Jessie didn't like him. Was it a misunderstanding because she was so shy?

Next, I help Summer edit a few words for spelling. We focus on the rule "change the *y* to an *i* and add *ed*." She edits *marryied* and *tryed*.

While I help Summer with this specific piece, I also help in a more general sense. I direct Summer to some of the fiction books on our shelf to point out that stories can be a bit longer, with more details about the problem and how the characters try to solve or deal with it. I also model and engage the whole class in shared writing to show how writers develop plot in fiction stories.

This modeling—along with conversation about character, plot, problem, and solution—begins with read-alouds in first grade. We talk about what happens in the beginning, middle, and end of stories. The beginning introduces us to the character. In the middle this character often tries to solve a problem. Sometimes she tries several different ways. As the story moves toward its end, the character resolves her problem (or sometimes doesn't).

As students move into second and third grade, like Summer, I encourage them to replicate the stories they read, in their writing. Copy a structure. Use a formula such as trying three ways to solve a problem, with the third one working. Describe the setting and make it an important part of your story.

Assessing Robbie's Writing (First Grade)

Robbie is a first-grade student. In September, he joins my class with little to no writing experience. Figure 9.3 shows his first piece of independent writing. This is what I observe:

- Robbie has a topic he knows and likes.
- His picture shows some wonderful detail.
- He writes an idea and a detail.
- He matches some letters to sounds (even though he does not write with conventional spelling).
- He seems to have spelled the word *fun* correctly.
- He uses some spacing between words.

Robbie is just beginning to develop confidence as a writer, and I am delighted that he is taking some risks. I encourage this confidence by praising him for his wonderful idea and detailed picture. I also compliment Robbie for sounding out the words in his two sentences. I don't point out that he has used a lowercase for *I,* forgotten to add the word *are,* and omitted periods at the end of his sentences. These are things I will teach when Robbie is ready—when he has been writing confidently for a while. For now, I celebrate with Robbie. He is a writer!

Figure 9.3 *Robbie's First Piece of Writing*

How Can I Monitor Each Child? Daily Observations at Work

After my minilesson, the children head off to begin their work. This is a time when I often take a moment to observe my students. I grab my assessment notebook and let my eyes wander around the room. I notice that Ryan quickly takes out his writing workshop folder and begins working on a story he started yesterday. He rereads his work and then starts writing.

Annie drifts around the room. She sharpens a pencil. She slowly finds her poetry journal. She heads for a small chair and then decides to join two friends who are working at a table. Finally, after looking over her classmates' work, Annie gazes into space, as though she is thinking. I watch her take a deep breath. She turns to a friend and says, "I don't know what kind of poem I want to write."

Claire suggests, "How about writing an animal poem or one about winter?"

Annie announces, "Oh, I know what I will do." She gets up and goes to the bookshelf. She flips through an animal nonfiction basket and selects a book about turtles, which she brings back to her table. Annie looks at one of the pictures in the book and then begins writing.

As Annie works her way into writing workshop, I also notice Kylie and Hanna. They have brought their clipboards over to a corner, where they are sharing their pieces with one another. Kylie asks Hanna, "Could you help me think of a way to end my poem?"

Hanna answers, "Sure. I can do that." They each read their poem aloud. Hanna suggests,"You could repeat the first line of your poem at the end. I think that would be good." Kylie nods in agreement.

What I Learn from Observations

I learn something from each of these observations. Ryan is a self-starter. He is focused and confident as he begins his writing for the day. Ryan knows that good writers reread their work before they continue writing. He is comfortable working alone.

Annie takes her time settling into writing workshop. I know that Annie has a lot of energy. Annie is a mover. It takes her time to decide on her writing. She understands that other writers can be helpers, so she asks for advice from a classmate. Annie also understands that books can help with ideas. Once Annie has a chance to settle in, she writes.

Hanna and Kylie are friends and good writing partners. They support one another as they write. Both feel comfortable asking for help and sharing with each other. When Hanna offers advice to Kylie ("You could repeat the first line of your poem at the end"), it shows that she is confident enough to give writing advice, and it shows she understands that sometimes poets repeat important words and lines in their poems.

Today I record my observations in my assessment notebook. I don't always write down what I see, but when I can, it serves as documentation and helps me note if there is progress and/or any patterns in the processes students follow as they write. Some of the things I look for as I observe are:

- Do students begin writing right away?
- Do students work alone or with a partner?
- Do students find partners helpful or distracting?

- Do students prefer to make books, write in notebooks, or write on pieces of paper?
- Do students write quietly? Do they need to talk with others before they write?
- How long can students sustain writing?
- Do students work on the same piece from day to day or do they start something new every day?
- Do students reread their writing before they continue a piece?
- Do students revise and/or edit? Do they use spelling resources?
- Where do students like to write? At a table, on the floor, or in a small chair with a clipboard?
- Do students ask other writers for help? Do they offer help?

Each of my observations gives me important information I can't get from a writing sample or even, in most cases, a writing conference. My observations are vital as I assess my students. Otherwise, how would I know that Ryan is a self-starter or that Kylie and Hanna offer revising help to one another? How would I know that Annie looks to books for writing ideas and finds comfort writing alongside others? Some of this information might eventually come out in a writing conference, but observations give me crucial support.

In addition, observations allow me to monitor my students frequently. I can note several observations in the span of a few minutes. A writing conference often takes much longer, with my focus centered on one student only. My observations allow me to celebrate what students do well and support them in their areas of need. If I see that Annie writes more successfully alongside others, I can provide that option for her. If I notice that John and Eduardo distract each other as they write, I can ask them to separate. And when I realize that Lacey misspells high-frequency words like *when* and *saw*, I can remind her about when and how we use our spelling cards as we write. My observations give me precious information that helps me monitor my students' achievement and progress (Figures 9.4 through 9.6).

Writing Conferences

The writing conference is a critical method for assessing and teaching my young writers. The word *assessment* actually comes from the Latin word *assidere,* which means "to sit beside." This is when I slow down and focus on

Figure 9.4 *Observation: Katherine Rereads Her Work as She Writes*

Figure 9.5 *Observation: Three Students Write and Share Together*

Figure 9.6 *Observation: Peer Editing in Progress*

one student at a time. Side by side we work together to improve a student's writing. Donald Graves (1994) explains, "The purpose of the writing conference is to help children teach you about what they know so you can help them more effectively with their writing" (59). I love Graves' description, because he emphasizes that the child is in charge during the conference, not the teacher.

Where do I hold writing conferences?

Conferences can happen anywhere in the classroom. I tend to find a spot next to a child who is working and we hold our conference right there: at a table, on the floor, in small chairs sitting next to one another. If we are going to publish a piece together during our conference, we move over to the computer, sitting side by side so both of us can access the screen and the keyboard.

What does a writing conference look like?

A writing conference is really a conversation between the writer and the teacher. (There are also student-student conferences, but I will focus on student-teacher conferences here.) During a student-teacher conference, I focus

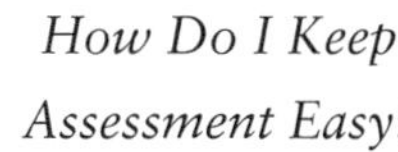

Figure 9.7 *Student-Teacher Conference*

more on the writer than on the writing. How is he learning to take life experiences and write about them? What ways is he learning to elaborate? Does he sense when his piece is unclear and needs more explanation? I don't want to help students "fix" their writing; I want them to grow as writers through the work we do on this one piece. And although I ask questions during conferences, I don't want to turn the meeting into an interrogation—a question-answer-question-answer experience. It should really be a dialogue, a sharing of ideas, which ultimately nudges the writer forward.

While I try to be flexible during writing conferences, it is helpful to follow a structure. Students start by sharing their writing. They read what they have so far, or if there is little or no writing, I say, "Tell me about your picture." I begin by noticing something done well. I praise students for a detailed picture, the wonderful use of language, or an inviting lead. Perhaps students write with a sense of organization, or they work to match letters to the sounds they hear. I want to pump them up, letting them know they are writers.

Next I often ask, "What do you need from me to help you with your writing today?" I want students to identify where they need assistance. Would they like to add another detail? Do they need help revising their ending sentence?

Are they stuck on where to take their story next? Sometimes students don't know how they need help. This is okay. I can gently nudge them.

The second part of a writing conference includes a teaching point. I try to show students something I notice in their writing, and work with them on ways to improve. For example, a young writer may come to the conference with a picture and one sentence: *I love hiking.* I admire the picture. The student reads the sentence and I offer praise again for writing an idea to go with the picture. If this child wants to add a detail, I might say, "You know, sometimes writers elaborate by *telling more.* They often tell *why*, or tell *how.* Sometimes they tell *who*. I notice in your story you say: *I love hiking.* You might add a detail by telling *where*. Where do you like to hike? You could also tell *who* goes hiking with you."

This sparks a conversation in which the child tells me, "We go to Wallace Falls. I go with my mom and dad." At this point, I encourage the student to add those two sentences.

After the student adds the details and reads back the revised piece of writing, I say, "Oh, I love the two details you added. It makes your story so interesting. Writers add details all the time to make their stories interesting. I would love for you to make this a new goal. Whenever you draw a picture and write a sentence, for instance about something you like to do or enjoy, think about how you can tell more (tell *how* you do it, tell *who* is with you, tell *why* you like it, tell *where* you are). Then try to add a couple of details." This is the third part of my writing conference: setting a goal with a student.

Three Parts of a Writing Conference

1. Praise the student for something well done.
2. Teach something based on the writing, or process, and give the student a chance to try it out.
3. Set a goal with the student.

Helpful Hints for Successful Writing Conferences

Through trial and error, I have developed a set of guidelines that contribute to successful writing conferences.

1. Keep conferences short. How short? Sometimes two minutes is enough. Sometimes three to five minutes is necessary. Once in a while, they need to be a bit longer. Let the time meet the need of the writer.

2. Build on students' strengths. Start with what they do well and move forward from there.

3. Focus on one or two teaching points. These should be attainable. Don't overwhelm students.

4. Keep it as a conversation. Don't get into a question-answer-question-answer pattern. Rather, make comments such as, "Tell me more about this" or "How fascinating; I didn't know that about your cat."

5. Encourage students to stay in charge. Let students talk. They read to you. They hold their own book, paper, or notebook.

6. Listen. Show interest. Let students know you believe in them as writers. Carl Anderson (2000) says, "The success of a conference often rests on the extent to which students sense that we are genuinely interested in them as writers—and as individuals" (22).

7. Meet with each student on a regular basis. Like other assessments and teaching moments, one size does not fit all. However, a good rule of thumb is to meet formally at least once every week and a half. For some students it will be more often.

Are All Conferences the Same? Exploring Different Kinds of Teacher-Student Conferences

Writing conferences vary because student strengths and needs vary. Sometimes the conference is a celebration of writing well done. Sometimes the conference focuses on the content of the writing, with work on elaboration, leads, or word choices. Beginning writers often need help matching text with picture, sounding out words, or adding a detail. There are times I help students with topic choice. And sometimes we concentrate on editing or getting a piece ready for publication. I focus on the student. What does the writer need from me to improve the writing?

There are times when the conference focuses on process. Our conversation centers on ways to gather ideas, how to take notes before writing, or choosing a place in the room that will support, rather than distract, this student writer. Process lessons are as important as content lessons.

Cole: Celebrating picture as part of the story

Cole is in Julie Filer's first-grade class. Julie sits down next to Cole and says, "I would love to hear your book. Would you read it to me?"

Cole agrees and begins reading:

The Rocket Ship Alien

One day it was rocket ship day.
Those were my favorite days

My rocket ship.
Wow.

10-9-8-7-6-5-4-3-2-1
Blast off.

Julie begins by telling Cole, "Wow, I love that you wrote about your pictures. Read your first page again."

Cole reads, "The Rocket Ship Alien. One day it was rocket ship day. Those were my favorite days."

Julie says, "I love your line: *Those were my favorite days.*" How did you think of that?"

Cole answers, "I just thought he might be thinking about those days."

Julie prods, "Tell me about your pictures."

Cole explains how his character, the alien, is lying in bed and another alien is looking in the window. The first alien is thinking about Rocket Ship Day.

When Cole turns to the second page, Julie says, "Tell me about this picture. What is this part?"

Cole begins, "Well, he's making a rocket ship underground and [pointing to the line at the top] this is the ground. Right here [pointing to the darkened part of the line] is where the ground retracts so the rocket ship can blast off."

Julie responds, "I love that word, *retract*. Can you explain that?"

Cole answers, "You know, it will move apart to make room for the rocket ship."

Cole turns to the last page of his book. He explains all the details of his picture. "This is where the ground is retracting and you can see the sun over the horizon. The rocket ship is going to blast off. These things [pointing to the lines on the rocket] are energy boosters. They make the rocket go fast."

Julie ends her conference by telling Cole, "I love that your book has a beginning, middle, and end. I love that your pictures are so detailed, and the words you use to describe, like *retract* and *horizon,* make your story really interesting. Your first page really made me want to read on when you said, *Those were my favorite days*."

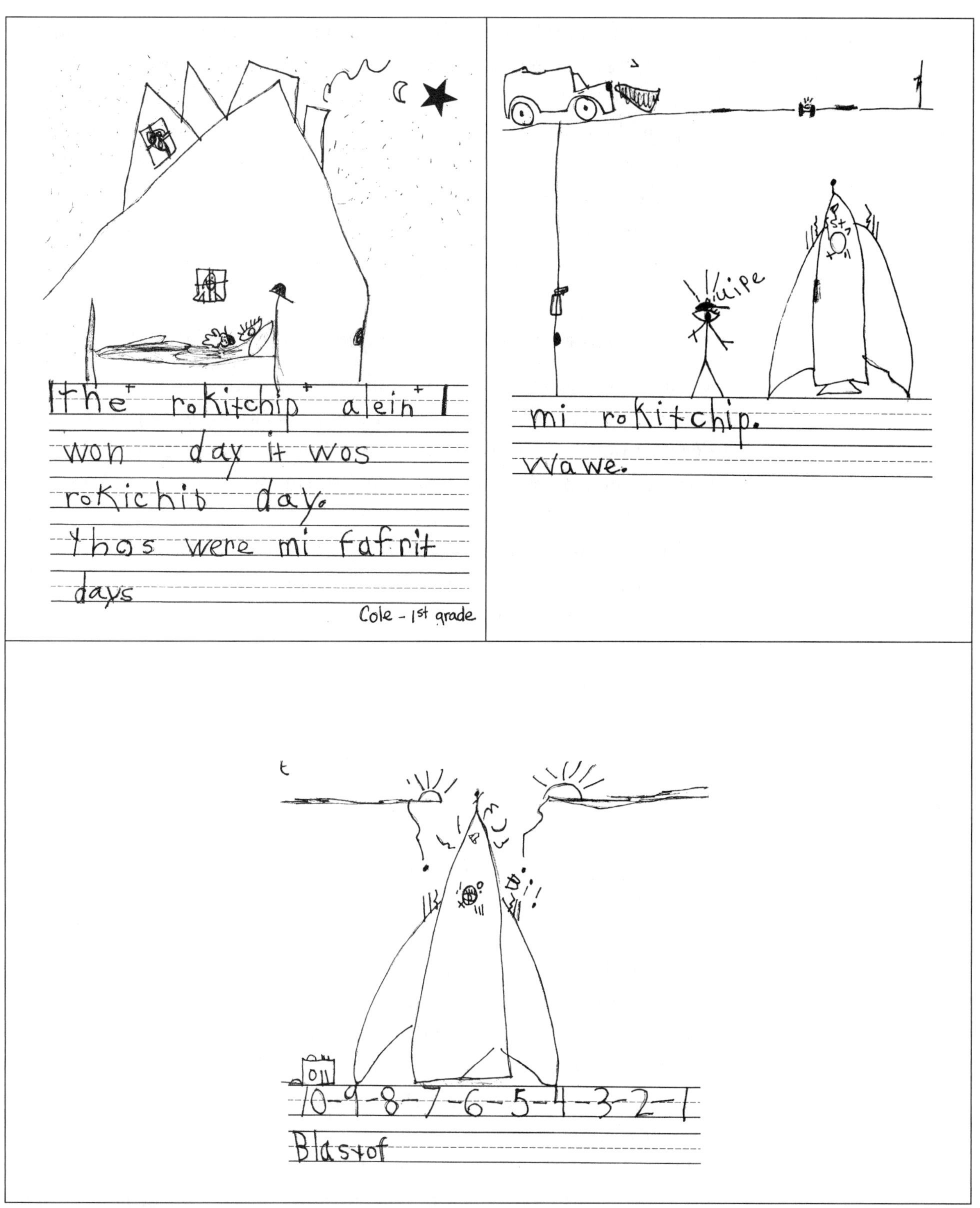

Figure 9.8 *Cole's Rocket Ship Book*

Cole is a writer beyond what we see in his transcription. Even though he did not represent them in text, his word choices are fabulous. This is a wonderful example of how we cannot separate the picture from the writing for young children. The picture is the detail, the word choices, the organization of the piece. Julie's wonderful invitation, "Tell me about your picture," opens up a story beyond what we see in the text. It allows Cole to tell his story with all the grandeur he imagined when he wrote and drew it. I never underestimate the words "Tell me about your picture."

Hunter: Revising and publishing conference (adding details)

Hunter is a second grader. It is November and up to this point he has not done much writing. Today Hunter starts writing workshop by getting several pieces of paper from our writing center. He works on a story independently. Near the end of the workshop I sit down next to Hunter, ready for a conference. I begin by saying, "Tell me what you wrote today."

Hunter answers, "I wrote a story about my cat."

"I would love to hear it. Would you read it to me?"

Hunter begins reading:

My Cat

My cat is lazy.
My cat is still.
My cat is sleepy.
Once I seen her drink out of the toilet.
And she sun bathes in the sun.
And she is 16 or 12.

Hunter has drawn lines between each sentence. He has also included a small picture for each idea (Figure 9.9).

I respond, "Wow. I love all the details you wrote about your cat. I notice you include a story in a story when you say, *Once I saw her drink out of the toilet.* Did you really see her do that?" Hunter nods. "That really helps me feel like I know your cat. Is this a story you would like to publish?"

Hunter says, "Yes. Can you type it?"

I ask Hunter to join me at the computer. We sit side by side in front of the keyboard and monitor. I am creating a moment in which I can nudge Hunter to elaborate a bit on the ideas in his story. I first say, "I notice you put lines between each sentence. Tell me about that."

Hunter answers, "This is a book. I want each of these parts to be different pages in my book."

"Okay. Let's begin with the title." I type *My Cat*. I ask Hunter, "Do you like the font—the way the letters look? Do you like the size of the words?" Hunter agrees that he likes the way it looks.

I type as Hunter reads the first page: "My cat is lazy."

Then I say, "What does your cat do that shows she is lazy?"

Hunter answers, "She just sits by the fire and sleeps all day."

"Oh, I love that detail. Would you like to add that? I can type it right after your first sentence." Hunter agrees.

Next, Hunter reads, "My cat is still." Then he says, "Wait. I want to add a simile." We have been learning about similes since September, and Hunter is really interested in them. Hunter continues, "She is as still as ice."

I show how impressed I am. "Hunter, you just stretched your moment by adding a simile. That is great." I type his words.

Figure 9.9 *Hunter Writes About His Cat*

Next, he reads, "My cat is sleepy."

I ask, "When does he sleep?"

Hunter answers, "All day." There is a pause and then he says, "Can I add that?" We do.

Hunter continues, "Once I saw her drink out of the toilet."

"You did? Anything else you want to add?" I ask.

"Yes: *Except my dog took out all the water.*"

"This is really shaping into a great story," I tell Hunter.

Hunter reads again, "And she sunbathes in the sun."

I ask, "Why does she do that?"

"She is cold sometimes in the house." I continue typing.

Hunter reads his last sentence. "And she is 16 or 12." Then he adds, "Cats are a lot older than dogs."

I type this last part. Then I ask Hunter, "Do you think your reader knows you are finished? Does this feel like the end of your book?" Hunter thinks. I ask, "How do you feel about your cat?"

Hunter says, "I love my cat. Her name is Oreo."

"That would make a great ending page for your story. Do you agree?" As I type, I praise Hunter for his ending page. He rereads his story and I print off the pages of his book. Hunter illustrates and shares his book with the class (Figure 9.10). Then we place it in a basket of student-published books for others to read.

This is a turning point for Hunter. He successfully wrote his own story, revised by adding details, and published his book. I now see a more confident and independent writer.

Emma: Revising for clarity

We have been learning about Harriet Tubman in social studies and reading. Some students, including second-grade student Emma, have chosen to write about her. Now she is ready for a conference. Emma reads her piece to me:

> *Harriet Tubman was a brave woman. She was a risk taker. She was the conductor. Harriet ran away when she was 29. Harriet Tubman was a special person.*

I praise Emma for her worthy choice of topic and for all of her wonderful details. I tell her, "I especially like that you used the words *risk taker* and *conductor* in your piece." Then I ask, "Would you mind reading your piece

Figure 9.10 *Hunter's Published Book About His Cat* *(continues)*

Once I saw her drink out of the toilet. Except my dog took out all the water. 	And she sunbathes in the sun. She is cold sometimes in the house. 
And she is 16 or 12. Cats are a lot older than dogs! 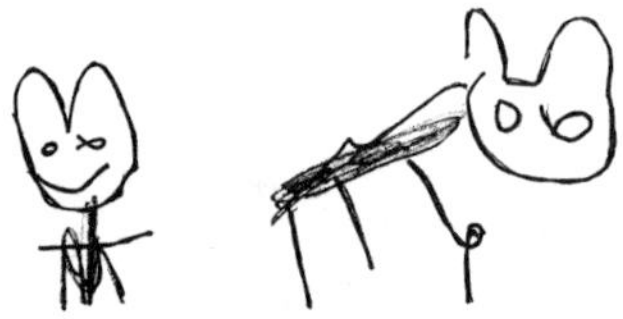	I love my cat. Her name is Oreo. 

Figure 9.10 *Continued*

another time to me? There were a few spots where I was confused. May I stop you as you read to ask a few questions?"

Emma says, "Sure." She begins to read, "Harriet Tubman was a brave woman. She was a risk taker. She was the conductor."

I interrupt, "Okay, I have a question. What was she the conductor of?"

Emma answers incredulously, "The Underground Railroad."

"Oh. Could I write that down for you? That makes it so much clearer." I record Emma's idea.

Emma continues reading: "Harriet ran away when she was 29."

I interrupt again. "Okay, stop. Where did she run away from or whom did she run away from?"

Emma explains, "From being a slave."

Again, I ask Emma, "Can we add that in? It helps me understand better."

Emma agrees and continues reading, "Harriet Tubman was a special person."

I praise Emma for her ending sentence. "I love your ending. It really sums up your piece and lets the reader know you are finished. I do have one more question for you, though. If you could tell me the most important thing about Harriet Tubman, something you think everyone should know, what would it be?"

Emma answers, "She went back and helped over three hundred slaves run away."

I answer with enthusiasm, "Oh, that is a wonderful detail. It would be great if you added that. You know, I love your ending sentence. Do you think we could put that detail right before your ending sentence?"

Emma agrees and I record her new detail (Figure 9.11). I ask Emma, "Would you like to publish this piece?" Emma says, "Yes." I suggest we work on typing it tomorrow during writing workshop.

During this conference, I wanted to show Emma that sometimes our writing is unclear and leaves readers with questions, which we can answer by adding details. However, I knew that if I expected Emma to work on the revisions independently, she might feel overwhelmed. Instead, I recorded the additions for her so she could concentrate on her ideas.

Brooke: Revising to extend ideas

Brooke, a second grader, comes to me one day with a piece about her mom (Figure 9.12). I ask Brooke, "What gave you this idea today?"

She answers, "I just love my mom and thought I would write about her."

"Okay. I would love to hear your piece."

Emma

Harriet tubmen was
a brave woman She
was a Risk taker She
was the kinDuckter
on the Underground Railroad
Harriet ran a way
from being a slave.
Win She wus 28
She went back and helped over 300 slaves
run away.
Harriet tubman
Vus a specia per Son.

Figure 9.11 *Emma's Draft*

Brooke reads:

I love my mom. My mom's name is Jane. She has brown hair and my mom has green eyes. She is beautiful. She is not such an animal lover but we still have animals. My mom does lots of activities with me like skiing and reading and lots of other things.

I begin, "Wow, Brooke. I love your piece. You give lots of details about your mom. I especially love the way you describe what makes her beautiful: her *brown hair* and *green eyes*. Nice description. I also love how you elaborate with examples when you say, *My mom does lots of activities with me like skiing and reading and lots of other things*. I point to these places in her piece.

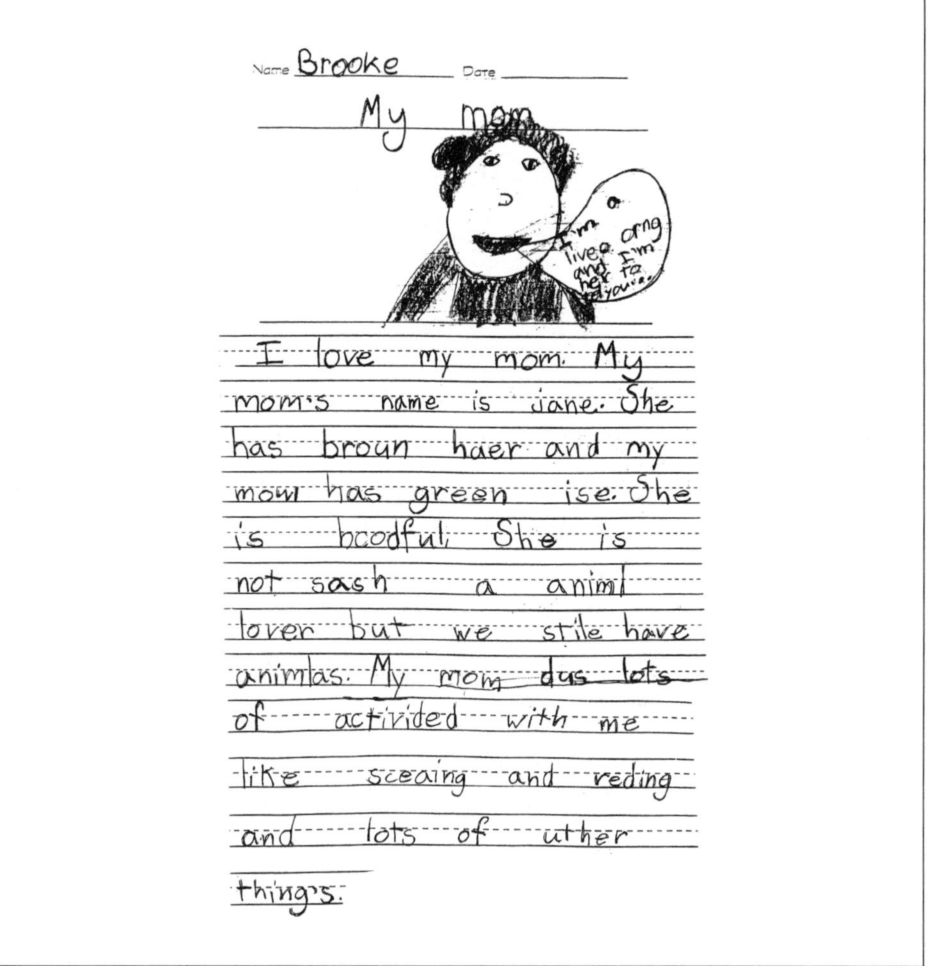

Name Brooke Date

My mom

I love my mom. My mom's name is Jane. She has broun haer and my mow has green ise. She is bcodful. She is not sash a animl lover but we stile have animlas. My mom dus lots of actrivided with me like sceaing and reding and lots of uther thing's.

Figure 9.12 *Brooke's Draft About Her Mom*

Brooke agrees. "I tried to elaborate."

"Well, you did. You know, I know something about your mom that I bet a lot of your readers won't know. Isn't she acting in a play right now in Woodinville?"

Brooke answers, "Yes."

I continue, "That's really interesting. Not many people can say their mom is an actress. Maybe you could add that to your piece."

Brooke agrees, "Okay."

"And you know how we have been working on adding an ending sentence that will satisfy our readers and let them know we are finished with our piece. Maybe you could think of a sentence to end your piece."

We have focused on just a couple of things, which I believe Brooke can tackle on her own. I leave Brooke to revise her piece (Figure 9.13). She keeps the first page intact but adds:

> *My mom is an actress too! But she is not a big star, but I think she should be one though because she is very good. I love my mom more than a pot of gold!*

Emelia: Editing conference

Conferences can be very short and focused. As I roam the room between conferences, I decide to check in with Emelia. I ask her, "How is it going today? It looks like you are writing a piece about your weekend. Is that right?" Emelia explains what her picture shows and then reads her piece to me (Figure 9.14).

I say, "I notice you have circled the word *aquarium* in two places. Is that because you are unsure about the spelling?"

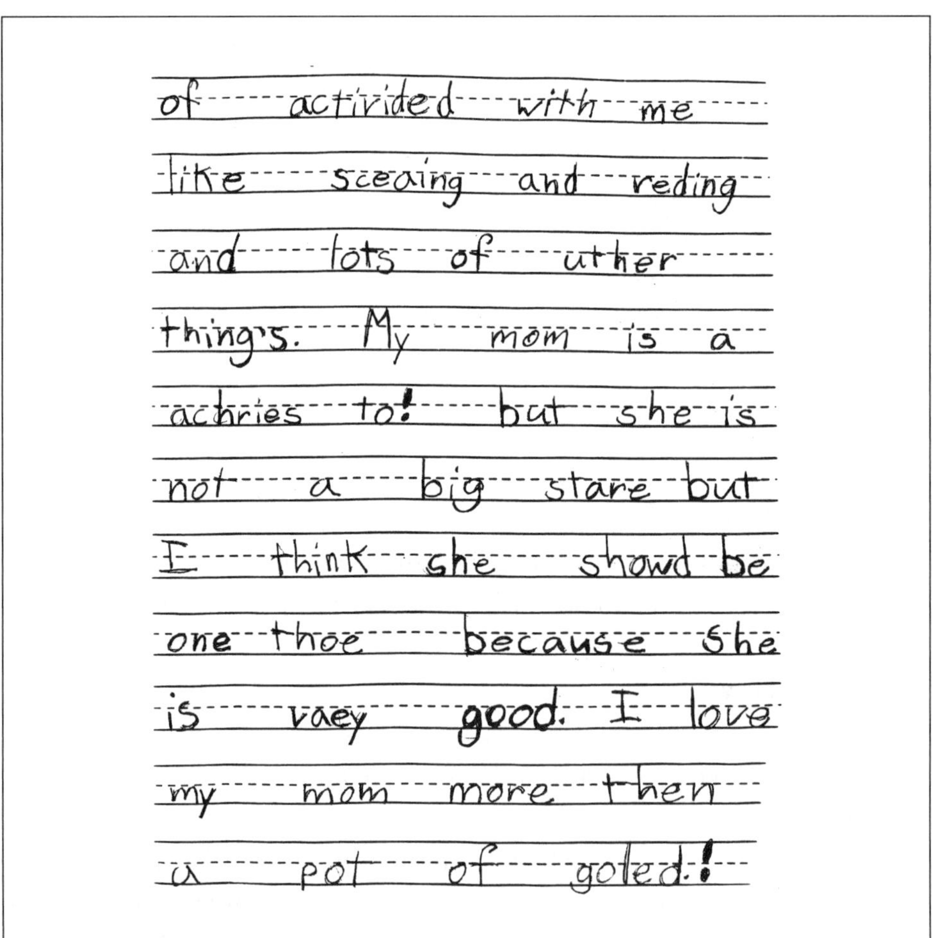
of actirided with me
like sceaing and reding
and lots of uther
thing's. My mom is a
achries to! but she is
not a big stare but
I think she showd be
one thoe because she
is vaey good. I love
my mom more then
a pot of goled!

Figure 9.13 *Brook's Revision*

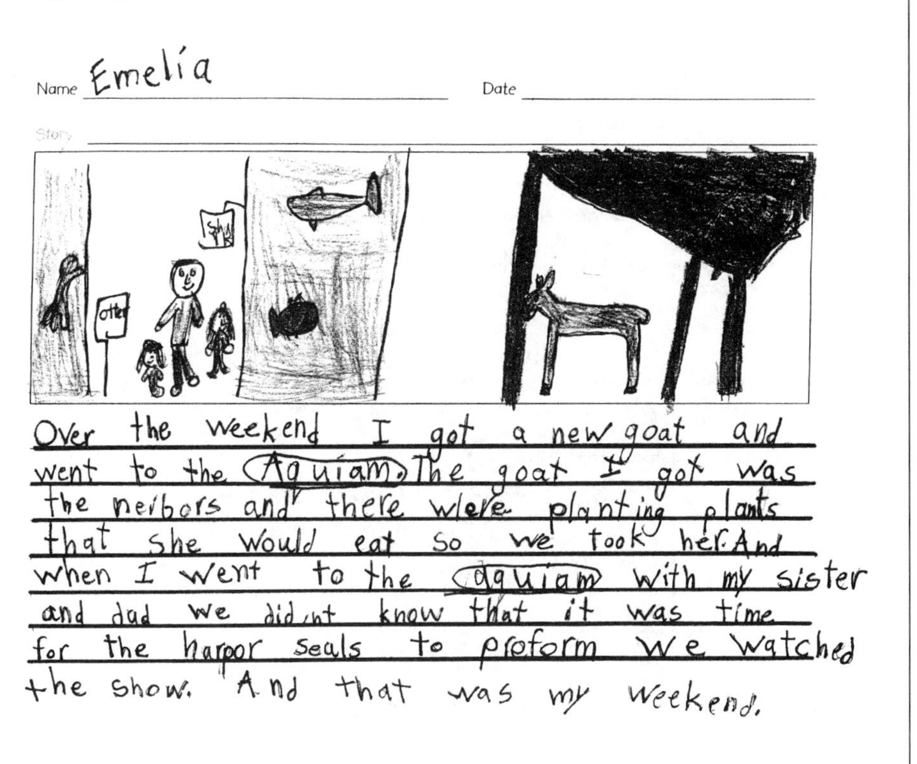

Figure 9.14 *Emelia Writes About Her Weekend*

Emelia answers, "Yes. Could you tell me if it's right?"

I answer, "Actually, you are very close. Let me write it on this sticky note for you and you can make the editing changes. I like how you circled the word and kept writing. That way you didn't interrupt your ideas, but you remembered to come back and edit the word. Good thinking."

I often teach students to underline or circle words when they would like help with spelling. This seems to alleviate their need to get the correct spelling right away. Instead, students feel free to continue writing, knowing they will get editing help later on.

Although this conference was brief and informal, I was able to praise Emelia's strategies and provide the support she wanted.

Recording Notes from Conferences

During conferences, I take notes to record my observations (Figure 9.15). What does this child know about writing? What are the writer's strengths? What are some appropriate next steps? These notes document progress and support my planning for future instruction. They also serve as evidence during parent-teacher communications.

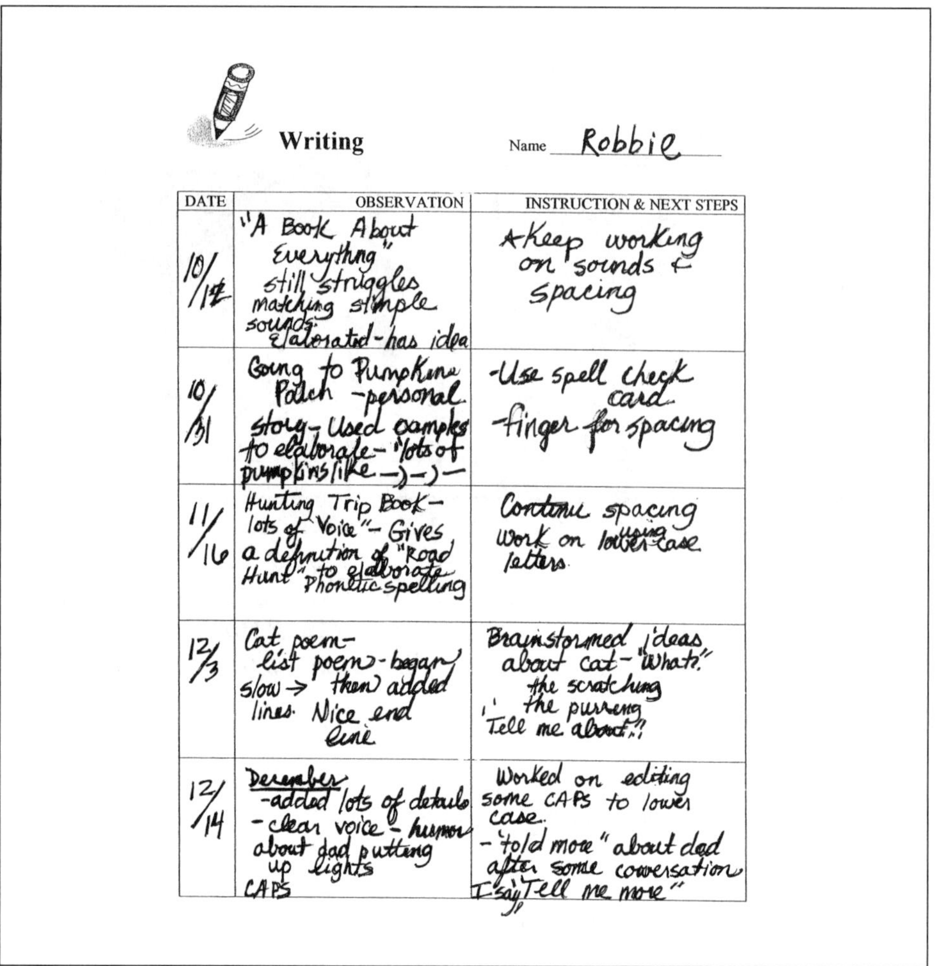

Writing Name Robbie

DATE	OBSERVATION	INSTRUCTION & NEXT STEPS
10/12	"A Book About Everything" still struggles matching simple sounds. Elaborated - has idea	*Keep working on sounds & spacing
10/31	Going to Pumpkin Patch - personal story - Used examples to elaborate - "lots of pumpkins like —)—)—	-Use spell check card. -finger for spacing
11/16	Hunting Trip Book - lots of "Voice" - Gives a definition of "Road Hunt" to elaborate. Phonetic spelling	Continue spacing. Work on using lower case letters.
12/3	Cat poem - list poem - began slow → then added lines. Nice end line	Brainstormed ideas about cat - "What?" the scratching, the purring. "Tell me about."
12/14	December - added lots of details - clear voice - humor about dad putting up lights CAPS	Worked on editing some CAPS to lower case. - "told more" about dad after some conversation. I say "Tell me more"

Figure 9.15 *Notes About Writing Conferences from Megan's Assessment Notebook*

How do I manage the rest of the class during conference time?

This may be the biggest question I am asked, and wrestle with myself, as I think about holding one-on-one writing conferences. What are the rest of the students doing? Since I hold the conferences during drafting time of the writing workshop, my answer is, "The other students are writing."

When I teach students about writing workshop at the beginning of the year, we practice developing stamina (see Chapter 2). I introduce students to the concept of independence. We review what will help them write independently (finding a good spot to write, choosing a topic they like, writing quietly, using resources) so that I can confer with students during drafting time.

When we begin drafting time, I roam around the room for the first five or six minutes. I observe students to make sure everyone is set to start. After I hold a couple of conferences, I roam the room for another five minutes. I check in with students who might need assistance or redirection, and I make observations again. I am then free to hold a few more conferences. If students are having a tough time working independently, I cut conferences short. I observe for the rest of the time, and I explain that I am looking for students who show they are independent writers. We debrief afterward and share strategies for independence.

All students want to meet with me; they want me to hold conferences. This desire to share their work one-on-one motivates them to write quietly and independently, perhaps getting help from a classmate or waiting until I'm free. Students know that after a couple of conferences I will roam the room, which is a great time for them to ask me for assistance. Often, by the time I am available, students have figured out their problem. And this is what I want. Most times, when students are nudged to solve a challenge on their own, or with the help of another student, they are able to do it. This is how they learn independence.

Teaching Students to Self-Reflect on Their Writing

In Chapter 2, I explain my system for holding onto student work. Whether students collect writing in large folders or in notebooks, I encourage them to look through their writing frequently to reflect on what they are learning to do well, and on how they have grown as writers.

We also create portfolios from one-inch, three-ring notebooks filled with transparent page protectors. These serve as holders for student-made books, papers, or copies of journal pages. The students decorate the portfolio covers with their name, photograph, and year in school (Figure 9.16).

Every four to six weeks, students take out their work and choose a piece for their portfolio (Figure 9.17). They read over their writing and select a piece they feel proud of. Sometimes I direct the genre or type of writing, such as when I ask students to choose a poem, personal narrative, nonfiction piece, reading journal entry, page from a science unit journal, and so on. I also ask students to write about why they are choosing this piece of writing on a portfolio reflection sheet. Then we slip the student work and the reflection sheet into the page protector, back to back. I sometimes make portfolio picks as well. If I see a student piece that shows great writing skill or progress, it becomes a "teacher pick."

Figure 9.16 *Student Portfolio*

Figure 9.17 *Students Choose "Portfolio Picks"*

Modeling Self-Reflection

Like anything else, students need to learn how to write self-reflections. I teach them by modeling one myself. I open my folder or writer's notebook and choose a piece I have written. I think aloud for students, saying things like, "I think I will pick this piece to show I am a good writer because I like all the details I included and I really think I used some interesting words, such as *fluttered* and *brilliant.*"

Then I model writing this on my self-reflection sheet. I tell students, "Today, you will be doing the same thing. I want you to go through your folders or notebooks and choose any piece of writing that really shows you are a good writer. You may choose it because you elaborated. You may choose it because you used interesting words. If so, write down the words you think are interesting. Maybe you think you really had an inviting lead or a satisfying ending. Maybe you added words to your picture for the first time."

"Don't say, 'I picked this piece for my portfolio because it is good' or 'I chose this piece because I liked it.' Of course it is good and of course you liked it. You are choosing it for your portfolio. Tell why it shows you are a good writer."

Using "Portfolio Picks" and Self-Reflection Sheets

After I model, students find a spot to spread out their work, or they flip through their journals. Emelia chooses a piece called "My Garden" (Figure 9.18). Then she writes on a self-reflection sheet to explain why she chose this piece for her portfolio (Figure 9.19). Emelia also selects a poem (Figure 9.20) and completes another self-reflection sheet (Figure 9.21).

Setting goals

Some children take the opportunity to reflect on their pieces and set goals for future work. Eric is a student who struggles with writing. He is just finding his voice and confidence as a writer. Eric has never written more than one sentence during writing workshop. He chooses his piece about the Mariners for his portfolio.

> *I'm going to the Mariners. They have to win. If they win then my whole bus gets a sucker. I'm going to watch. The Mariners will hopefully win. Ken Griffey Jr. hit a grand slam when they get to go away to the Angels. The Mariners against the Angels. The Mariners won.*

This is my garden.
My garden has... roses, strawberries, rassberries, beans, tamatos, tulips, daises dafidils and painses. In the summer all this is alive with bright butueful colors. The flowers are the pretteiest, But the berries are the yummest! In the Summer somtimes I sit in the garden but now I know that my bottom gets dirty. thats my garden

Figure 9.18 *Emelia's Piece, "My Garden"*

Name Emelia Date ____________

Portfolio Self-Reflection

I chose this piece for my portfolio because it shows lots of details and a story with in a story.

Figure 9.19 *Emelia's Self-Reflection on "My Garden"*

Figure 9.20 *Emelia's Poem, "Fall Tree"*

The amount of writing in Eric's story is very important to him, and he sets a goal to write one that is even longer. In his self-reflection (Figure 9.22) Eric writes:

> *I chose this piece for my portfolio because this was the longest story I have ever written in my life. Today I will write one longer but I do not know how long it will take me to write a longer story.*

When students self-reflect on their writing, they take a huge step toward becoming better writers. It encourages them to read their work like writers, and it allows them to see how much they have grown as writers over the year. When students self-reflect, they see all of the good things they are doing, and it motivates them to grow even more.

Students often read their work during times other than portfolio picks. They share and enjoy each other's stories, poems, and books throughout the year. It's delightful to see students spontaneously flip through their journals,

Name Emelia Date ____________

Portfolio Self-Reflection

I chose this piece for my portfolio because it shows A Turn around part at the end. And a Simpathy.

Figure 9.21 *Emelia's Self-Reflection on "Fall Tree"*

Name Eric Date ____________

❖❖ ***SELECTION FOR MY PORTFOLIO*** ❖❖

I chose this piece for my portfolio because
this Was the
logist Storei hav
ovrr rot hi mi
lif today i Will
rit one logor

Bot ido not oh hat log rit will toke mi to rit a logr IStorier!

Figure 9.22 *Eric's Self-Reflection Sheet*

writing folders, and portfolios. They giggle at funny stories, revel in how they "used to write," and share their "best" work.

Scoring Writing Samples and Writing Prompts

Formal assessments are part of life in the classroom today. Students participate in state, district, and schoolwide writing assessments at various grade levels. In our state, papers are scored for their content and conventions on a 4-3-2-1 scale. A score of 3 means a student meets the standard. 4 means the student exceeds the standard. 2 means the student is approaching the standard, and 1 means the child is in need of much assistance.

In the primary grades we give writing prompts to our students and score their papers three or four times a year. Our grade levels agree on prompts, which, in the past, have included:

- Tell us about an interesting animal. Explain why this animal is interesting.
- Write about your favorite season. Explain why this season is your favorite.
- Tell about a favorite time you spent with your family. What made this a special time?

We agree on how we will administer these prompts, deciding what kind of rehearsal or prewrite students will engage in, and then we come together and read our students' papers. This is the rich part of the assessment. When colleagues come together and read aloud student papers, scoring and discussing the strengths and needs of writers, we learn so much—not only about our students' writing skills but also about what we are teaching well, and what we need to focus on next.

On my recording sheet I not only score my students in content and conventions; I write short anecdotal notes about their writing as well. For instance, I give Jane's writing a score of 3 for content and 4 for conventions. In my notes, I explain that she has a "great lead/examples" but is also "a bit repetitive." I give Ryan a score of 4 for content and 4 for conventions. I write "voice*, word choice*—*slithering, floating*." And I give David a score of 2 for content and 2 for conventions. My notes say, "a couple of ideas, letters strung together." (See Figure 9.23.)

These extra notes help me see potential patterns in student writing. I recognize the students' strengths as well as their needs and then direct my instruction accordingly. For example, I notice that many students still need work on elaboration, so I continue to teach all students about elaboration. I also notice

Writing

	date	topic/prompt		date	topic/prompt		date	topic/prompt	
				10/07	Favorite Season			Open- Favorite Season, Sport, What I Like/Did Over Weekend	
	COS	CON	comment/teaching point	COS	CON	comment/teaching point	COS	CON	comment/teaching point
Adam				3	3	Lead + End * Kind of a list	3-	3	Add some details okay end.
Anna				1	3	Add more details (one sentence)			
Avery				2	3-	Repetitive sentence but adds 3 reasons	2+	2	gave 1 example Add more.
Boyd							3-	3-	some examples Caps/Periods in sentences
Daesha				4	4	Very detailed + poetic *spelling	3-	4	Nonfiction about Pilgrims
David				2	2	a couple ideas. -letters string together			
Eddy				1	1	sound/symbol corr. *high freq words	2	1	a few ideas Spelling difficult
Garrett			off top!	2	2	Lead + End spelling low a bit confusing *poetic			
Gavin				2	2+	off topic - 2 sentences	2	2+	1 long sentence a list
Garrity				3-	3	gives a few reasons One cap missing	3	4-	word choice "sly" miss one cap
Geneva				4	3+	Gave examples Nice spelling	3	3-	bad day for Denetry 1 sentence
Hanna				3	3+	poetic/word choice → caps/spelling	4	3	voice filled. Nice sentences
Henry				2	3	No lead sentence Had end sent. (brief)	2+/3-	2	More details needed "was" No end. Work on spacing
Ibi				3-	3	No last sentence. A couple details			
Izzy				2-	3	No periods Elaborate more	3-	2+	Needs flow/org Needs periods/spell good
Jason									
Jane				4	4	Very poetic + fluent language	3	4	Great lead/examples A bit repetitive.
Kylie				3	3	Some spelling errors	3-	3+	Add more details (a few)
Laurelle							3		Thanksgiving details No end.
Nolan				3	3	Nice examples	2+/3-	3	good spelling need periods/caps for send.
Ryan H.				4	3	word choice* voice *	4	4	voice * lead * end *
Bobby				4		Voice-filled messy	3	2+	a long list- voice some spelling/periods
Ellen				2-	2-	few details spelling/H.W.	3-		some details Spelling hard/H.W hard
Eleanor				3	3	like a poem	3	3+	like a poem Great lead

Figure 9.23 *Scoring Sheet for Student Writing*

that three students need help with spacing between words. Rather than teaching this convention to the entire class, I gather these specific students and reteach lessons by modeling and engaging them in shared practice.

Using Anecdotal Notes for Student Feedback

Other than the formal assessments our grade level agrees to administer, I do not put scores on primary writing. I give students lots of oral feedback when I roam around the room and when we confer together. I also give specific written feedback about what I see students doing well and what I want them to work on next.

Ricky wants to write a book entitled "My Puppy." He gets the idea from his poem "Roxy Girl" (see Chapter 4). However, Ricky does not know where to begin. He explains that he wants to write a book but he cannot figure out how to start. I confer with Ricky and help him discover ideas for his book (Figure 9.24). He writes:

Title: My Puppy
Page 1: My puppy's name is Roxy. Roxy is a chocolate lab.
Page 2: My puppy likes to play with her dragon.
Page 3: When Roxy goes to sleep, Roxy wiggles her tail.
Page 4: My puppy turns her head like "What the heck?"

Ricky works so hard to write this story. It is not easy. I help him write the word *dragon.* He labors over the details and often needs assistance, but he does it! He writes his first book. I want Ricky to know how much I appreciate his writing, so I write a short message on a sticky note to let him know, "Job well done."

These short notes mean the world to students. Written feedback provides tangible evidence that they are writers. Someone has noticed they write well. I also encourage students to write notes to each other when they read their classmates' books. I say, "Tell others what you like about their books or poems. Write it down. Let them know you enjoyed their writing and why."

Final Notes

Donald Graves (1994) argues, "We've underestimated what children can do" (xvi). I believe this is true. I am constantly astounded at the talent and skill of my young writers. They are truly amazing. Teachers often ask me, "Do your students really understand *simile* and *metaphor*? Do they really elaborate using anecdotes and statistics? Did a second grader really write that free verse poem?" The answer to all of these questions is "Yes."

I know that if we believe in our young writers and teach intentionally, they will rise to a level of greatness. Assessment plays a huge part in this climb. Through our observations and conversations, we learn from students how to better teach and stretch their minds. When we sit beside our colleagues, student writing in hand, and read aloud their words and look at the stories in their pictures, we gain greater understanding of students' strengths. We learn to plan our lessons better to meet their needs and challenge their thinking. Through thoughtful assessment, we understand our students and become better teachers.

Figure 9.24 *Ricky's Book* My Puppy

Figure 9.24 *Continued*

APPENDIX A

Anecdotal Notes Conference Form

Name ____

Writing

Date	*Observation*	*Instruction & Next Steps*

APPENDIX B

Writing Scoring Form

	date	*topic/prompt*		*date*	*topic/prompt*		*date*	*topic/prompt*	
student	COS	CON	*comment/teaching point*	COS	CON	*comment/teaching point*	COS	CON	*comment/teaching point*

REFERENCES

Professional Books

Anderson, Carl. 2000. *How's It Going? A Practical Guide to Conferring with Student Writers*. Portsmouth, NH: Heinemann.

Angelillo, Janet. 2002. *A Fresh Approach to Teaching Punctuation*. New York: Scholastic.

Boushey, Gail, and Joan Moser. 2006. *The Daily 5: Fostering Literacy Independence in the Elementary Grades*. Portland, ME: Stenhouse.

Calkins, Lucy. 1994. *The Art of Teaching Writing*. Portsmouth, NH: Heinemann.

Calkins, Lucy et al. 2003. *Units of Study for Primary Writing*. 7 vols. Portsmouth, NH: *first*hand, Heinemann.

Calkins, Lucy, and Abby Oxenhorn. 2003. *Small Moments: Personal Narrative Writing*. In Units of Study for Primary Writing, 7 vols. Portsmouth, NH: *first*hand, Heinemann.

Fletcher, Ralph. 2006. *Boy Writers: Reclaiming Their Voices*. Portland, ME: Stenhouse.

———. 1993. *What a Writer Needs*. Portsmouth, NH: Heinemann.

Fletcher, Ralph, and JoAnn Portalupi. 2001. *Writing Workshop: The Essential Guide*. Portsmouth, NH: Heinemann.

———. 1998. *Craft Lessons: Teaching Writing K–8*. Portland, ME: Stenhouse.

Flynn, Nick, and Shirley McPhillips. 2000. *A Note Slipped Under the Door: Teaching Poems We Love*. Portland, ME: Stenhouse.

Fox, Mem. 2001. *Reading Magic: Why Reading Aloud to Our Children Will Change Their Lives Forever*. Orlando, FL: Harcourt.

———. 1993. *Radical Reflections: Passionate Opinions on Teaching, Learning, and Living*. San Diego: Harcourt Brace.

Graves, Donald H. 2003. *Writing: Teachers and Children at Work, 20th Anniversary Edition*. Portsmouth, NH: Heinemann.

———. 1994. *A Fresh Look at Writing*. Portsmouth, NH: Heinemann.

———. 1991. *Build a Literate Classroom*. Portsmouth, NH: Heinemann.

———. 1983. *Writing: Teachers and Children at Work*. Portsmouth, NH: Heinemann.

Harvey, Stephanie, and Anne Goudvis. 2007. *Strategies That Work*. Portland, ME: Stenhouse.

Harwayne, Shelley. 1992. *Lasting Impressions: Weaving Literature into the Writing Workshop*. Portsmouth, NH: Heinemann.

Heard, Georgia. 1999. *Awakening the Heart: Exploring Poetry in Elementary and Middle Schools*. Portsmouth, NH: Heinemann.

Hoyt, Linda. 1999. *Revisit, Reflect, Retell*. Portsmouth, NH: Heinemann.

Johnson, Nancy J., and Cyndi Giorgis. 2007. *The Wonder of It All: When Literature and Literacy Intersect*. Portsmouth, NH: Heinemann.

Keene, Ellin Oliver, and Susan Zimmermann. 1997. *Mosaic of Thought: Teaching Comprehension in a Reader's Workshop*. Portsmouth, NH: Heinemann.

Newkirk, Thomas. 2002. *Misreading Masculinity: Boys, Literacy, and Popular Culture*. Portsmouth, NH: Heinemann.

Pearson, P. David, and M. C. Gallagher. 1983. "The Instruction of Reading Comprehension." *Contemporary Educational Psychology* 8: 317–344.

Ray, Katie Wood, and Lisa B. Cleaveland. 2004. *About the Authors: Writing Workshop with Our Youngest Writers*. Portsmouth, NH: Heinemann.

Ray, Katie Wood, and Lester Laminack. 2001. *The Writing Workshop: Working Through the Hard Parts (and They're All Hard Parts)*. Urbana, IL: National Council of Teachers of English.

Routman, Regie. 2005. *Writing Essentials*. Portsmouth, NH: Heinemann.

———. 2003. *Reading Essentials*. Portsmouth, NH: Heinemann.

———. 2000. *Kids' Poems*. New York: Scholastic.

Serafini, Frank. 2001. *The Reading Workshop: Creating Space for Readers*. Portsmouth, NH: Heinemann.

Sloan, Megan. 2008. *Teaching Young Writers to Elaborate: Mini-Lessons and Strategies That Help Students Find Topics and Learn to Tell More*. New York: Scholastic.

Spandel, Vicki. 2005. *The Nine Rights of Every Writer: A Guide for Teachers*. Portsmouth, NH: Heinemann.

Taberski, Sharon. 2000. *On Solid Ground: Strategies for Teaching Reading K–3*. Portsmouth, NH: Heinemann.

Trelease, Jim. 2006. *The Read Aloud Handbook*, Sixth Edition. New York: Penguin.

Zinsser, William. 2001. *On Writing Well: The Classic Guide to Writing Nonfiction, 25th Anniversary Edition*. New York: HarperCollins.

Children's Books

Adler, David. 1992. *A Picture Book of Harriet Tubman*. New York: Scholastic.

Arnosky, Jim. 1996. *All About Deer*. New York: Scholastic.

Avi. 2000. *Ereth's Birthday*. New York: HarperCollins.

———. 1995. *Poppy*. New York: HarperCollins.

Baylor, Byrd. 1981. *Desert Voices*. New York: Macmillan.

Bennett, Elizabeth. 2007. *Powerful Polar Bears*. New York: Scholastic.

Brenner, Martha. 1994. *Abe Lincoln's Hat*. New York: Scholastic.

Bruel, Nick. 2006. *Who Is Melvin Bubble?* New Milford, CT: Roaring Book Press.

Burleigh, Robert. 1997. *Hoops*. San Diego: Harcourt.

Cannon, Janell. 1993. *Stellaluna*. San Diego: Harcourt Brace.

Clarke, Ginjer L. 2007. *Cheetah Cubs: Station Stop 2 (All About Science Reader).* New York: Grosset & Dunlap.
———. 2006. *Gross Out! Animals That Do Disgusting Things.* New York: Penguin.
Cleary, Beverly. 1975. *Ramona the Brave.* New York: Scholastic.
Cooper, Wade. 2007. *Night Creatures.* New York: Scholastic.
Creech, Sharon. 2001. *Love That Dog.* New York: Joanna Cotler Books.
Cronin, Doreen. 2005. *Diary of a Spider.* New York: Joanna Cotler Books.
———. 2003. *Diary of a Worm.* New York: Joanna Cotler Books.
DeCesare, Angelo. 1999. *Flip's Fantastic Journal.* New York: Penguin.
DePalma, Mary Newell. 2005. *A Grand Old Tree.* New York: Scholastic.
Edwards, Pamela Duncan. 1999. *Barefoot: Escape on the Underground Railroad.* New York: HarperCollins.
Ehlert, Lois. 1995. *Snowballs.* New York: Harcourt Brace.
Faulkner, Matt. 1965. *Jack and the Beanstalk.* New York: Scholastic.
Fleming, Denise. 2001. *Pumpkin Eye.* New York: Henry Holt.
———. 1997. *Time to Sleep.* New York: Henry Holt.
———. 1996. *Where Once There Was a Wood.* New York: Henry Holt.
Gibbons, Gail. 2001. *Polar Bears.* New York: Holiday House.
———. 2000. *Bats.* New York: Holiday House.
———. 1996. *Deserts.* New York: Holiday House.
———. 1992. *Recycle!* Boston: Little, Brown, & Company.
Guiberson, Brenda Z. 1991. *Cactus Hotel.* New York: Scholastic.
Howker, Janni. 1997. *Walk with a Wolf.* Cambridge, MA: Candlewick Press.
Johnston, Tony. 1994. *Amber on the Mountain.* New York: Penguin.
Khanduri, Kamini. 1992. *Polar Wildlife.* New York: Scholastic.
Kline, Suzy. 1996. *Horrible Harry and the Dungeon.* New York: Viking Press.
Levenson, George. 1999. *Pumpkin Circle: The Story of a Garden.* Berkeley, CA: Tricycle Press.
London, Jonathan. 1993. *Red Wolf Country.* New York: Scholastic.
———. 1996. *The Eyes of Gray Wolf.* San Francisco: Chronicle.
MacLachlan, Patricia. 1994. *All the Places to Love.* New York: HarperCollins.
Mansfield, Massachusetts, St. Mary's Catholic School. 2005. *Haiku Hike.* New York: Scholastic.
McGovern, Ann. 1973. *The Pilgrim's First Thanksgiving.* New York: Scholastic.
Munson, Derek. 2000. *Enemy Pie.* San Francisco: Chronicle.
Nicholas, Christopher. 1999. *Know-It-Alls: Wolves!* New York: McClanahan Book Company.
O'Brien, Robert C. 1971. *Mrs. Frisby and the Rats of NIMH.* New York: Simon & Schuster.
Parker, Kim. 2005. *Counting in the Garden.* London: Orchard Books.
Parker, Steve. 1999. *It's an Ant's Life: My Story of Life in the Nest.* Pleasantville, NY: Reader's Digest Children's Books.
Pilkey, Dav. 1999. *The Paperboy.* New York: Scholastic.
Polacco, Patricia. 1995. *My Ol' Man.* New York: Philomel.
———. 1993. *The Bee Tree.* New York: Trumpet.
———. 1991. *Appelemando's Dream.* New York: Philomel.
Ring, Susan. 2007. *The Great Barrier Reef: An Undersea Adventure.* New York: Scholastic.

Ryan, Pam Munoz. 2001. *Hello Ocean.* Watertown, MA: Talewinds.
Rylant, Cynthia. 2000. *In November.* San Diego: Harcourt.
———. 1985. *The Relatives Came.* New York: Scholastic.
———. 1982. *When I Was Young in the Mountains.* New York: Penguin.
Scholastic Children's Dictionary. 1996. New York: Scholastic.
Seuss, Dr. 1960. *One Fish, Two Fish.* New York: Random House.
Simon, Seymour. 2006. *Amazing Bats.* New York: Scholastic.
Stepanek, Mattie J. 2001. *Heartsongs.* New York: Hyperion.
Teague, Mark. 2002. *Dear Mrs. LaRue: Letters from Obedience School.* New York: Scholastic.
Watt, Melanie. 2006. *Scaredy Squirrel.* Toronto: Kids Can Press.
White, E. B. 1952. *Charlotte's Web.* New York: Harper & Row.
Wild, Margaret. 2006. *Fox.* La Jolla, CA: Kane/Miller.
Willem, Mo. 2008. *The Pigeon Wants a Puppy.* New York: Hyperion Books.
Winter, Jeanette. 2005. *The Librarian of Basra.* Orlando, FL: Harcourt.
———. 2002. *Emily Dickinson's Letters to the World.* New York: Farrar, Straus, and Giroux.
———. 1999. *Sebastian: The Story of Bach.* Orlando, FL: Harcourt.
Wong, Janet S. *You Have to Write.* 2002. New York: Simon & Schuster.
Wood, Lily. 2000. *Bats.* New York: Scholastic.
Worth, Valerie. 1994. *All the Small Poems and Fourteen More.* New York: Farrar, Straus and Giroux.
Yolen, Jane. 2003. *Color Me a Rhyme: Nature Poems for Young People.* Honesdale, PA: Boyds Mills Press.
———. 1987. *Owl Moon.* New York: Scholastic.
Zolotow, Charlotte. 1992. *The Seashore Book.* New York: Hyperion.

INDEX